Ground Crew

Ground Crew

THE FIGHT TO
END SEGREGATION AT
GEORGIA STATE

Maurice C. Daniels

The University of Georgia Press
Athens

© 2019 by the University of Georgia Press
Athens, Georgia 30602
www.ugapress.org
All rights reserved
Designed by Kaelin Chappell Beoaddus
Set in 10.75/13.5 Bulmer MT Std by Kaelin Chappell Beoaddus

Most University of Georgia Press titles are
available from popular e-book vendors.

Printed digitally

Library of Congress Cataloging-in-Publication Data

Names: Daniels, Maurice Charles, 1952– author.
Title: Ground crew : the fight to end segregation at Georgia State / Maurice
  C. Daniels.
Description: Athens, Georgia : University of Georgia Press, [2019] | Includes
  bibliographical references and index.
Identifiers: LCCN 2019018153| ISBN 9780820355955 (hard back : alk. paper) |
  ISBN 9780820355962 (e-book) | ISBN 9780820355979 (pbk. : alk. paper)
Subjects: LCSH: Georgia State College of Business Administration—
  History. | Segregation—Georgia—History—20th century. | African
  Americans—Civil rights—Georgia—History—20th century. | Civil rights
  movements—Georgia—History—20th century.
Classification: LCC LD1965 .D34 2019 | DDC 379.2/6309758—dc23

  LC record available at https://lccn.loc.gov/2019018153

*To my father, Eddie Daniels Sr.,
my mother, Maggie C. Daniels,
and the descendants of
Bill and Margie Bogan and
Doc and Lucinda Daniels*

Every time I take a flight, I am always mindful of the many people who make a successful journey possible—the known pilots and the unknown ground crew . . . without whose labor and sacrifices the jets flights to freedom could never have left the earth.

—DR. MARTIN LUTHER KING JR.

CONTENTS

ACKNOWLEDGMENTS xi

INTRODUCTION 1

CHAPTER 1 Breaking the Color Line 11

CHAPTER 2 Renewing the Struggle:
The Alliance with Atlanta's Black Institutions
and the NAACP 34

CHAPTER 3 Laying the Groundwork:
The Challenge and the Backlash 53

CHAPTER 4 *Hunt v. Arnold*: The Trial Begins 72

CHAPTER 5 "The Higher Dictates of Justice and Equity":
Judge Sloan's Verdict 96

CHAPTER 6 The Struggle Continues 118

NOTES 129

BIBLIOGRAPHY 161

INDEX 169

Illustrations follow page 71

ACKNOWLEDGMENTS

This volume is part of a series of books and documentaries produced by the Foot Soldier Project for Civil Rights Studies (FSP) that includes the book *Saving the Soul of Georgia: Donald L. Hollowell and the Struggle for Civil Rights* and the public television documentaries *Hamilton Earl Holmes: The Struggle Continues* and *Mary Frances Early: The Quiet Trailblazer.*

The FSP chronicles the lives and stories of those "foot soldiers for equal justice" whose names may not be familiar but whose activism helped bring about sweeping social change in our nation's history. Such work helps to illustrate how social change and social reform result from the hard work and dedication not only of the few celebrated historical figures whose names are preserved but also of the countless individuals whose contributions, though unrecognized, are nevertheless crucial.

In many ways, I was influenced to help create the FSP by my father, Eddie Daniels Sr., and the black community in my hometown of Rochelle, Georgia. My dad served as principal of the Excelsior Elementary and High School in Rochelle—the segregated school for black children. In solidarity with other local black citizens, he successfully circumnavigated the barriers of the Jim Crow system and led the transformation of an under-resourced, moribund, two-room wood-clad school, which used hand-me-down books and recycled buses, to develop one of the great bastions of education in Georgia during the 1950s and 1960s.

The heroic, unsung activism and great moral courage of my father and other citizens of my hometown in the midst of blatant racial oppression helped shape my understanding and appreciation of the power of everyday people to achieve social change. My recollections of their powerful activism, magnificent spirit, and bold determination to improve their lot inspired me to chronicle the stories of unsung activists in the black freedom struggle.

I am indebted to a number of friends and colleagues who contributed directly to making this book possible. Diane H. Miller's perceptive editorial direction, sharp eye, and meticulousness played a pivotal role in the organization, writing, and completion of this book. I am deeply grateful for her highly skillful editing and wise counsel. I am also appreciative of the editorial guidance of Charles Duncan, who helped me develop the conceptual framework of this manuscript during the writing of my book *Horace T. Ward: Desegregation of the University of Georgia, Civil Rights Advocacy, and Jurisprudence*. His depth of knowledge of civil rights history and superb editorial assistance have been invaluable.

I owe a great deal to Derrick P. Alridge for his encouragement, stewardship, and generosity with his time and talents in reviewing drafts of this manuscript. He provided indispensable recommendations and guided me to primary and secondary sources that enriched this study. I also thank Maurice J. Hobson and Dwight D. Watson for their scholarly insights and helpful commentary.

Christopher Strickland, FSP graduate research associate, made tremendous contributions to my research for this book. He spent many hours in libraries and archives unearthing historical documents. Christopher's expert research skills, resourcefulness, and creativity greatly enhanced this research endeavor.

In 2000, the FSP completed the production of the documentary film *Horace T. Ward: Foot Soldier for Equal Justice*, which chronicled the struggle of Horace T. Ward and the NAACP to break the mantle of segregation in higher education in Georgia. In the research process for this film, my interviewees included NAACP stalwart and business leader Jesse Hill; civil rights lawyers Donald L. Hollowell, Constance Baker Motley, Horace T. Ward, and Vernon E. Jordan Jr.; and Myra Dinsmore, one of the plaintiffs in the lawsuit to end segregation at Georgia State. Those interviews provided my initial insight into the significance of the *Hunt v. Arnold* case. I am grateful for the valuable information these individuals shared, which became the foundation of my research for this book.

I am especially grateful to Crystal Freeman, the daughter of Barbara

Hunt, who was the lead plaintiff in the *Hunt* case. Crystal has been a one-person band trumpeting the importance of acknowledging the efforts of plaintiffs and activists in the struggle to desegregate Georgia State. She provided a number of primary- and secondary-source documents that were invaluable in the research process.

I greatly appreciate the support and assistance of a number of archivists and librarians. Archivists at the Atlanta History Center, Emory University's Robert W. Woodruff Library, the Georgia Department of Archives and History, Georgia State University's Special Collections, the National Archives—Southeast Region, and the University of Georgia Libraries were especially instructive and helpful. Special thanks to Jill Severn, Christian Lopez, and Sheryl Vogt of the University of Georgia Richard B. Russell Library for Political Research and Studies; Courtney Chartier of the Stuart A. Rose Manuscript, Archives, and Rare Book Library; Derek Mosley and Anita Martin of the Auburn Avenue Research Library on African American Culture and History; Victoria Fox of Farrar, Straus and Giroux; Kayla Jenkins of the NAACP LDF; Amber Anderson of the Atlanta University Center, Robert W. Woodruff Library Archives Research Center; and Phyllis A. Perry, daughter of trailblazing photographer and journalist Harmon G. Perry.

My deepest gratitude to Mick Gusinde-Duffy, the University of Georgia Press's executive editor, who read my initial draft of this manuscript, for his encouragement and editorial recommendations. I also appreciate the reviews and tremendously helpful suggestions of the press's anonymous reviewers of this manuscript. Their cogent editorial recommendations helped me develop a more in-depth scholarly study.

I am grateful for the collective and expert work of Beth Snead, Jon Davies, Lea Johnson, and other able staff of the University of Georgia Press in the publication process. I also thank Barbara Wojhoski for her skillful copyediting and Pamela Gray for her excellent indexing work.

This research was funded, in part, by the J. Alton Gregory Support Fund, created by a gift from chief justice emeritus Hardy Gregory Jr. (Georgia Supreme Court) and Toni Gregory to the Foot Soldier Project for Civil Rights Studies. Many thanks to Chief Justice Gregory and Toni for their generous support.

My deepest thanks to my wife, Renee, and our daughters, Carrin, Lauren, Nicole, and Maya, for their editorial assistance, love, and support. I thank them for their patience and grace as I burdened them with questions about this book, especially during family vacation time.

Ground Crew

INTRODUCTION

On January 9, 1961, civil rights pioneers Hamilton Holmes and Charlayne Hunter broke the 175-year-old color line at Georgia's flagship university, the University of Georgia, after Judge William Augustus Bootle ordered their admission to the state's most cherished all-white institution (*Holmes v. Danner*). Holmes and Hunter were the first black students to enter a white public school, college, or university in the state, a watershed moment that represented a major turning point in Georgia history. Judge Elbert Tuttle of the Fifth Circuit Court of Appeals, as well as the U.S. Supreme Court, ultimately affirmed Bootle's decree, and the two brilliant and courageous students rightly became icons of the civil rights movement.[1]

Holmes and Hunter's epic battle was won by the nation's most elite civil rights lawyers—Thurgood Marshall, Robert Carter, Constance Baker Motley, Jack Greenberg, and emerging civil rights barrister Donald L. Hollowell.[2] Heightening the historic significance and drama of the groundbreaking legal case were the contributions of local attorneys Horace T. Ward and Vernon E. Jordan Jr., whom Hollowell involved in the case. Ward had lost his own protracted legal fight (*Ward v. Regents*) to enter the University of Georgia School of Law in 1957, after law school dean J. Alton Hosch declared that Ward "didn't show the type of mind . . . to successfully pursue the study of law."[3] Despite Hosch's condescending contention, Ward subsequently earned his law degree at the prestigious Northwestern University School of Law. In an epic moment of poetic justice, during Holmes and Hunter's trial Hollowell directed University of Georgia president O. C. Aderhold to reveal to the court that the man Hosch had described as lacking the mind to be a lawyer had not only graduated from Northwestern University law school and passed the bar but was now seated at the lawyer's table as counsel to Holmes and Hunter.[4]

Vernon Jordan helped the Hollowell legal team examine the admissions records of white students and found a document demonstrating a significant discrepancy in the treatment of Hunter's application and that of Bebe Brumby. Brumby was the daughter of Otis A. Brumby, a former prominent member of the General Assembly and also a relative of U.S. senator Richard Russell.[5] Both Hunter and Brumby were transfer applicants interested in journalism. Brumby was courted for entrance and admitted to the university, in contrast to the categorical rejection of Hunter's and Holmes's applications, purportedly due to "limited dormitory facilities."[6] However, Jordan discovered that Brumby had applied to the university *after* Holmes and Hunter submitted their applications. This finding provided incontrovertible evidence supporting Holmes's and Hunter's claims of discrimination and figured prominently in Bootle's triumphant ruling in favor of Holmes and Hunter and the cause of desegregation.[7]

The struggle to desegregate the University of Georgia that culminated in 1961 was covered by America's most prestigious print and broadcast media outlets and has been chronicled in scholarly and trade publications as well as documentary films.[8] Yet two years earlier, in *Hunt v. Arnold*, Barbara Hunt, Myra Dinsmore, and Iris Mae Welch won a groundbreaking federal injunction against the all-white Georgia State College of Business Administration (now Georgia State University) in downtown Atlanta. In contrast to the widespread coverage of the University of Georgia case, the plaintiffs in *Hunt v. Arnold*, along with local activists involved in the case and the court victory itself, have been virtually ignored in civil rights history. Although the three "hidden figures" and their local comrades who won the first NAACP victory against segregated education in Georgia helped to establish important legal precedents that figured prominently in the subsequent *Holmes* case, *Holmes* has largely overshadowed the *Hunt* triumph.

In a number of scholarly histories chronicling the struggle for racial equality in Georgia, the *Hunt* case has been omitted entirely; in those instances where it is examined, the narrative is by and large a mere footnote. This book sheds light on the Georgia State applicants' arduous struggle and tremendous sacrifices, which established vital groundwork for the

Holmes case—the breakthrough that led to the removal of state-sanctioned legal barriers to desegregation in higher education. Not only did the legal precedents established in the *Hunt* case figure prominently in the *Holmes* decision, but one year later, in *Meredith v. Fair*, the U.S. Fifth Circuit Court of Appeals cited the *Hunt* ruling in upholding the injunction against racial discrimination at the University of Mississippi. The historic *Meredith v. Fair* ruling led to the admission of James Meredith to the University of Mississippi in 1962.[9]

Notably, the Fifth Circuit specifically declared that to the extent that the University of Mississippi relied on the requirement of alumni certifications and recommendations from white alumni, which were ruled unconstitutional in the *Hunt* case, "Meredith was discriminated against in violation of the equal protection clause of the Fourteenth Amendment and was unlawfully denied admission."[10] The court went on to declare that the University of Mississippi's "continued insistence" on the requirement of white alumni recommendations represented "demonstrable evidence of a State and University policy of segregation that was applied to Meredith."[11]

Meredith made his original inquiry to seek admission just two weeks after Bootle's federal court order to enroll Holmes and Hunter, a court order that also cited the *Hunt* decision.[12] Constance Baker Motley, who played a key role in laying the groundwork that led to the *Hunt* and *Holmes* legal triumphs, was Meredith's chief counsel. Motley recounts that Meredith was emboldened by the actions of Holmes and Hunter.[13]

Ground Crew illustrates how the Georgia State case fit into the NAACP's grand strategy to defeat segregation in higher education. It discusses a number of cases that preceded *Hunt*, including several U.S. Supreme Court victories the NAACP won against segregated colleges and universities in states outside the Deep South. Despite these triumphs, as the narrative relates, white supremacists in Georgia blatantly ignored the court's rulings, and many of Georgia's high-profile politicians led a campaign to sustain segregation in Georgia and across the South.

The narrative also traces how NAACP Legal Defense and Educational Fund (NAACP LDF) lawyers worked with local attorneys to chip away at segregation plaintiff by plaintiff, case by case, and state by state.[14] Motley, for example, in addition to representing plaintiffs and working with local counsel in the *Ward*, *Hunt*, and *Holmes* cases in Georgia and the *Meredith* case in Mississippi, also served as counsel for Autherine Lucy in her epic battle to enter the University of Alabama, shortly before the black applicants initially sought admission to Georgia State.

The book also relates how many of the same key activists and local lawyers who achieved victory in the *Holmes* case participated in the *Hunt* case and the earlier *Ward* case. Importantly, it illustrates the trajectory of the NAACP's collaboration with local black lawyers and activists, from filing its first lawsuit against segregated education in Georgia in the *Ward* case to establishing significant legal groundwork in the *Hunt* victory, to winning the *Holmes* case, which resulted in the admission of Holmes and Hunter to the University of Georgia.

The narrative elucidates the close ties between local black lawyers and NAACP LDF attorneys and explores the details of their strategies to desegregate higher education in Georgia. The story of race relations and legal segregation in modern America led black attorneys to civil rights work,[15] and their collective efforts helped bring about sweeping social change. This book reveals that most of the handful of Atlanta's black lawyers in the 1950s had some involvement in civil rights litigation and illustrates how they worked together against racial injustice.

Though attorneys A. T. Walden and Donald Hollowell, both of whom were involved in the *Hunt* case, dedicated their practices largely to civil rights work in Atlanta and across the state, others within the small band of black attorneys also stepped up to take on civil rights cases. In her book *Courage to Dissent: Atlanta and the Long History of the Civil Rights Movement*, historian and legal scholar Tomiko Brown-Nagin notes that "by uncovering the rich history of civil rights lawyering at the local level and the world of practitioners like Walden," we can expand our understanding of how local civil rights lawyers "shaped the course of the long civil rights movement."[16] This book provides insight into the challenges faced by local lawyers advancing the cause of civil rights in the Georgia State case, including their encounters with racial discrimination by the bar itself.

Notably, local counsel E. E. Moore, who engaged in the general practice of law, emerged as lead counsel in the *Hunt* case. Archival records reveal that nearly all the black lawyers in Atlanta at the time worked on the litigation in its formative stages. The narrative also covers the small group of black attorneys who joined in solidarity with Hollowell and Walden to defend the NAACP against legal attacks by the state around the time of the *Hunt* case.[17] The state's actions to ban the venerable civil rights organization demonstrated the vehemence with which Georgia officials sought to thwart any challenge to Georgia's segregated way of life.

The book illuminates in particular the significant contributions of the trailblazing black female lawyer Constance Baker Motley, who worked closely with local lawyers on the *Hunt* case. Though Motley fit even more uneasily into the white-dominated legal system than her black male counterparts, she effectively represented Marshall and the LDF during the *Hunt* trial and provided an important role model and great source of inspiration to the black women plaintiffs.[18]

Brown-Nagin notes that narratives about the legendary Thurgood Marshall and the tactics and techniques of the NAACP LDF dominate much of the legal history of the civil rights movement.[19] However, a new generation of scholars has broadened its focus from chronicling the achievements of nationally renowned figures to illuminating the stories of lesser-known activists such as Hunt, Dinsmore, and Welch.[20] For example, in historian Emilye Crosby's edited volume *Civil Rights History from the Ground Up: Local Struggles, a National Movement*, Crosby discusses the importance of historians focusing on the movement's meaning for the local people who stepped up to "directly challenge institutional white supremacy."[21]

Hunt, Dinsmore, and Welch, and the grassroots activists who supported them, were significant albeit unsung activists who helped advance the black freedom struggle through their challenge to institutional racism at Georgia State. Historian and legal scholar Kenneth Mack observes that "grassroots protest and authenticity" remain the "strongest impulse in civil rights history," leading scholars to focus on the "organizing traditions of local southern black communities that developed their own organic forms of protest."[22] This book illuminates, in great detail, how local activists and lawyers developed organic forms of protest, banded together to resist oppression, and mounted a successful strategy to eliminate state-sanctioned obstructions to the admission of black students to a public college in Georgia in the late 1950s.

The narrative also illustrates the solidarity of largely autonomous black institutions and individuals, who did not depend on whites for their economic survival, in the fight that led to the first legal victory against segregated education in Georgia. The book brings to light the significance of black economic independence in mounting the challenge against Georgia State. Most of the applicants were employed by black businesses, and their jobs were therefore not in jeopardy due to their activism. Historian Maurice Hobson, in his book, *The Legend of the Black Mecca: Politics and Class in the Making of Modern Atlanta*, traces the history of black Atlantans building a strong foundation in business and education, which was crucial in undergirding the desegregation efforts of the Georgia State applicants.[23] Building on this narrative, *Ground Crew* specifically discusses how successful black businesses and black institutions of higher education in the "black mecca" provided encouragement and support to the applicants seeking to enter Georgia State. For example, the narrative examines the influence of community leaders such as prominent businessman Jesse Hill and Morehouse professor Samuel Williams, who were key advisers to the applicants and plaintiffs.

Chapter 1 introduces the six black students who bravely sought to enter the Georgia State College of Business Administration in March 1956. It discusses the institution's founding in 1913 as an evening division of the Georgia Institute of Technology and its evolution into an independent unit of the University System of Georgia. The chapter describes the racially charged environment in Georgia and the layers of white supremacy that buttressed Jim Crow policies. It focuses on how inflammatory political rhetoric and racial hysteria incited violent acts to deter blacks from seeking racial justice and explores white officials' support for black colleges as a strategy to thwart the desegregation movement.

The story that follows contextualizes the black struggle to end segregation at Georgia State within the framework of the NAACP's groundbreaking legal victories against segregation in education in southern and border states, including its U.S. Supreme Court wins. It examines how these triumphs enraged whites and describes how rebellious Georgia officials engaged in state action that openly defied federal court actions. The chapter also highlights the first legal challenge to segregation in higher education in Georgia, mounted by Horace T. Ward in 1950. It emphasizes how many of the civil rights lawyers, community leaders, and grassroots activists who supported Ward were able to apply lessons they had learned from his struggle to enter the University of Georgia to help secure rights for the Georgia State applicants. Conversely, the chapter also describes how state officials recycled ploys they had created to block Ward's admission to obstruct the Georgia State applicants.

In chapter 2, the narrative chronicles the renewed efforts of two of the original group of black students and three new black students seeking admission to Georgia State. The chapter focuses on the milieu of black Atlanta and describes its immersion in a culture of racial uplift and educational attainment. It discusses the evolution of Atlanta's successful black businesses and its center of black higher education. It explores the relationships between the black applicants to Georgia State, grassroots activists, key leaders of Atlanta's black businesses and educational institutions, and black attorneys. It underscores the advocacy of these civil rights activists and shows how they embraced and inspired the black applicants to persevere in their efforts to overcome the barriers mounted to block the admission of blacks to white institutions.

This chapter also explores white resistance and the absurd tactics of the regents, Georgia State officials, and high-profile public officials who sought to impede the admission of black students to so-called all-white educational institutions. It illustrates the importance of black economic independence in the struggle and highlights how most of the applicants depended on black enterprises for their employment. The chapter sheds light on how the alliance forged between the black applicants and key sectors of the local black community culminated in a federal lawsuit challenging racial discrimination at Georgia State. With the help of Thurgood Marshall, Robert Carter, and the NAACP LDF, local attorney E. E. Moore Jr. filed the lawsuit on September 28, 1956, on behalf of Barbara Hunt, Myra Dinsmore, Russell Roberts, and Iris Mae Welch.

Chapter 3 explores details of the legal complaint against Georgia State, which centered on the newly adopted alumni certification requirement, which gave white alumni the authority to certify or not certify black applicants. It reveals the intransigent response to the complaint by Georgia officials, including Attorney General Eugene Cook, who stood out as a leading public spokesman for white supremacy. Cook and other white leaders, ensconced in segregationist mores, railed against the NAACP and its campaign for racial equity. White leaders vilified the NAACP, labeling it a Communist-influenced organization and characterizing efforts to admit blacks to Georgia State as Communist inspired. Taking a cue from Georgia's white political leaders, the *Georgia State Signal*, Georgia State's student newspaper, penned editorials that espoused racist sentiments and featured inflammatory language. The *Signal* sought to exploit views expressed in Booker T. Washington's 1895 Cotton States and International Exposition address to justify its opposition to racial justice.

Notwithstanding the NAACP's brilliant record of working with local attorneys to successfully litigate cases against segregation, a careful analysis of this body of work reveals the overwhelming obstacles, setbacks, and even missteps in the journey to end segregation. For example, the narrative points out that the plaintiffs' lawyers failed to thoroughly vet plaintiff Russell Roberts, while the state's attorneys probed deeply into his private life. The state's investigation revealed serious concerns about Roberts's background. Because by this time the federal courts had ruled against obstructing black students due to race, such investigations had become a stratagem of civil rights opposition lawyers seeking to disqualify applicants on other grounds. Despite arguments by plaintiffs' attorneys that the information was irrelevant, the damaging evidence became a stumbling block for the plaintiffs' case. The chapter also discusses state officials' efforts, shortly before the *Hunt* trial, to enact legislation to harass or ban the NAACP outright.

Chapters 4 and 5 cover details of the *Hunt v. Arnold* trial, which took place December 8–12, 1958. The narrative provides a glimpse of some of the tense exchanges that transpired before a wide array of print media outlets and a crowded courtroom filled with Board of Regents' members, leading Georgia State officials, and prominent black leaders. The trial was replete with dramatic arguments and counterarguments, from a question about Atlanta NAACP president John Calhoun's alleged membership in the Communist Party to an assertion about defense attorney B. D. Murphy's membership in the Ku Klux Klan.

Chapter 4 shows how Moore, Hollowell, and Motley homed in on the authentic desire of Hunt, Dinsmore, and Welch to earn a college degree and attacked hastily developed Jim Crow policies such as the alumni certification requirement. The defendants' attorneys countered with a parade of regents and university officials who swore that such policies were nondiscriminatory, adopted in good faith to improve the quality of education. The discussion includes intimate details from the courtroom testimony that reveal the strategizing of Moore, Hollowell, and Motley to secure the rights of the plaintiffs, as well as the legal maneuvering of Cook and Murphy in their effort to sustain educational segregation in Georgia. The chapter further explores how the state delved into the plaintiffs' private lives, seeking to disqualify them on grounds of moral turpitude.

Chapter 5 tells the story of how the civil rights lawyers surmounted massive resistance to win the first case against segregated education in Georgia. It reviews Judge Boyd Sloan's decision, which not only declared segregation at Georgia State unconstitutional but also issued a broader injunction against racial discrimination in Georgia's public colleges and universities. The chapter explores how the groundwork laid by activists in the Georgia State case yielded important legal precedents and a major victory on the road to ending segregation in higher education in Georgia. It underscores the tremendous challenges the plaintiffs endured, and how in removing substantial obstacles from the path of future black applicants, the case set the stage for the historic *Holmes v. Danner* decision in January 1961.

The chapter also examines the limitations of Sloan's decision, in that none of the plaintiffs were able to enroll as a result of his ruling. In fact, despite the significant precedents established in *Hunt v. Arnold*, its importance is often overlooked, and some have viewed the case as unsuccessful because it did not lead to the immediate desegregation of Georgia State. Certainly this case study does not fit easily into the "top-down" historical view that focuses so heavily on nationally celebrated civil rights figures and major events. Nevertheless, the largely unremembered plaintiffs, local lawyers, and community leaders at the heart of this story shed light on the importance of grassroots activists coalescing with the larger civil rights movement to effect positive social change.[24] The chapter also reveals how the defense attorneys' intrusive examination of the plaintiffs' private lives affected Sloan's ruling.

Chapter 6 covers the immediate aftermath of the trial, including the pervasive white backlash and state leaders' circumvention of Sloan's order. Despite this intransigence from Georgia's governor and General Assembly, building on the triumph of *Hunt*, Atlanta's black leaders in collaboration with the NAACP LDF meticulously planned and mounted another fierce legal attack on segregated education that ultimately led to a U.S. Supreme Court victory less than two years later. Through another protracted struggle, this legal victory forced the desegregation of the University of Georgia and the admission of its first two black students. Finally, the chapter provides a window into the admission of the first black students to Georgia State University and a glimpse of the institution's emergence from a college with a bitter segregationist history to an institution with an enviable record of diversity in terms of its number and percentage of black students.

This book records an important chapter in the history of civil rights and higher education in Georgia. It outlines the story of unsung black applicants and plaintiffs and their impact on the desegregation of Georgia State University. The narrative explores the collaboration between local activists and lawyers and the NAACP LDF in the struggle to defeat Jim Crow. It also highlights how many of the same key activists and lawyers who championed the Georgia State case and the earlier *Ward* case continued their fight against segregated education and won the landmark victory that led to the desegregation of the University of Georgia.

Although the federal court injunction against state-sanctioned racial discrimination at Georgia State did not result in the immediate desegregation of Georgia State or other institutions of higher education, the narrative describes how the groundwork laid in the case dismantled some of the most significant barriers to racial justice at public colleges and universities in Georgia. At the same time, the narrative reflects how state officials viciously attacked the character of the black applicants, erected racist barriers, and even enacted new legislation to obstruct their admission to Georgia State University. Finally, this study provides the backdrop of the sacrifice and struggle of the applicants, local activists, and NAACP lawyers who challenged layers of white supremacy to win a precedent-setting case, forging a path for Georgia State University today to pride itself as a leader in diversity among research universities.

CHAPTER 1

Breaking the Color Line

The struggle that led to the *Hunt v. Arnold* (*Hunt*) case began in March 1956, when six black students, determined to obtain a college degree and weary of the exclusion of blacks from so-called white colleges and universities, sought to break the color barrier in Georgia's institutions of higher education. In a racially charged environment exacerbated by the 1954 *Brown v. Board of Education* decision and local and regional challenges aimed at ending segregation, Russell T. Roberts, Myra E. Dinsmore, Mae Thelma Boone, Edward Jacob Clemons, Rosalyn Virginia McGhee, and Charlie Mae Knight sought to gain entrance to the all-white Georgia State College of Business Administration (Georgia State) in Atlanta. These six were the first black students to apply for admission to the institution, which was founded in 1913 as the Evening School of Commerce of the Georgia Institute of Technology.[1]

Atlanta businessmen who desired a night school for their employees were the principal proponents who helped create the school. The institution was renamed the University System of Georgia Evening School in the early 1930s, and in 1947 became the Atlanta Division of the University of Georgia. On July 13, 1955, the Georgia regents "approved the separation of the Atlanta Division from the University of Georgia and designated it as an independent unit of the University System of Georgia." The institution was renamed the Georgia State College of Business Administration. In 1956, the year in which the first black applicants sought admission, the college enrolled approximately 5,600 students, 2,200 for daytime classes and 3,400 for evening courses.[2]

Despite Mayor William B. Hartsfield's characterization of Atlanta in 1955 as the "city too busy to hate," in response to the *Brown* decision and black advocacy for social justice, state and university leaders sought to preserve the centuries-old racial caste system and stiffened their resistance to racial equality in Georgia and its capital city.[3] Led by then-governor Marvin Griffin, one of the political leaders who formed the States' Rights Council of Georgia in 1955 to preserve segregation, Georgia officials vehemently opposed any efforts to alter segregation. On May 18, 1954, Griffin, then serving as lieutenant governor, reacted to the *Brown* decision in firebrand inflammatory style, adamantly declaring, "I will maintain segregation in the schools and the races will not be mixed, come hell or high water.... The meddlers, demagogues, race baiters and Communists in the United States are determined to destroy every vestige of states' rights."[4]

Griffin affirmed his ingrained position on segregation in his January 11, 1955, inaugural address, stating, "So long as Marvin Griffin is your governor there will be no mixing of the races in the classrooms of our schools and colleges of Georgia."[5] One year later, demonstrating the recalcitrance and solidarity of Georgia's public officials in opposition to federal desegregation mandates, Georgia's General Assembly enthusiastically applauded Griffin nine times in his State of the State message, affirming his declaration that Georgia "must never surrender" in the fight to safeguard its racial traditions.[6]

In a later gubernatorial campaign, before a "howling crowd" in Washington, Georgia, Griffin crudely instructed his audience on how to deal with civil rights protesters and "law violators" such as Martin Luther King Jr. Griffin advised, "There ain't but one thing to do and that is to cut you a black-jack sapling and brain them, and nip 'em in the bud to begin with."[7] Though Griffin claimed the threat was only a figure of speech and shouldn't be taken literally, he warned King to "get out of Georgia or stop leading Negro protests." He quipped, "If he is still here in January violating the law, I'll put him so far back in jail you'll have to pipe air to him."[8] Like many southern politicians of his time, Griffin drew on inflammatory political rhetoric and exploited racial hatred to rile whites against equal justice for blacks.

In some cases, this racist hysteria incited violent acts.[9] A savage example occurred during longtime governor Eugene Talmadge's bid for a fourth term. Talmadge, one of the South's most "notorious demagogues and race baiters," fiercely berated blacks in his campaigns.[10] In one of his stump speeches he observed, "I was raised among niggers and I understand them.... I want to see them treated fairly and I want to see them have justice in the courts. But I want to deal with the nigger this way: He must come to my back door, take off his hat, and say, 'Yessir.'"[11] Though Talmadge made a point of noting that "he had never joined the Ku Klux Klan," he nevertheless "bragged of beating and flogging the black people who worked on his farm in south Georgia."[12]

On July 25, 1946, nine days after Talmadge's Democratic primary victory following a racially polarizing campaign, a mob of white men lynched four black young people, George Dorsey, Dorothy Dorsey Malcom, Mae Murray Dorsey, and Roger Malcom, on the Moore's Ford Bridge in Walton County, Georgia.[13] Though there is no record of a direct link between Talmadge and the lynching, Talmadge's overtly racist campaign unquestionably exacerbated racial tensions, and he had delivered a racially polarizing stump speech on Monroe's courthouse square in Walton County less than a month before the lynching.[14]

Seeking to distance their town from the gruesome murders, some of the well-to-do white citizens of Monroe blamed the lynching on "Talmadge's supporters . . . the rabble rousers, the low class folks."[15] As one white businessman noted, "I hold Eugene Talmadge guilty of murder. . . . You can't sow the seeds of racial hatred without bearing a crop."[16] Nonetheless, in keeping with the widespread immunity granted to lynch mobs despite their savagery, "no charges were ever brought against any of the twenty men rumored to have participated in the lynching," and Talmadge was subsequently elected to his fourth term as governor.[17]

Hard-line as well as more-progressive white political leaders espoused racial hatred in their campaigns, setting a menacing tone that undermined any advances toward racial equality. Mirroring his father's racial politics, Herman Talmadge, who immediately preceded Griffin as governor, "openly sought support from the Ku Klux Klan."[18] Even Ellis Arnall, who served as Georgia's governor from 1943 to 1947 and was relatively moderate compared to Talmadge, was not opposed to employing violent and reprehensible political rhetoric toward blacks.[19] On August 9, 1942, in a stump speech, Arnall warned, "If a Negro tried to enter a white school down his way [Newnan], the Negro would not live to see the sun set and there would be no need to call out the militia."[20] Similarly, with regard to blacks entering white institutions of higher education, Arnall quipped, "Any nigger who tried to enter the [University of Georgia] would not be in existence [the] next day."[21]

In December 1955 and January 1956, only months before the six students tried to enroll at Georgia State, Georgia's intolerance for desegregating its schools and colleges was dramatized in Governor Griffin's efforts to prevent Georgia Tech from playing the University of Pittsburgh in the Sugar Bowl. Griffin opposed Georgia Tech's participation because Bobby Grier, a black fullback, was a student-athlete on the Pittsburgh team.[22] Griffin's reaction to a single black student on a team competing with one of Georgia's all-white colleges left no doubt about the pervasive wall of segregation facing black students who attempted to enroll at Georgia State. Griffin stressed that he could not publicly support accepting the bowl bid due to the presence of a black player on the team, although he had privately given his approval to Georgia Tech's coach Bobby Dodd.[23] However, Griffin quickly reversed even his private approval in response to public controversy after representatives of the States' Rights Council, of which Griffin was a member, denounced Georgia Tech playing in the bowl game.[24]

Rabid segregationist Roy V. Harris, who served as president of the States' Rights Council as well as the (white) Citizens' Councils of America, argued that the state's racial mores and customs should be preserved no matter the cost. Harris, a longtime Georgia legislator representing Augusta, was first elected to the Georgia House of Representatives in 1921. He served more than twenty years, including tenure as Speaker of the House. Harris propagated his scathing opposition to racial equality by excoriating blacks and riling whites in his personal newspaper, the *Augusta Courier*.[25]

Drawing a line in the sand and threatening cataclysmic disaster if the federal courts forced desegregation, the belligerent Harris wrote in an editorial:

> There is another thing the negroes ought to consider, if they have any sense at all. When the time comes for the white and negro children to attend the same schools there is [*sic*] going to be a lot of people killed in this state. If that day ever comes we will have bloodshed, race riots, a race war and the most terrible time this state has ever known.
>
> The negroes cannot hope to gain anything by this thing happening. The negroes will be the losers in the long run. If this ever happens there are going to be a lot of negroes hurt and hurt bad in Georgia.[26]

Harris cautioned that "blacks were trying to undermine segregation in the state by attacking it in the areas of entertainment and sports."[27]

Once the matter of Georgia Tech's bowl bid became public and threatened Griffin's position as Georgia's most outspoken high-ranking state official espousing segregation, he reverted to the demagoguery of his gubernatorial campaign, vowing to sustain segregation. "Warning in apocalyptic terms of impending doom" to cherished southern traditions if Georgia Tech played in the game, Griffin proclaimed, "We cannot make the slightest concession to the enemy in this dark and lamentable hour of struggle. There is no more difference in compromising the integrity of race on the playing field than in doing so in the classroom. One break in the dike and the relentless seas will rush in and destroy us."[28] Griffin's declaration inflamed controversy among Georgia Tech students, faculty, and administrators, as well as media outlets and the state's diehard segregationists.

On December 2, 1955, the controversy reached a fever pitch when approximately two thousand unruly Georgia Tech students, asserting their right to accept the Sugar Bowl bid, burned an effigy of Griffin, then marched to the capitol and hung another effigy of the governor.[29] Not surprisingly, in the 1950s environment of racial prejudice and bigotry, the outcry centered not on discrimination against the black student-athlete but rather on the governor's meddling in internal matters of the university and prohibiting the college from competing in the prized bowl game. In fact, George Harris, president of the student government, pointedly informed the press that Georgia Tech students were "not against segregation but against political forces which are trying to prevent [them] from going to the Sugar Bowl."[30]

After considerable political haggling by Georgia's most powerful segregationist leaders, the Georgia Board of Regents met and approved Georgia Tech's participation in the Sugar Bowl. However, to ensure that their actions were not mistaken for a retreat from racial segregation, the regents declared that "Georgia teams would participate in no integrated contests upon Georgia soil, nor in any contests where segregation was not maintained in the stands."[31] Despite this fairly minor concession, Griffin remained undaunted in his racial demagoguery and continued to spearhead unequivocal resistance to desegregation throughout his tenure as governor.[32]

Oddly enough, it should be noted that Griffin and his brother Cheney Griffin enjoyed a personal relationship with the fearless civil rights leader Hosea Williams and even helped put him through college. The Griffins began their personal relationship with Williams when he was elected president of the black American Legion post in the Griffins' hometown at the same time Cheney Griffin served as president of the white post.[33] Similarly, and paradoxically, Roy Harris, who openly endorsed violence against blacks in his personal newspaper, maintained congenial relationships with some blacks in his hometown of Augusta, Georgia. Harris, a successful attorney, represented a number of black clients, including the prominent black-owned Pilgrim Life Insurance Company.[34]

Roy McCracken, Harris's former law partner, recalled, "I think black people knew him as a man of power; they respected him and they knew that if he served as their attorney he could get results."[35] Ed McIntyre, Augusta's first black mayor, pointed out that Harris "may not have been the true segregationist he portrayed," explaining, "Georgia politics in the early days was based on race and I think if you were going to get elected, the politicians who could holler 'nigger' the loudest and vowed to keep down black folks in this state were the persons who would maintain their political positions."[36] The personal relationships some racist political leaders established with blacks do not lessen the politicians' deleterious impact in obstructing racial justice, but they do reveal the complexities of white racism and the nuances of black life in the Jim Crow era.

The outspoken Griffin championed the "massive resistance" movement, which sought "to restore and protect time-honored traditions." The movement emerged in response to a series of U.S. Supreme Court decisions that culminated in the 1954 *Brown v. Board of Education* ruling, which "struck directly at the institutionalized framework of the southern social system."[37] The NAACP, led by Charles Hamilton Houston, won a number of lower federal court and U.S. Supreme Court cases preceding the *Brown* ruling in southern and border states.[38] Houston was a Harvard Law School graduate, the first black elected editor of the *Harvard Law Review*, and a former dean of Howard University School of Law. He was also the first full-time lawyer to head the NAACP's legal department and the visionary chief architect of the NAACP's legal program to defeat Jim Crow.

Thurgood Marshall, Houston's star pupil from Howard University law school, joined him in the NAACP's battle for equal justice. Notably, between the late 1930s and early 1950s, the NAACP in collaboration with local civil rights lawyers and activists won landmark cases across the South, including major voting rights cases such as *Smith v. Allwright* in Texas and *King v. Chapman* in Georgia, which declared the all-white primary unconstitutional.[39] Darlene Clark Hine observes that "black southerners" and the NAACP demonstrated "unwavering commitment to fight every infringement on their right to vote."[40] In 1944, following a long, hard struggle, with the help of local activists, the NAACP won a unanimous U.S. Supreme Court decision that nullified "the claims of the Democratic Party to be a private organization open only to white members."[41]

Leading up to the Georgia State case, the NAACP also won a string of U.S. Supreme Court cases in higher education, including *Gaines v. Canada*, *Sipuel v. Board of Regents of the University of Oklahoma*, *McLaurin v. Oklahoma*, and *Sweatt v. Painter*. The rulings in these cases affirmed, in the states of Missouri, Oklahoma, and Texas, the constitutional rights of blacks as guaranteed by the Fourteenth Amendment.[42]

In the *Gaines* case, Missouri resident Lloyd Gaines, a black applicant, sought to enter the University of Missouri to study law in 1936. Intent on sustaining racial segregation in its institutions, Missouri officials denied Gaines admission solely on the basis of his race. The state subsequently offered Gaines a scholarship to attend a law school outside the state, which he refused. With the help of Houston and Marshall and in collaboration with Sidney Redmond and Henry Espy, leaders in the St. Louis Branch of the NAACP, Gaines filed a lawsuit.[43]

Houston and his co-counsels triumphed in the case. In 1938, in the first U.S. Supreme Court ruling regarding race, higher education, and equal justice, the court ruled that the State of Missouri could not evade its Fourteenth Amendment obligation by sending its black students out of state.[44] Though Gaines exemplified courage and grit in the protracted litigation and the ruling established a significant judicial precedent against segregated education, inexplicably, after winning the suit Gaines vanished, and his disappearance remains shrouded in mystery.

Unmoved by the NAACP's Supreme Court victory in the *Gaines* case, Oklahoma officials denied Oklahoma resident Ada Lois Sipuel admission to the Oklahoma School of Law based on her race. Thurgood Marshall, aided by Oklahoma lawyers Amos T. Hall and Roscoe Dungee, prevailed in a lawsuit that declared Oklahoma was constitutionally obligated to provide her with an equal education. However, forced to admit her, officials "roped off a space in the state capitol building to serve as her law school."[45]

Oklahoma resident G. W. McLaurin, who sought to enter the University of Oklahoma Graduate School of Education, and Texas resident Heman Marion Sweatt, who applied for admission to the University of Texas, met a similar fate. After a legal fight, Oklahoma officials admitted McLaurin but restricted him "to sit in an alcove in the back of the classroom and at a separate table in the library and cafeteria."[46] Taking a cue from Oklahoma officials, the University of Texas opened a law school for blacks in the basement of a building in downtown Austin.[47] Local counsel W. J. Durham, who was active in the Dallas branch of the NAACP, worked with Marshall and NAACP LDF attorney James M. Nabrit Jr. to mount a legal challenge against such disparate treatment that eventually found its way to the U.S. Supreme Court.[48]

On June 5, 1950, the NAACP won two precedent-setting U.S. Supreme Court victories against racial discrimination in higher education. The court found that the basement law school provided for Heman Sweatt was in no way equal to the facilities available at the University of Texas and for the first time "ordered the admission of a black student to an all-white educational institution."[49] On the same day, the court declared that the "separate dining facilities, bathrooms, classrooms, and housing facilities on the University of Oklahoma campus were unconstitutional."[50] White reaction to the NAACP's vigorous campaign for human justice and its Supreme Court victories was swift, defiant, and at times laced with calls for mob action. Senator Theodore G. Bilbo of Mississippi, for example, "advocated for mob violence against Negroes who dared to vote." Mississippi governor Fielding Wright pronounced, "We shall insist on segregation regardless of the consequences."[51]

In a similar vein, in a speech delivered to the South Carolina Legislature in response to the *Smith v. Allwright* voting rights decision, Governor Olin D. Johnston recommended widespread legislative action and other measures to circumvent the court's decision. He declared: "We will have done everything within our power to guarantee white supremacy in our primaries and in our State in so far as legislation is concerned. Should this prove inadequate, we South Carolinians will use the necessary methods to retain white supremacy in our primaries and to safeguard the homes and happiness of our people. White supremacy will be maintained in our primaries. Let the chips fall where they may!"[52]

Ominously, less than a month before the six black applicants sought to enter Georgia State, Georgia legislator and States' Rights Council cofounder Roy Harris, also a member of the University System's Board of Regents, reaffirmed the views of the state and the regents on segregation. This influential regent, who spearheaded the state's efforts to sustain segregation and incite whites to fight "outside agitators" who threatened Georgia's cherished traditions, made it abundantly clear that any attempt to overturn segregation would be met with harsh resistance. Harris likened the NAACP's efforts to achieve equal justice to the actions of the carpetbaggers, a derogatory term for northern opportunists who moved south after the Civil War to profit from Reconstruction.[53]

In February 1956, speaking at a dedication ceremony for two new campus buildings at Savannah State College, a black college under the regents' control, Harris vowed again that there would be racial hostility and violence if the federal courts ordered desegregation in the South.[54] The *Atlanta Journal*, the *Savannah Evening Press*, and the black-owned *Savannah Tribune* covered the dedication ceremony. The *Savannah Evening Press* printed Harris's speech in its entirety. As quoted in an article dated February 19, 1956, the powerful regent and leader of state and regional white supremacist organizations warned the audience: "Ninety years ago there came into the South from the Northern and Midwestern states a group of adventuresome people whom we have come to know as carpetbaggers. They came for the sole purpose of enriching themselves and taking advantage of the members of your race. . . . The old-time carpetbaggers used the members of your race. They used them as the sacrificial goats in order to secure their election to office and the stealing of what little business and industry which was left in the South."[55]

Blaming blacks for the racial strife in the South, Harris declared that as a result of Negroes being duped by the carpetbaggers, "ill feeling developed" between blacks and whites. He continued:

> Bitterness, strife, and the spilling of blood resulted. . . . Finally we, by mutual consent, evolved a pattern of life in the South, whereby the two races could live together in peace and harmony and are building a state in which we can live and prosper. . . .
>
> After we have pulled ourselves up by our bootstraps and after all of the hardships we have endured, there comes into our areas a new group [the NAACP]. . . . They come seeking to divide the people of the South again. They come seeking to destroy the friendly relations which we have tediously built up over the years. They come seeking to enlist your aid in the enforced integration of the races. They come seeking your aid to return to the old days of bitterness, strife, and bloodshed. For as surely as the sun rises and sets, if the power of the federal courts is ever used to enforce the integration of the races in the South, there will be a long period of bitterness, hatred, and bloodshed. . . .
>
> The way of the modern-day carpetbagger leads to bitterness, to hate, to strife, to turmoil and bloodshed. . . . So I submit to you that the way of life that has brought to us peace, understanding, progress, prosperity, and happiness and which holds so many promises for the future is worthy of continuing."[56]

In closing his no-holds-barred address, Harris prophesied, "The white people of this state will not voluntarily surrender that [segregated] way of life. They will fight for its continuance and its preservation."[57]

Harris's references to the peace, understanding, and even happiness of blacks in the context of a segregated way of life that relegated them to second-class citizenship, while patently absurd, were nevertheless common among white southerners, who blamed black aspirations for equal justice on "outside agitators." Harris condemned the NAACP for its interference and efforts to destroy the "understanding and happiness" he erroneously attributed to relationships between blacks and whites. Preposterously, Harris claimed that by mutual consent blacks and whites had evolved a pattern of life in the South characterized by peace and harmony, with prospects of prosperity for both races. In reality, blacks in the South were far from equal partners in the pattern of life that emerged following Reconstruction. Whites unilaterally established black codes that undergirded a racially oppressive society reminiscent of slavery. The Ku Klux Klan and other hate groups terrorized violators, who risked being cruelly punished or even lynched for any breaches of these codes.[58]

The two new buildings at Savannah State College represented important expenditures in its mission to educate blacks. The Board of Regents' funding, however, was not solely a gesture to help the black college. As historian Joy Ann Williamson observes in her work *Radicalizing the Ebony Tower*, Mississippi governor James L. Alcorn and other white officials recognized the need to support the education of blacks dating back to the establishment of Alcorn University, the first black land-grant institution, in 1871.[59] However, Williamson notes further that "their motives . . . were not purely altruistic since they also wanted to stall the growing movement to integrate the University of Mississippi."[60]

In a 1955 *Journal of Negro Education* article, Atlanta University professor R. O. Johnson points out that "it was not until it became clear that segregation itself was in imminent danger of being destroyed by decisions of the Supreme Court" that Georgia "ever made any effort to provide equality of educational opportunities between whites and Negroes."[61] In light of the mounting legal victories against segregated education, white officials increased support for black educational institutions to try to halt the movement to desegregate.[62] However, even with this additional money, funding allocated to black colleges represented a pittance in comparison to expenditures for white colleges and universities. James D. Anderson has documented the historic underfunding and poor conditions of black colleges in his definitive work *The Education of Blacks in the South, 1860–1935*. Observing that "the material and financial status of black higher education was bad," Anderson describes black colleges as "understaffed, meagerly equipped, and poorly financed."[63]

Similarly, scholars Marybeth Gasman and Christopher Tudico note that public black colleges "received less funding than their white counterparts and thus had inferior facilities."[64] Such observations were reflected vividly in the disparities at Georgia's three public historically black colleges—Albany State College, Fort Valley State College, and Savannah State College. The Board of Regents' funding for these colleges was minuscule compared to its support for all-white institutions, and the black colleges' facilities were grossly inferior as a result. In 1938, according to a state-sponsored study, of the university system's budget, which exceeded $1.5 million, only $65,500 was allocated for the three black colleges.[65] By 1953-54, the state appropriation to the university system for higher education was more than $11 million; however, the system continued to disproportionately allocate funds for the education of blacks. Georgia spent less than 10 percent of the $11 million appropriation on its three black colleges.[66] Moreover, although blacks constituted more than one-third of the state's population, Georgia Board of Regents' policies, buttressed by state laws, restricted attendance at sixteen of the state's institutions of higher learning to "white students" only.[67] The regents limited black students aspiring to higher education to attending the state's underfunded black colleges. Additionally, graduate and professional opportunities for blacks were virtually nonexistent throughout the South.[68] Nonetheless, Harris, in his speech, magnanimously extolled the virtues of these gross disparities as evolving by "mutual consent."

Westley Wallace Law, president of the Georgia Conference of NAACP branches and an unbridled crusader for civil rights in Savannah and across the state, strongly urged blacks to boycott Harris's speech. Law charged that Harris was a "foe of racial integration and human rights" who espoused "schemes for forestalling integration in the public schools and was the prime mover in the formation of the States' Rights Council."[69] In calling for the boycott, Law contended that Harris's appearance represented "an affront to the hopes and aspirations of the Negro people."[70]

Responding to Law's call for protests, Savannah State College president William K. Payne doubled down and renewed his invitation to Harris to speak at the dedication, while issuing a statement that the NAACP did not speak for him or the institution.[71] It is not known whether Payne invited Harris because Payne himself subscribed to segregation and second-class citizenship for blacks, or whether he simply buckled under to pressure from the regents, who controlled the purse strings at Savannah State and had provided funding for the two new buildings. Nevertheless, despite the controversy, an *Atlanta Journal* article covering the speech reported that there was no demonstration whatsoever among "a standing room only audience of about 900" attendees.[72] Similarly, the *Savannah Tribune* observed that although there was considerable speculation in the community about how Harris would be received, "no untoward incidents occurred and [Harris] was applauded at the conclusion of his address" by the "over capacity crowd."[73]

In reporting on Harris's speech, the *Savannah Tribune* emphatically took issue with many of his specious and inflammatory remarks, observing that "hatred, bitterness, strife, and bloodshed" would occur only "if it is initiated and carried out by white people at the suggestion and encouragement or predictions of demagogues."[74] Moreover, the paper reported that Payne, displaying utter disregard for the views of students and faculty, openly discouraged dissent. The paper also provided a rationale for the large crowd, reporting that students and faculty were forced to attend the dedication and prohibited from protesting.

In a reprehensible example of suppression at a public college, Payne and other college officials warned that if students did not attend the ceremony they would be given two demerits.[75] The *Tribune* reported that this was a severe penalty. To monitor students' presence, "each student was given a yellow slip of paper with his name on it, which was to be placed in a box near the stage at the conclusion of the program."[76]

Sadly, black college officials' suppression of student demands for civil rights was not uncommon. For example, in 1961 William Dennis, the president of Albany State College, expelled Albany State students for participating in the Albany civil rights movement.[77] Dennis was likely forced into this action by the regents, as undoubtedly resistance to regents' pressure would have cost him his presidency. Joy Ann Williamson provides context for the actions of Presidents Payne and Dennis. According to Williamson, state officials and their allies demanded that black colleges "distance themselves from the black freedom struggle and promised to mete out harsh penalties if they did not."[78]

To discourage activism, campus officials banned civil rights organizations and sought to purge activists from campuses, in some cases denying students financial aid or suspending or expelling them. College officials who supported civil rights efforts or refused to punish student activists faced termination, and governing boards threatened to withhold funding.[79] Williamson explains that some college presidents justified their role in obstructing the movement on campuses as "a necessary compromise that secured the future of black higher education."[80]

Anderson notes the concerns of black intellectuals such as W. E. B. Du Bois and Carter G. Woodson that black college officials and students "had forsaken their obligation to become socially responsible leaders of their people."[81] Anderson relates Woodson's argument that the "miseducation" of black students had resulted in the creation of a "highly educated bourgeois that was estranged from ordinary black people." Likewise, writer and poet Langston Hughes denounced the "cowards from colleges" and the "meek professors and well-paid presidents" who acquiesced to racism and the oppression of black people.[82]

Although the actions of black college administrators and students in some cases reflected a rejection of the black freedom struggle, scholars have underscored that the responses of black college officials and students to white pressure to distance themselves from the black freedom struggle varied widely. For example, although a large number Savannah State students acquiesced to President Payne's demand not to protest against Roy Harris, many Albany State students embraced and participated in the Albany movement, despite President Dennis's extreme efforts to thwart their involvement.[83] In contrast to the actions of Payne and Dennis, when North Carolina A&T students initiated their historic sit-ins, "their college president refused to curtail student actions despite pressure from state officials."[84] Similarly, Morehouse president Benjamin Mays created a campus environment that denounced segregation and fostered a spirit of activism among students and faculty. Mays openly and fervently supported legal challenges to segregation and even admonished students for patronizing segregated establishments.[85]

Dating back to the late 1930s, a number of students and some officials from predominantly black schools, including Mays, championed the black freedom struggle through their involvement with the Southern Negro Youth Congress (SNYC). Founded in 1937, the SNYC encouraged young blacks to take a militant stance against racial oppression, extralegal violence, and black disenfranchisement.[86] Although scholars have paid little attention to the SNYC, it was a major civil and human rights organization supported by such luminaries as W. E. B. Du Bois, Paul Robeson, Esther Cooper Jackson, Adam Clayton Powell Jr., and Eleanor Roosevelt. On October 20, 1946, speaking to an audience of more than eight hundred "militant young southerners" at an SNYC conference in Columbia, South Carolina, Du Bois urged the youth to fight for democracy and resist Jim Crow.[87]

Although some white students supported the SNYC, the organization's membership was primarily composed of black students from public and private historically black colleges and universities concerned about ending the poll tax and overcoming racial oppression, including lynching and mob violence. The SNYC's influence on civil rights attorney Donald Hollowell, one of the local counsels to the Georgia State students, is but one example of its significant impact on the black freedom struggle. As a student at Lane College in Jackson, Tennessee, Hollowell was elected president of the student council, which allowed him to attend an SNYC conference on the campus of predominantly black Allen University in 1946. He credits his exposure to Du Bois, Robeson, and other black activists at the conference as a key factor in his decision to pursue the profession of law and use it as his weapon of choice in the struggle for social justice.[88]

Hollowell recalled being especially inspired to join in the fight against racial injustice by the words and songs of Paul Robeson, who delivered a keynote address and sang at the conference. Hollowell remembered: "He was a big man. A big dark-brown-skinned, heavy-voiced, beautiful-voiced man who loved what he did. Who was smart—when at Rutgers was an honor roll man. He was smarter than the average man. Therefore, he saw no reason for himself to be subjugated because of his color. . . . When he sang 'Climbing Up,' it just made your soul feel the need, and your mind to understand that this is a man who believed that you have to work at eliminating those things that stand in your way."[89] Despite notable examples of black militancy on college campuses, however, all-white or predominantly white boards controlled black colleges and often selected black administrators "who would not encourage agitation against the racial hierarchy" but instead acquiesce to pressure from white authorities.[90]

Roy Wilkins, the NAACP executive director, felt no such pressure. After reading the *Atlanta Journal*'s account of Regent Harris's white supremacist speech, Wilkins sent a telegram to Board of Regents chair Robert O. Arnold the following day. Wilkins asked the Board of Regents "to make possible the appearance of an authorized spokesman for the NAACP to address the student body of an institution in the university system, preferably the University of Georgia." He stated, "We think you will agree that the college men and women of Georgia should have the right to hear both sides of this question. Just relations between the races can be realized only after sober conclusions are reached following free and open debate."[91] No record could be found of a response to Wilkins from Arnold. It is safe to conclude, however, that an "NAACP spokesman" would have been unwelcome by the regents even at the state's black colleges, let alone at the University of Georgia.

In 1955, less than a year before the black applicants challenged segregation at Georgia State, federal district court judge J. Harlan Grooms issued a declaratory judgment and injunction against defendant William Adams, dean of admissions of the University of Alabama, for denying admission to Autherine Lucy and similarly situated black applicants "on account of their race and color."[92] NAACP lawyer Constance Baker Motley argued the case before the Supreme Court. Though the University of Alabama did not have a written policy barring blacks from admission, the court ruled, "There is a tacit policy to that effect. Defendant Adams has pursued such policy in denying applications for admission."[93] Grooms prohibited Adams and other Alabama officials from denying Lucy and "others similarly situated the right to enroll in the University of Alabama and pursue courses of study thereat, solely on account of their race and color."[94]

The NAACP victory in Alabama further aroused the leading "defenders of white supremacy," who mounted executive, legislative, and judicial efforts to sustain the subordination of blacks. In addition to these actions, some of these defenders continued to advocate or incite violence.[95] Civil rights opponents sought "to mobilize white southerners to block all federal efforts to implement the *Brown v. Board of Education* ruling" and its precedents.[96]

A key stratagem of the massive resistance to racially mixed schools was to prevent desegregation by closing publicly funded schools and shifting to some form of private schools.[97] In particular, "Georgia was a leader in the regional effort to prevent enforcement of the *Brown* decision."[98] On February 6, 1956, Griffin, intensifying his obstruction of racial justice, presented an interposition resolution to a joint session of the general assembly that sought to deny the Supreme Court the authority to enforce constitutional rights guaranteed to blacks. The defiant resolution stated that the Supreme Court had no authority to declare segregated public schools unconstitutional, expressly calling for Georgia to interpose "her sovereign power between the Court and her public schools" and to declare the Supreme Court decisions to abolish segregation "null, void and of no effect."[99]

The Georgia Commission on Education, which was created by the

Georgia Senate and House of Representatives to "recommend courses of action for consideration by the General Assembly" and more specifically to preserve "separate education of the white and colored races," published Governor Griffin's interposition resolution.[100] Griffin rebelliously contended "that the State of Georgia in ratifying the Fourteenth Amendment to the Constitution, did not agree, nor did the other states ratifying the Fourteenth Amendment agree, that the power to operate racially separate public schools and other facilities was to be prohibited."[101] The general assembly approved the resolution on March 9, 1956, less than two weeks before the six applicants attempted to enroll at Georgia State. Segregationists banded together to forestall indefinitely the admission of blacks to white schools.

The context in which the six applicants sought to enter the all-white college included not only the intractable determination of Georgia state and local officials to ignore Supreme Court decisions abolishing segregation but also an equally obstinate refusal among federally elected political leaders across the South to abide by such decisions. Led by Georgia U.S. senator Richard Russell, three days after the interposition resolution and about ten days before the black applicants sought admission to Georgia State, Georgia's congressional delegation unanimously endorsed the Southern Manifesto. The manifesto, signed by 101 U.S. senators and members of the House of Representatives, openly defied the 1954 *Brown v. Board of Education* decision and sought to thwart civil rights.[102] With the exceptions of Senate majority leader Lyndon B. Johnson and Tennessee moderates Albert Gore Sr. and Estes Kefauver, every other southern senator, including Georgia's Walter F. George and Russell, signed the document.[103]

When questioned about his commitment to Jim Crow, Senator Russell of Georgia, a die-hard segregationist, publically espoused his extreme racist views. "Any southern white man worth a pinch of salt would give his all to maintain white supremacy," he observed. "I am willing to go as far and make as great a sacrifice to preserve and insure [sic] white supremacy in the social, economic, and political life of our state as any man who lives within her borders."[104] In accordance with state and regional segregationist leaders, regents and university officials would use all lawful and even extralegal means to sustain segregation.

Civil rights leader Julian Bond described the racial environment in Atlanta in the late 1950s, about the time the six black students challenged segregated education at Georgia State:

Even though Atlanta was a modern segregated city, and the burden of segregation didn't fall as heavily on black people in Atlanta as it did, say, in rural Mississippi, nonetheless, the Atlanta I found in 1957 was a complete apartheid society. There were some chinks in that apartheid armor. The Atlanta University Center where I was a student at Morehouse had white teachers teaching black people, probably against the law in Georgia, and there were the occasional white exchange students at Spelman, Morris Brown, Clark, Morehouse, or Atlanta University . . . but in all public places—restaurants, lunch counters, movie theaters, every place in life—there was a rigid divide enforced by law between black and white.[105]

Civil rights activist Mary Frances Early, who grew up in Atlanta in the 1940s and 1950s, also recounted how the Jim Crow system oppressed blacks. Early recalled, "We were living in a city that [officials] said was too busy to hate, but that wasn't what I observed. And I was tired of the demeaning system of segregation. The system was designed to humiliate you, to subjugate you, and to make sure that any degree of largesse that would come from overall society, you would get less of it. We had to smile when we felt like crying."[106]

Likewise, in 1960 the *New York Times* observed that Atlanta was a city "where black college graduates often had to find work as postal clerks, where supermarkets would not hire black workers even in black neighborhoods, and where 'a Negro may not ride in a "white" taxi or eat in a downtown restaurant or see the touring company of "Sunrise at Campobello" except from a segregated seat.'"[107]

Though Hartsfield and some of Atlanta's key business leaders, such as Coca-Cola president Robert Woodruff, were considerably more forward thinking and moderate on racial issues than officials in rural Georgia or in other southern cities such as Birmingham, Atlanta too was entrenched in Jim Crow mores.[108] Even with Atlanta's reputation as the "mecca" of black-owned businesses and despite its progressive black middle class, its cadre of elite black institutions of higher learning, and its large number of black physicians, dentists, real estate brokers, and other professionals, Atlanta remained a thoroughly segregated city. Whitney M. Young Jr., founding dean of the Atlanta University School of Social Work and director of the National Urban League in the 1960s, noted that although the city bragged about its racial progress in comparison to Mississippi, "nothing was really integrated, not even the library or the buses, but the people were beginning to believe their own press clippings—even the Negroes."[109]

Despite Mayor Hartsfield's promotion of Atlanta as progressive on racial issues, state leaders, including Governor Griffin and Georgia's general assembly, were unwavering in their insistence on racial segregation. In the face of intransigent efforts to sustain racial oppression, blacks in Georgia were becoming increasingly frustrated with the inequities of Jim Crow. Their challenge to segregation in higher education began as early as 1950, when Horace T. Ward, a Morehouse College and Atlanta University honor graduate, sought admission to the University of Georgia School of Law. Ward became the first African American to sue for admission to an all-white college or university in Georgia.[110] Ward's quest to enter the law school was met with strong opposition from Griffin's predecessor, Herman Talmadge, who had been elected governor on a platform of maintaining segregation.

In addition to strongly contesting Ward in federal court, state officials, in a relentless effort to deter Ward, tried surreptitiously to doom his lawsuit. Benjamin Elijah Mays, president of Morehouse College, recalled that a "distinguished white man" came to his office to request that he advise Ward to withdraw his lawsuit. Mays said the man assured him that Atlanta University could secure funding "to build a law school for Negroes" as recompense for his help. Mays, a staunch civil rights advocate, told the man firmly that he could find "no honorable way" to "persuade Mr. Ward to withdraw."[111]

Herman Talmadge's views reflected those of his father, longtime governor Eugene Talmadge, who was unequivocal in his intolerance of any threat to end segregated schools. In 1941, for example, in an attempt to remove "foreign professors trying to destroy the sacred traditions of the South," Eugene Talmadge forced the Board of Regents to fire Walter Dewey Cocking, dean of the College of Education at the University of Georgia, for his alleged advocacy of "social equality" and "race-mixing."[112] Charging that Cocking supported educating black and white children together, Talmadge made good on his threat that "he would see to it that any person" in Georgia's colleges and universities who stood for "communism or racial equality" would be quickly dismissed.[113] He avowed, "I'm not going to put up with social equality in this state as long as I'm Governor.... They can't slip through no crack and they can't crop up in no funds coming into this state. We don't need no Negroes and white people taught together."[114]

With the younger Talmadge at the helm of state government replicating his father's racial intolerance and schemes to obstruct social equality, state and university officials erected numerous barriers to keep Ward out of the law school, including formulating new admissions requirements. However, with the help of Thurgood Marshall, the LDF, and Atlanta civil rights attorney Austin Thomas Walden, Ward filed a lawsuit in 1952 contending that he had been denied admission on the basis of race and color. Ward's case was eventually "tried in federal court and dismissed on technical grounds," without ever addressing the reasons he had been denied admission.[115]

Because the University of Georgia School of Law refused to admit Ward and his legal case was ultimately dismissed, the Georgia State applicants, if admitted, would become the first black students to enter a white educational institution in Georgia. Georgia State offered classes in business administration, education, and the liberal arts for white students, most of whom enrolled in evening classes, which provided an opportunity for working persons to earn a degree. This opportunity was unavailable, however, to blacks—who constituted at least 20 percent of Atlanta's population—due to Georgia's policy of segregated education.[116]

NAACP officials and other black community leaders who rallied to support the black applicants anticipated less resistance to black students entering Georgia State, as opposed to the University of Georgia, because of its urban location and the fact that it was a commuter college and not the state's flagship institution.[117] The University of Georgia was the alma mater of Georgia's most prominent white citizens, including U.S. senator Richard Russell and governors Eugene and Herman Talmadge. "By 1950, fifteen UGA alumni had been elected governor, and nine had been elected to represent Georgia in the U.S. Senate."[118] The university was thus considered the pride of Georgia education.

The University of Georgia also had a strong relationship with the rural counties in Georgia through its extensive agricultural program. A strong football tradition added to the affection many Georgians felt for their flagship institution, which the Georgia State College of Business (Georgia State) did not evoke. Consequently, the black community leaders promoting desegregation believed the resistance mounted against Ward's efforts to enter the University of Georgia might be less intense for students seeking to enter Georgia State. The leaders also thought they could offer greater support and protection for the students and better manage any problems because the college was located in the midst of Atlanta's large and progressive black community.[119]

Most of the legal experts advising and assisting in the Georgia State case, including NAACP attorneys Marshall, Carter, and Motley and local attorneys Hollowell and Walden, had been involved in Ward's case and were able to apply what they had learned to help the Georgia State applicants. Civil rights warrior and Atlanta NAACP branch president John Calhoun had identified three potential applicants to Georgia State as early as January 1956 and had appealed to Thurgood Marshall for help.[120] On March 23, 1956, Boone, Clemons, Dinsmore, Knight, McGhee, and Roberts tried unsuccessfully to enroll at Georgia State.

Despite support from Marshall, America's premiere civil rights attorney, and activists such as the venerable Austin Thomas Walden, the dean of the small number of black lawyers in Georgia who had practiced civil rights law since 1911, Georgia State and Board of Regents officials insisted on an abundance of racially discriminatory technical requirements that stymied the applicants. The applicants encountered a morass of formidable obstacles, mostly related to the Board of Regents' alumni certificate requirements. These requirements made the following stipulations:

> Any resident of Georgia applying for admission to an institution of the University System in addition to meeting other requirements shall submit certificates from two citizens of Georgia, alumni of the institution he desires to attend, which shall certify that each of such alumni is personally acquainted with the applicant and the extent of such acquaintance; that the applicant is of good moral character, bears a good reputation in the community in which he resides, and in the opinion of such alumnus is a fit and suitable person for admission to the institution and able to pursue successfully the courses of study offered by the institution he desires to attend.
>
> In addition the applicant shall submit a certificate from the Ordinary or Clerk of the Superior Court of the county in which he resides that such applicant is a bona fide resident of the county, is of good moral character, and bears a good reputation in the community in which he resides.[121]

Presumably to assist white students in large counties, who were unlikely to be known to the clerk or ordinary, in complying with the additional stipulations, the Board of Regents amended the requirements on May 9, 1956. Under the new requirements, in lieu of a certificate from the ordinary or clerk of the Superior Court, applicants residing in a county with a population of one hundred thousand or more could submit a certificate from a third alumnus of the institution they desired to attend. The new requirements stipulated that the third alumnus must be chosen from a list of alumni provided by the president of each institution's Alumni Association. The amendment also likely resulted from the complaints of some clerks or ordinaries that the certification requirement increased their workload.

The hastily developed alumni certification requirements had been adopted by the regents shortly after Ward applied to the University of Georgia School of Law to block his application.[122] Admissions director George Blair asserted that he had denied the six black applicants consideration for admission because their applications lacked the necessary character recommendations.[123] As reported in the *Atlanta Daily World*, "a maze of complications and red tape" rebuffed the applicants' determination to begin spring classes at the college.[124]

In the unlikely event that a black applicant obtained good character recommendations from two white alumni of the institution, the Board of Regents' additional requirement of "good moral character and good reputation certified by the ordinary or Superior Court clerk" or by a third alumnus from a list specifically compiled by the president of the Alumni Association posed an additional impediment.[125] Walden, however, was friendly with Fulton County ordinary Eugene Gunby and hoped to help the applicants obtain certifications from the superior court. Walden therefore accompanied the applicants to Gunby's chambers on the morning of March 23, 1956, prior to the applicants' visit to the college.[126]

Walden was one of only a handful of black lawyers in Georgia in the 1950s, a number that remained in the single digits until 1962.[127] He had an alliance with Thurgood Marshall and served for several years as president of the Atlanta branch of the NAACP and Atlanta's black bar association (Gate City Bar), which fought against racial injustice. Walden was an effective advocate in the black freedom struggle over the course of a career that featured "epic battles against the Ku Klux Klan, hostile judges, and courtroom opponents," winning a number of historic civil rights cases in the state.[128] For example, in 1945, less than a year after the *Smith v. Allwright* decision, Walden joined forces with Marshall to represent Primus King, an itinerant preacher from Muscogee County, Georgia, and won a groundbreaking federal district court case that forced the opening of the all-white Democratic primary in Georgia to black citizens.[129]

Even with his pro–civil rights stance and success in battling the segregationist system, Walden had an uncommon entrée to the white power structure, and "he used it effectively to try to uplift the black community."[130] Constance Baker Motley observed that Walden was part of what many Atlantans called the "old guard" or the "black cabinet," and Walden often negotiated with the white power structure to try to improve conditions in the black community.[131] Walden's links with the establishment as head of the "Negro old guard," however, frustrated some black leaders who pushed for a more militant approach to attacking segregation. Ruby Hurley, Southeast director of the NAACP, for example, recommended that the Atlanta office of the NAACP relocate away from Auburn Avenue to distance the organization from the "Negro old guard," who objected to a "vibrant branch" of the NAACP.[132]

Despite Walden's connections with the establishment and friendly relationship with Gunby, he was unsuccessful in helping the applicants obtain the required judicial certification. Gunby declined to certify the applications of the six black applicants, advising them that the court provided character certificates in batches directly to the institution after applications were "processed and approved" by the college.[133] The duplicity here by college officials and Gunby was simply outrageous. The college would not accept applications from black students until they received certificates from the court, and the court would not certify their applications until the college approved them. Though the college rejected the applicants and Gunby refused to certify them, Walden vowed that the six applicants would continue their efforts and "do what they could to gain admission."[134] Walden also declared that filing a federal lawsuit loomed as a next step.[135]

The Board of Regents' approval of new application regulations, purportedly to limit admission to better-qualified students, shortly after the six black applicants tried unsuccessfully to enroll on March 23, 1956, affirmed Walden's contention that legal action would be necessary. In a private session on May 9, 1956, the regents approved a new screening program that empowered the president of any college or university controlled by the regents "to refer an application to the Board of Regents for assignment . . . if he believed that the educational needs of the applicant could be best met at some other institution in the system."[136]

In addition to the relatively new policy requiring character certificates and the hastily set-up screening program, the applicants also faced a long-standing Board of Regents' policy designed to keep blacks out of white colleges and universities. On August 11, 1943, five years *after* the *Gaines* decision outlawed the practice, the regents had approved a resolution to offer out-of-state scholarships to blacks. Since that time, the regents had forestalled challenges to the segregated system by providing out-of-state aid to black students seeking to enter white institutions.

The Board of Regents' policy stipulated that the regents would provide scholarships for "post-graduate work for qualified negroes [*sic*]" that would "be measured by the difference in cost to the applicant in the institution to which he [was] sent and the cost to white students obtaining similar work in the University System."[137] The program continued to grow and reached its height in the late 1950s, when it provided nearly $300,000 a year to more than 2,700 black students.[138] Similar to the out-of-state funding offered to Lloyd Gaines, Georgia provided financial support for black students to attend school out of state if the state's black colleges did not offer the program of study in which they were interested.

The regents hoped to dissuade the black applicants from seeking to enter Georgia State by offering them such assistance. Interestingly, demonstrating their intention to uphold segregated education and guarantee that out-of-state funding was readily available to the six black Georgia State applicants, at their board meeting on May 9, 1956, the regents increased the annual allocation for "scholarships for Negroes" from $250,000 in 1955–56 to $275,000 for the fiscal year beginning in July 1956.[139] The Georgia officials' decision to essentially ignore the U.S. Supreme Court ruling in *Gaines* was just one of numerous examples of their defiance of the court, in accordance with their Interposition Resolution and the Southern Manifesto.[140]

Nonetheless, imbued with a spirit of activism and determined to enter Georgia State, which was convenient to their jobs on Auburn Avenue and offered a number of night courses, the applicants flatly refused the regents' offer to pay their tuition and defray expenses to attend a college out of state. Dinsmore, for example, believed it was shameful that blacks were barred from entry to Georgia State and asserted that it was her "right as a Georgia citizen to attend the college."[141] Accepting the out-of-state aid would also have disrupted the applicants' households, as four of the six had started families by that time. Despite the pervasive racially obstructive policies the applicants faced and their unsuccessful attempt to register on March 23, the venerable Walden promised "he would continue his fight to have them enrolled."[142] Yet with generous and ardent support from Governor Griffin, the States' Rights Council, and a plethora of high-ranking public officials, and undergirded by an Interposition Resolution and the Southern Manifesto, the Board of Regents and university officials were primed to continue their unwavering resistance.

CHAPTER 2
Renewing the Struggle
*The Alliance with Atlanta's
Black Institutions and the NAACP*

Less than three months after their initial attempt to enter Georgia State, Russell Roberts and Myra Dinsmore, along with new prospective black applicants Barbara Hunt, Marian McDaniel, and Iris Mae Welch, again sought admission to the college. Mae Thelma Boone, Edward Clemons, Rosalyn McGhee, and Charlie Mae Knight had ended their efforts to enroll. Although the reasons for their withdrawal are not known, the inflammatory statements by high-profile political leaders, threatening phone calls, and pervasive resistance by Georgia State and Board of Regents officials might have influenced their decisions.[1]

The newly formed group of five prospective applicants knew one another and frequently lunched together at various locations on historic Auburn Avenue, including Yates and Milton Drugstore and Henry's Grill. During one lunch discussion, the group considered the possibility of renewing the efforts to enter Georgia State initiated by the six original black applicants.[2] Like the original group, they concluded that enrolling at Georgia State would be more affordable than attending the Atlanta University Center's black private colleges, and Georgia State's evening program would enable them to retain their day jobs and attend college at night. Though the students' reasoning reflected Georgia State's original mission of providing an evening school for employees of Atlanta businesses, black employees were not the intended beneficiaries.[3]

The prospective applicants also reasoned that if they were admitted to the urban campus to attend the commuter college in the evenings, they would not have to reside in dormitories, which might put their personal safety at risk. These fears were not unfounded; only a few years later, on Charlayne Hunter's first night in a dormitory at the University of Georgia, "rioters set fires in the woods near Hunter's dormitory, threw bricks and other missiles at the dorm windows, tossed rocks and firecrackers at reporters, and scuffled with police."[4] Historian Robert Cohen observes that UGA earned "bragging rights" as the first campus in the 1960s "to produce violent resistance to racial equality."[5] Cohen describes how UGA students waving a "Nigger Go Home" sign rioted outside Hunter's dormitory room, intent on forcing the removal of Hunter and Holmes from the University.

After suppressing the riot outside Hunter's dormitory room, university officials suspended not the perpetrators of the violence but Hunter and Hamilton Holmes. Dean of Students J. A. Williams stated in a letter to Holmes, "Last night the events which took place on the University campus were due to the enrollment of you and Charlayne Hunter at the University of Georgia. These events placed in jeopardy the lives of you and Charlayne as well as university students, university officials and city police."[6]

It is bitterly ironic that officials suspended Holmes and Hunter while allowing most of the rioters to remain in school.[7] Hunter (now Hunter-Gault) chronicled her experiences as one of the University of Georgia's first two black students in her memoir, *In My Place*. Reflecting on her hostile introduction to dormitory life, she recalled, "The first two nights I stayed on campus, I was serenaded by students chanting words ['Nigger Go Home'] I had a hard time relating to myself."[8] In Maurice Daniels and Derrick Alridge's documentary, *Hamilton Earl Holmes: The Legacy Continues*, Holmes and his mother, Isabella Holmes, recount in vivid detail the emotional toll these events took on Holmes, who traveled home to Atlanta every weekend to escape the hostile environment of the UGA campus and seek social and emotional support from family and friends.[9]

Jesse Hill Jr., a central figure in the Atlanta branch of the NAACP and prominent business leader of the Atlanta Life Insurance Company, along with other black activists pushing for desegregation, were understandably wary of placing young people in danger. They therefore favored efforts to break the stranglehold of segregation first at Georgia State instead of at the University of Georgia or other all-white colleges outside Atlanta. Moreover, the black leaders also preferred the commuter college because it eliminated any potential problems associated with black students residing in dormitories. Given concerns about Holmes and Hunter's personal safety at the university in Athens, black community leaders had initially tried to persuade them to attend Georgia State.[10] Hill noted that the black leaders also sought to recruit older students to attend night school, as "people hesitated to send a seventeen-year old kid into that hostility."[11]

Georgia State was also very close to the Auburn Avenue community, where several of the applicants lived and worked.[12] Auburn Avenue was an enclave for progressive blacks and an area where community leaders orchestrated civil rights efforts. Several prominent black-owned establishments and black civic organizations, including the *Atlanta Daily World*, the Atlanta branch of the NAACP, the historic Ebenezer Baptist Church, the Atlanta Life Insurance Company (one of the largest black-owned insurance companies in the nation), and an array of lawyers, educators, intellectuals, and ministers were assembled along "Sweet" Auburn Avenue. *Fortune* magazine christened Auburn Avenue the "richest Negro street in the world."[13] Tomiko Brown-Nagin notes that the Auburn Avenue elite shared values of "racial uplift ideology premised on autonomous black institutions, social respectability, the pursuit of education, and economic self-sufficiency."[14] Several of the economically self-sufficient institutions on "Sweet Auburn," steeped in a culture of racial uplift and educational advancement, employed the prospective applicants and insulated them from the reprisals and intimidation of an unsympathetic white power structure.[15]

In his comprehensive narrative of the history of black Atlanta, Maurice Hobson helps illuminate the origins of black Atlanta's progress in business and education. Dating back to the Emancipation Proclamation, Hobson explains, "Atlanta, Georgia has boasted a history of black people thriving through the establishment of black-owned businesses and black education."[16] The emergence of the successful black middle and upper classes can be traced to events tied to the aftermath of the Civil War. Hobson notes that during and after the Civil War, Atlanta was "occupied by Union troops and it housed the district headquarters for the Freedmen's Bureau, which aided blacks."[17] Large numbers of blacks migrated to the city to escape oppression, seek refuge from racial violence, and benefit from the economic opportunities and legal protection of the Freedmen's Bureau. Blacks migrating to Atlanta "asserted themselves by building institutions that promoted autonomy."[18]

However, even with Atlanta's history as the district headquarters of the Freedmen's Bureau and its occupation by Union troops, it was far from being the promised land for blacks. Mark Bauerlein, in *Negrophobia: A Race Riot in Atlanta, 1906*, and Gregory Mixon, in *The Atlanta Race Riot: Race,*

Class, and Violence in a New South City, describe terrorism against blacks in Atlanta at the turn of the twentieth century. In September 1906, a white mob attacked blacks, allegedly due to unsubstantiated reports of assaults by black men on white women. More than twenty blacks and two whites were killed in the riot, and hundreds more were seriously injured.[19] Ironically, and sadly, although whites blamed the riots on black men assaulting white women, historian Allison Dorsey contends that the cause of the riot was whites' visceral response to blacks' economic progress.[20] Similarly, Hobson argues that the riot was sparked by economic competition between blacks and whites.[21]

Tomiko Brown-Nagin correctly posits that "myth shrouds the extent of violence" in Georgia, "especially in Atlanta and other urban areas." Although the Atlanta riot "is considered a deviation from Georgia['s] racially moderate history" as compared to other Deep South states, white terrorism toward blacks was common in Georgia during this time, including other incidents in Atlanta and its suburbs.[22] For example, a few years before the Atlanta riot, Sam Hose was lynched in Newnan, Georgia, for allegedly murdering his landlord and raping the landlord's wife. Less than two months before the Atlanta riot, in Atlanta's Lakewood suburb, Floyd Carmichael was "literally shot to pieces . . . by a hundred bullets" for allegedly assaulting a fifteen-year-old white girl.[23] Despite the prevalence of racial violence in Atlanta and the white backlash, Hobson asserts that black Atlanta flourished because significant numbers of blacks educated themselves and established prosperous business enterprises. However, while it is clear that blacks banded together to build a strong foundation in business and education, they did so in an unquestionably hostile environment.

The cadre of black institutions of higher education in Atlanta founded after the Civil War played a pivotal role "in establishing and maintaining Atlanta's thriving black upper and middle classes."[24] According to James Anderson, blacks were determined to develop systems of education to prepare them for full and equal participation in a democratic society and support their resistance to racial subordination.[25] Graduates and faculty of Morehouse College (established in 1867), Spelman College (1881), Atlanta University (1869), Clark College (1870), Morris Brown College (1885), and Gamma Theological Seminary (1866) were critical to black Atlanta's social, economic, and political progress.

William Madison Boyd is a notable example of a scholar/activist at a black institution who advocated for equal justice for blacks in Atlanta and across the state. Boyd chaired the Political Science Department at Atlanta

University and served as president of the NAACP Georgia Conference of Branches. He worked closely with Thurgood Marshall and was a central figure who orchestrated several Georgia civil rights cases challenging racial discrimination, including Horace T. Ward's quest to enter the University of Georgia.[26] It is important to underscore that key figures from the cluster of black institutions of higher education, such as Morehouse professor Reverend Dr. Samuel Williams, fervently resisted racial subordination and played integral roles in supporting the applicants and litigants in the Georgia State case.

The premiere black-owned business on "Sweet Auburn" was the Atlanta Life Insurance Company. Hill, then chief actuary of the company, was a leader in civil rights efforts and worked with a delegation of community activists to battle segregation in Georgia.[27] Hill also became a leader of the Atlanta Committee for Cooperative Action (ACCA), a progressive civic club comprised of black men under forty who were dissatisfied with the pace of Atlanta's progress toward equality. The ACCA advocated a more militant stance against racial discrimination.[28] Hill was the "man from the ACCA who was most concerned with school integration."[29]

The black applicants to Georgia State were aware of Hill's civil rights efforts, and the Atlanta Life Insurance Company employed three of the initial applicants—Myra E. Dinsmore, Rosalyn Virginia McGhee, and Charlie Mae Knight. Dinsmore recalled, "Atlanta Life was a big business operation as black businesses went back then. But still, it was small, and everybody knew everybody. So it didn't take very long for [Hill] to become aware of what we were doing. And of course when he discovered it, he was very encouraging."[30]

In *An Education in Georgia: Charlayne Hunter, Hamilton Holmes, and the Integration of the University of Georgia*, Calvin Trillin describes the genesis of efforts to desegregate Georgia State, based on an interview with Hill, that differs from Dinsmore's recollections. While Dinsmore stated that Hill learned of the applicants' efforts to enter the college after their initial attempts to enroll, Trillin indicates that Hill enlisted the help of other black leaders and campaigned to recruit black applicants in an effort to desegregate Georgia State. Hill recalled, "We tried to get some of the people in our own office" at Atlanta Life Insurance to seek admission to Georgia State, and "we got three girls to apply."[31]

Irrespective of whether Hill actually recruited the applicants, he was unquestionably at the forefront of civil rights activism in Georgia, working tirelessly to end segregation and often confronting harsh resistance from state officials. Hill was a strong-minded activist, and his financial independence as an executive with a black-owned company allowed him to persist in his advocacy undeterred by the white power structure. It is also worth noting that although Hill may or may not have specifically recruited Dinsmore, Knight, and McGhee, he created an environment at the company that encouraged them and other Atlanta Life employees to advocate for civil rights. For example, Knight and McGhee recalled that they obtained their admissions applications to the all-white college from a collection of applications Atlanta Life made available to its employees.[32] However, Knight, like Dinsmore, contended that she did not discuss her efforts to seek admission to Georgia State with anyone connected with the Atlanta Life Insurance Company, other than Dinsmore and McGhee, prior to submitting her application.[33]

Evoking the pattern of obstruction implemented by UGA officials to block Horace Ward, Georgia State set up formidable barriers to impede the black applicants. In a 1996 interview, Hill noted that Georgia State sometimes refused to give applications to interested black students. To elude this unequal treatment, Hill explained, applications were secured surreptitiously at night by (black) maintenance staff working at the college.[34]

The newly adopted Board of Regents' policy that was implemented after Ward's application, which required applicants to secure character recommendations from alumni of the institution, was still in effect. The regulation had stalled the six original black applicants to Georgia State and remained a formidable obstacle for the new group. Ward and his attorneys had viewed this requirement as simply a ploy to thwart his application.[35] The University of Georgia purportedly refused to admit Ward because he had refused to seek character recommendations from alumni of the all-white law school.

Having learned from Ward's experience, the newly formed group of black Georgia State applicants sought to prove that the obstacles mounted to block Ward's application were virtually impossible to remove or bypass in any routine way. Rather than assuming that the white alumni would not provide character certificates for black applicants, the applicants assertively asked alumni for character references.[36] Although the applicants knew none of the white alumni, they jointly drafted a letter to the alumni of the college residing in Fulton County requesting certifications regarding their character and reputation.[37]

Marian McDaniel, who had been office secretary for the Atlanta branch of the NAACP since September 1953, prepared the letters. McDaniel stated that she used the equipment in the NAACP office to prepare the stencil and mimeograph the letters. On behalf of Hunt, Dinsmore, Roberts, Welch, and herself, she mailed the following letter, dated June 11, 1956, to approximately one hundred Georgia State alumni.[38]

> Dear Friend: We, whose names are listed below, are desirous of attending Georgia State College of Business Administration in Atlanta during the 1956 Summer Quarter. Your name has been furnished as a graduate of the school, and as you may know, each applicant is required to secure a certificate from "two citizens of Georgia, alumni of the institution to which application is being made, that the applicant is personally known, that he is of good moral character, bears a good reputation in the community in which he resides, and that he is a fit and suitable person for admission and able to pursue successfully the course of study for which he desires to register." If you would be willing to certify one or more of us, kindly advise either of us at the address indicated below . . . so that you may be contacted for an appointment. Inasmuch as the registration dates are June 14–15, an immediate response would be appreciated.[39]

Even if the alumni had been favorably inclined toward the admission of black students, the carefully and restrictively worded requirement made it extremely unlikely that an alumnus who did not know the applicant could honestly attest to all the stipulations. As expected, none of the applicants received a response from any of the white alumni.[40] It should be noted that McDaniel mailed the letters on June 11 and requested a response by June 14 or 15, a very short and perhaps unreasonable turnaround time.

Nonetheless, after failing to receive responses to their written requests for character recommendations, on June 14, 1956, the five students completed application forms for admission to Georgia State. Along with Rev. E. R. Searcy, the pastor of Mount Zion Second Baptist Church; Rev. Samuel Williams, the pastor of Friendship Baptist Church; and an *Atlanta Daily World* newspaper reporter, the students visited the Registrar's Office at Georgia State to submit their applications.[41] Given that the students visited the college to submit their applications only three days after mailing their letters to the alumni, it appears they had concluded in advance that the alumni would not respond favorably, and their request was merely a formality that enabled them to document the lack of response.

Dinsmore noted that the black applicants had asked Reverends Searcy and Williams to accompany them to vouch for their characters.[42] Williams himself confirmed that he accompanied Barbara Hunt to the college "to testify as to her character."[43] He stated that Hunt also asked him to escort her because "she wasn't sure how she would be received for she had been reading the [inflammatory] statements by the Governor of the State and the Attorney General."[44] Governor Griffin's demagoguery was especially repugnant, and Hunt was understandably concerned. The *Atlanta Daily World* (*ADW*) reported in a June 15, 1956, article that the ministers also accompanied the applicants to shield them from newsmen, in an effort "to keep their identity out of local papers to avoid further threatening telephone calls."[45] Though an *ADW* reporter accompanied the students to the college, the paper did not disclose the applicants' identities in the June 15, 1956, article.

Williams recalled that admissions director George Blair rejected Hunt's application because it did not contain the "required alumni signatures." Blair then asked the other four applicants, who were standing in line behind Hunt, if their applications contained the required signatures; all the applicants responded that their applications did not include the signatures. Blair subsequently refused to consider the applications of the other four applicants, indicating that they were incomplete as well.[46]

The same day, Williams accompanied Hunt to the offices of two individuals who were on the special list of alumni or college officials obtained from Blair's office and designated by the college to provide alumni certifications.[47] Reflecting the arbitrariness, lack of preparation, and capriciousness of the regents and Georgia State officials in their efforts to keep black students out of the college, "the applicants were given a handwritten list of names" of alumni approved to provide certifications.[48] The list included the names of about fifteen persons who were employed at the college, including some who were not alumni, which violated the Board of Regents' policy.[49]

Because the regulation had the unintentional outcome of obstructing some white applicants, college officials enforced the policy loosely, sometimes allowing employees who were not alumni to provide certifications. However, such lax adherence to the policy did not benefit the black applicants. Although Williams offered to attest to Hunt's character, both officials whom Hunt approached with her request stated that they could not sign Hunt's application because they did not know her.[50] Similarly, Searcy accompanied Roberts to try to obtain a signature from one of the officials on the list, but this employee also refused on the grounds that he did not know Roberts or Searcy.[51]

None of the five applicants were successful in obtaining alumni certifications during their June 14, 1956, visit to the college.[52] Staff writer Samuel

Adams of the *ADW* concluded in his June 15 article that the "young Negro women and a man" were denied admission to the "all-white Georgia State College of Business Administration in a bold attempt to complete admission procedures adopted by the Board of Regents." Adams asserted that the procedures had been adopted by the regents "to frustrate the efforts of Negro applicants."[53]

The persistent efforts of black applicants to enter Georgia State alarmed university officials. In preparation for a larger group than appeared at the Registrar's Office that day, "three officers of the Georgia Bureau of Investigation [GBI] sat quietly in a corner of the registration room."[54] Whether the GBI officers were on the scene to intimidate the black applicants or to try to gather evidence to block their applications, their presence revealed the extent to which Georgia officials considered the applicants a threat to the state's segregated system of education.

The GBI officers reported that they were present as "observers," and no untoward incidents occurred.[55] However, neither the students' persistence nor the clergymen's willingness to vouch for their character yielded favorable consideration of their applications. The registrar verbally rejected each of them for admission, on the grounds that their applications did not include the required certificates of character.

Because Georgia State had been a division of the University of Georgia from 1947 to 1955, a large number of Georgia State alumni were technically University of Georgia graduates. In their unyielding effort to obtain signatures, two of the applicants, Boone and Clemons, sought certifications from UGA alumni. With Walden's help they were able to secure good moral character certifications from two graduates of the University of Georgia, Rev. James L. Welden, pastor of Oak Grove Methodist Church, and Clarence Jordan of Americus, Georgia.[56] Welden had earned a BS degree in 1946. Jordan had earned a BS degree in 1933 and had gone on to further study at the Southern Baptist Theological Seminary in Kentucky.[57]

Though white southerners overwhelmingly espoused white supremacy, Jordan was a notable exception who manifested his commitment to racial equality through progressive social action. In 1942, he cofounded Koinonia Farm, a community of interracial Christian believers in southwest Georgia who shared faith and resources. Interracial communing in the Deep South was a huge anomaly in the 1940s. Not surprisingly, Jordan, his family, and the Koinonia community endured "arson, drive-by gunfire, personal assaults, harassment of their children, boycotts by local suppliers, the menace of a 90-car Ku Klux Klan caravan, and ouster by the local church—all for the offense of living in interracial fellowship."⁵⁸ True to form, Georgia officials impaneled a grand jury that declared Koinonia a Communist-front organization and found that the organization had staged the violence against itself to secure insurance money and gain publicity.⁵⁹ Jordan had risked his personal safety and the safety of his family on a number of occasions in rural Georgia. He had come face-to-face with the Ku Klux Klan in his quest for racial equality in southwest Georgia—perhaps the most racially oppressive area of the state.

Baker County, also commonly known as "Bad Baker County," and Terrell County, also known as "Terrible Terrell," were two of the southwest Georgia counties in which numerous incidents of lynching and other atrocities against black citizens had occurred.⁶⁰ Three years after Jordan established the Koinonia community, for example, Baker County sheriff Claude Screws, aided by policemen, lynched Robert Hall, a black citizen of Baker County. Screws and the officers savagely beat Hall with their fists and a two-pound blackjack, after the *handcuffed* Hall allegedly reached for a gun and tried to escape. Screws then tied Hall's lifeless body to a car and "dragged him around the county seat before beating him again and pouring acid on his face."⁶¹ Demonstrating the widespread acceptance of such cruelty to blacks, Screws was elected to the state senate less than a decade later.⁶² Yet despite this savagely racist environment, Jordan persisted and even thrived in his efforts to build the interracial Koinonia community.⁶³ Given the raw courage he displayed in rural Georgia, he had no qualms about helping black applicants try to break the chains of segregation at Georgia State in urban Atlanta.

Despite Jordan's and Welden's good character certifications for the black applicants, in yet another rejection, George Sparks, president of the college, determined the certifications to be ineligible. He declared, "Since [Georgia State] had been separated from the University of Georgia (UGA), the university alumni were not eligible to sign as endorsers for the applicants."⁶⁴ Sparks's action was extremely disingenuous, as the Georgia Regents had approved the separation of Georgia State from UGA less than a year earlier, in September 1955. According to Gene Britton, a writer for the *Atlanta Constitution* and the *Atlanta Journal*, Reverend Williams told Sparks that obtaining an alumni certification from Georgia State graduates was simply not feasible because the college "as a separate entity, did not then have a graduating class."⁶⁵ Blair, the lead enforcer of the alumni certification policy, even admitted to Clemons "that GSC had no alumni."⁶⁶

Having operated as the Evening School of Commerce of the Georgia Institute of Technology (Georgia Tech) from its inception in 1913 until the institution was renamed the University System of Georgia Evening School in the early 1930s, and as the Atlanta Division of the University of Georgia from 1947 until July 1955, when the black applicants sought admission in March and June 1956, all alumni who graduated prior to July 1955 were technically Georgia Tech, University System of Georgia Evening School, or University of Georgia graduates.[67] Even more to the point, the application form specified that any alumnus of the "University of Georgia or The Atlanta Division" could provide an alumni certification.[68] During the black applicants' visit to Blair's office, they pointed out that the application form indicated that University of Georgia graduates could provide the certifications. Clemons recalled that Welden had already signed his application and that Jordan told Blair he was ready and willing to endorse Clemons's application.[69]

Outrageously, Blair went into his inner office and returned to present the applicants with copies of revised applications with a "red line drawn through 'The University of Georgia.'"[70] Clemons said "he knew for a fact the phrase qualifying University of Georgia graduates to certify" applicants was "scratched out" after he successfully obtained Welden's signature and Jordan's consent to certify his good character.[71] Thus, in addition to the contrived schemes officials designed to obstruct black applicants, they also spontaneously created barriers to their entrance. The perseverance of the applicants, with the irrepressible Williams as their adviser and often spokesman, clearly exposed the state's charade and its willingness to go to any lengths to deny the black applicants admission, including imposing new rules on the spot.

Unyielding to such absurd obstacles, following the rejection of their applications the applicants immediately sought the counsel of E. E. Moore Jr., a local black attorney who was active in the NAACP. On June 15, 1956, the day after Blair rebuffed the five black applicants, Moore agreed to represent them. Moore was part of Atlanta's progressive black elite and one of a handful of black attorneys who delved into civil rights. Though Moore, unlike Hollowell, did not devote the majority of his time or practice to civil rights, like Hollowell he was a determined civil rights activist lawyer who had the confidence of Thurgood Marshall and the NAACP.[72]

Moore had distinguished himself as an able civil rights lawyer in the prolonged fight to desegregate Atlanta's public golf courses. In 1953, physician Hamilton Mayo Holmes and his two sons, Alfred "Tup" Holmes, a businessman, and Oliver Wendell Holmes, a minister, sued the city of

Atlanta in federal district court (*Holmes v. City of Atlanta*) to gain access for blacks to the city's municipal golf courses.[73] A family of race leaders among Atlanta's black elite, Hamilton Mayo Holmes was the grandfather of Hamilton Holmes, "Tup" was Hamilton Holmes' father, and Oliver was his uncle.

Local black attorneys R. Edwin Thomas, S. S. Robinson, and Moore guided the legal efforts through the federal courts with the help of Marshall and the NAACP national office.[74] In 1954, the federal district court restrained the City of Atlanta from refusing to allow blacks to play golf on its public courses. However, the court postponed the judgment to afford the city "a reasonable opportunity to promptly prepare and put into effect regulations for the use of the municipal golf facilities" while preserving segregation. Rejecting the court's decision to relegate black players to future segregated facilities, Thomas, Moore, and Robinson appealed to the Fifth Circuit U.S. Court of Appeals, which upheld the lower court's decision. However, in an appeal to the U.S. Supreme Court, their efforts led to a historic 1955 victory that declared the segregated recreational facilities unconstitutional.[75]

Though the golf courses in Atlanta became the first desegregated public facilities in Georgia, the victory over Jim Crow on these courses affected only a small number of economically successful blacks and did little to change the daily racial oppression experienced by blacks in Atlanta.[76] As Maurice Hobson has observed, if anything "set Atlanta's black community apart from other southern cities, it was the select few [blacks] who were able to achieve positions of political and economic power far beyond the expectations of the black masses in the rest of the South."[77] The historic golf-course case offers a prime example of how a select few blacks were able to win an important victory that nevertheless did not directly benefit the black masses.

Less than a year after the U.S. Supreme Court triumph overruling segregated public recreational facilities, Moore now sought to help the Georgia State applicants overturn segregation in public higher education, an effort that, if successful, would have a much broader impact on the black population across the economic spectrum. On June 15, 1956, Moore wrote a letter to President Sparks stating that Hunt, Dinsmore, McDaniel, Roberts, and Welch, "members of the Negro race," had made a diligent effort to comply with the policy requiring character certificates but were unsuccessful because they were not personally acquainted with any of the college's alumni.

Moore requested that Sparks allow his clients' applications to be considered as a result of their "complying with other valid and reasonable regulations of the institution and the Board of Regents."[78] Moore made the request on the basis that the black applicants had "no friends or acquaintances [among] and [were] not personally known to any member or members" of the (white) alumni of the institution.[79] Despite Moore's passionate plea, Sparks responded in a June 22, 1956, letter that he had no recourse but to "carry out [Board of Regents'] regulations."[80]

In an interview, long-serving Georgia State vice president George Manners contended that the institution's primary motivation for rejecting blacks was a law stipulating that state financial support would be withdrawn from any white school or college that admitted a black student.[81] Since state funding represented the majority of revenue for public colleges and universities, withdrawal of state funding basically meant closing those schools. In the event that Board of Regents or university officials considered admitting a black student to an all-white college or in the case of a federal court order, the Georgia General Assembly had enacted an appropriations bill in 1951 that required withholding state funds.[82] Even most liberal-minded whites buckled under the threat of the state shutting down a college if a black student enrolled. The hastily developed appropriations bill, approved by the legislature just six weeks after Horace Ward submitted his application, created yet another barrier to black access to all-white colleges.[83]

In 1956, the legislature passed a number of additional laws to maintain segregation in education, including bills that prohibited providing state funds to desegregated school districts and "a requirement that the governor close any school system maintaining a racially mixed school."[84] Manners later observed that he had "no prejudice against the admission of blacks," but insisted that if the institution had admitted "one black, all funds would have been withdrawn and [Georgia State] would have been closed."[85] Similarly, a few days after the original group of applicants sought admission, Sparks expressed alarm at the prospect of black applicants entering the all-white college, fearing that "one [Negro] person would jeopardize the educational opportunities of 5,000 others" as a result of the Georgia law stating that "all state appropriations would be cut off if segregation was dropped."[86] Tellingly, Sparks expressed no concern about the thousands of blacks who had been barred from educational opportunities at Georgia State and other all-white colleges and universities for decades.

Sparks's long service to the college dated back to 1928, when he began as director of the Evening School of Commerce, as Georgia State was then known.[87] He shepherded the school through the Great Depression, overseeing a major expansion of the college's curriculum, faculty, infrastructure, and student enrollment during his twenty-five-year tenure as director. Sparks's governance played a pivotal role in the school's evolution from a small evening program to a four-year college with graduate studies. Sparks also spearheaded the effort to establish Georgia State as a separate college, which won the Board of Regents' approval in 1955.

Recognizing the impact of Sparks's leadership on the growth and development of the institution, the regents rewarded him by appointing him the college's first president.[88] Sparks's personal views on racial discrimination are not known. However, although university officials such as Sparks and Manners claimed they had "no prejudice" and used the appropriations bill as their rationale for rejecting black applicants, they were no beacons of nondiscriminatory treatment of blacks. There is no record that either Sparks or Manners espoused equal justice for blacks or opposed the legislation designed to sustain white supremacy.

Sparks stated in his June 22, 1956, response to Moore that he "sent [Moore's] letter to Attorney General Eugene Cook who represent[ed] [the Georgia State College of Business] in such matters."[89] Shortly thereafter, Moore pursued the matter with the regents. In a letter dated July 5, 1956, Moore again requested a waiver of the alumni character certification requirement, reasserting that the plaintiffs were not personally known to any of Georgia State's all-white alumni. The regents responded to the request on July 12, 1956, refusing to waive the requirement. Their response reflected a hardened, calculated opposition that provided the applicants with no recourse but to pursue litigation.[90]

Roberts recalled that after Georgia State turned down his application, he talked to John Calhoun, Atlanta NAACP branch president, to request assistance from the NAACP.[91] Calhoun agreed to present his request to the NAACP's executive committee and later informed Roberts that the NAACP would help the applicants "finance the litigation."[92] Hunt recalled that she initially approached Moore about representing her in the case after Georgia State rejected her application and later met with Calhoun.[93] In a deposition taken on August 18, 1958, Hunt stated that she and her co-plaintiffs "didn't have the money" to pay Moore's fee, and they therefore discussed conferring with Calhoun about financial assistance.[94] Hunt noted that she met with Calhoun independently, as his office was "right across the street from where [she] worked and it was very convenient for [her] to go over and check with him" about financial help to pay for Moore's legal services.[95]

As he had with Roberts, Calhoun told Hunt he would consult with the NAACP's executive committee about possible assistance.

After securing Moore's legal representation and receiving a pledge of financial support from the Atlanta branch of the NAACP, and convinced that Georgia State would not admit them without a court fight, four of the applicants—Barbara Pace Hunt, Myra Elliott Dinsmore, Russell T. Roberts, and Iris Mae Welch—filed a lawsuit. Marian McDaniel, who worked for Calhoun, also discussed the financing of the litigation with him. However, in November 1956 she had ended her employment with the NAACP and moved to Springfield, Ohio, so she did not participate in the litigation as a plaintiff.[96]

Hunt, a native of Beaver Falls, Pennsylvania, was born in 1933. She excelled in her studies and graduated from Beaver Falls High School in 1951. With the goal of becoming a journalist, she enrolled in Clark College in Atlanta in the fall of 1951. In September 1952, after completing one year of study at Clark, she returned to Beaver Falls, where she married Eldridge F. Hunt Jr. Following the birth of two children and after separating from her husband in 1954, Hunt returned to Atlanta with her children.[97] Hunt then secured a job as a secretary in the Atlanta office of the *Pittsburgh Courier* (a black-owned newspaper), located on Auburn Avenue.[98]

Working closely with Paul Brown, the editor of the Georgia branch of the newspaper, Hunt reignited her interest in journalism and sought to enter Georgia State to take courses in "journalism" and "secretarial work."[99] Working for the *Pittsburgh Courier*, a national organ that promoted black uplift and advocated for the defeat of Jim Crow, Hunt was undoubtedly encouraged to advocate for her rights as a Georgia citizen in her quest to attend Georgia State.[100] In a front-page editorial, the *Pittsburgh Courier* demonstrated support for Hunt and the cause of racial justice, stating, "Jim Crow is still the South's leading pitcher, but the grizzled old vet is being rocked by some solid hits here and there by the opposing team, despite the fact that segregation's ace hurler still manages to slip over a fast one here and there."[101]

Although Hunt and her fellow black applicants were unsuccessful in their bid to enroll, the paper included their effort in its list of "play by play" actions across the South aimed at ending segregation. Following more than two years of employment at the *Pittsburg Courier*, at the time of the trial, Hunt was employed as a secretary in the Registrar's Office at Atlanta University.[102]

Myra Elliott Dinsmore was born in Temple, Georgia, in Carroll County on March 20, 1932. She moved with her parents to Atlanta when she was twelve years old. Dinsmore attended David T. Howard and Booker T. Washington High Schools in Atlanta; after her sophomore year at Washington High School, she entered Boggs Academy, a prestigious black Presbyterian-supported school in Keysville, Georgia.[103] After graduating as valedictorian at Boggs Academy in 1951, in 1952 she entered Spelman College in Atlanta, an elite institution founded in 1881 for the purpose of educating black women.

Two years later, after starting a family, Dinsmore dropped out of Spelman. According to court records, she married Adolphus Dinsmore Jr. in May 1954 and gave birth to Adolphus Dinsmore III in August 1954. She divorced Dinsmore in 1955 and married Robert Joseph Holland in October 1956.[104] Myretta June Holland and Jocelyn Elaine Holland were born to Dinsmore in 1957 and 1958, respectively.

In January 1955, Dinsmore started working as a maid and elevator operator for Thomas, Boland, and Lee Shoe Company. A few months later, she left the shoe company and was hired as an IBM keypunch operator for the Atlanta Life Insurance Company, where she met Jesse Hill and black co-workers who aspired to earn college degrees at Georgia State.[105] Though they did not join the lawsuit, Rosalyn McGhee and Charlie Knight worked as keypunch operators with Dinsmore during the time they initially sought to register at Georgia State in March 1956.[106] Dinsmore ended her employment at Atlanta Life in April 1958, three weeks before the birth of her third child, Jocelyn.[107] In a deposition taken on September 26, 1958, shortly before the trial, Dinsmore stated that she sought to enroll in business courses at Georgia State to "better [herself] in doing [her] work."[108]

The third litigant, Iris Mae Welch, was born in Auburn, Alabama. Welch graduated from Alabama State High School, a secondary school on the campus of Alabama State College, in 1940.[109] After completing high school, Welch taught elementary school for three years in Blanton, Alabama, and one year in Salem, Alabama. Aspiring to earn a college degree, Welch enrolled in summer courses at Alabama State College during the years she taught elementary school. In 1943, Welch moved to Columbus, Georgia, where she worked in a photography store owned by J. E. Jordan, an active member of the NAACP.

In 1945, Jordan moved his photography business to Atlanta's black business district on Auburn Avenue and expanded his enterprise to include

Jordan's Cut-Rate Drug Store. Welch moved to Atlanta to continue her employment with Jordan and worked as a bookkeeper and clerk for his businesses.[110] She stated that she was interested in enrolling at Georgia State to complete the college work she had begun at Alabama State College and to hone her skills in shorthand and bookkeeping for her work as a clerk.[111]

Russell T. Roberts, a U.S. military veteran and the only male among the plaintiffs, was a native of Terrell County, Georgia. He attended Dawson High School through ninth grade and completed tenth and eleventh grades at Tuskegee Institute High School. In 1943, after his eleventh grade year, he joined the Marine Corps, where he served three years before moving to Atlanta. Roberts, who worked as a salesman for the North Carolina Mutual Insurance Company for eleven years after moving to Atlanta, sought admission to Georgia State to take courses related to insurance and business.[112]

With legal counsel from Moore, the four plaintiffs proceeded with the lawsuit and sought expert legal help in civil rights litigation from the central office of the NAACP. The NAACP granted the request and attorneys Thurgood Marshall, Robert L. Carter, and Constance Baker Motley joined the case. With resolute determination to dislodge segregation and with expertise gained from his representation of Horace T. Ward, Atlanta civil rights attorney Donald Hollowell also joined the team.[113] With Moore serving as chief local counsel, Hollowell played a leading role as co-counsel for the plaintiffs in the Georgia State case.

Though Walden had played a central role in advising the applicants and had been at the vanguard of civil rights cases in Georgia for nearly fifty years, he did not play a principal role in representing the plaintiffs. In the wake of concerns among NAACP leaders about the retiring Walden's progress on civil rights cases, Hollowell had emerged as Georgia's chief civil rights attorney. As early as 1949, Georgia NAACP president William Madison Boyd had urged Thurgood Marshall not to allow an important civil rights case to "drag unnecessarily," and in 1951, NAACP Southeast director Ruby Hurley complained that Walden's "inactivity [was] killing [their effort] in Georgia."[114] Boyd expressed to Marshall concerns about Walden's progress on civil rights cases.[115]

Moreover, local civil rights leaders feared that "Walden had become too involved with the white political leadership to aggressively attack segregation."[116] Student activists charged that Walden was too moderate and behind the times. The criticism stemmed largely from his tendency to seek compromise with the white power structure and his skepticism about direct action due to concern for the protestors' safety.[117]

Ironically, Walden's disfavor with student activists resulted, in part, from students comparing him to attorneys he mentored, such as Donald Hollowell, who worked with the activists behind the scenes and supported direct action. Though Hollowell, Vernon Jordan, Horace Ward, Howard Moore, and other young activist lawyers recognized Walden's unparalleled contributions as Georgia's pioneering civil rights lawyer, the retiring Walden, in his seventies by the onset of the black militancy of the late 1950s and 1960s, was not viewed by student protesters as a part of the movement.

In contrast, as Tomiko Brown-Nagin notes, "The students lionized Hollowell, Howard Moore, Jr., and others as uncompromising advocates of racial justice."[118] As a new generation of civil rights activism emerged, some young activists lashed out, mistakenly characterizing Walden's approach as conservative "Uncle Tom" leadership.[119] Reflecting on the undeserved affront, a thoughtful Walden responded, "I can go a long way to overlook the impetuosity and impatience of youth. . . . People know I was fighting for these things way back when it took guts to do it."[120]

Though his tactics and approach to civil rights differed from those of the young activists, Walden was in no way an "Uncle Tom." On the contrary, the intrepid Walden, the son of slaves, was a determined civil rights leader with an unparalleled record as an agent of social change in Georgia, who often put his life on the line.[121] His daring crusade to challenge whites-only polling places in the face of Klansmen and his legal prowess in the case that shattered the all-white primary in Georgia are only two of the many examples of his singular courage and effectiveness. It is doubtful that any of his critics, though well meaning, displayed the valor or risked their personal safety to the degree that Walden did repeatedly in the struggle for civil rights during very dangerous times.[122]

Beginning in the mid-1950s, Hollowell served as chief counsel in most of Georgia's civil rights cases, replacing Walden as the chief lawyer who collaborated with the NAACP and Marshall. Walden, however, continued to champion the cause of social justice and served as co-counsel or adviser in civil rights cases until the 1960s, including his role as legal adviser in the *Hunt* and *Holmes* cases, as well as his enormously successful and effective work in the Atlanta student sit-in cases.

Local counsel Moore, Thurgood Marshall, and Robert Carter, with support from the local NAACP, filed the class action suit *Hunt v. Arnold* against the University System of Georgia in federal court, on behalf of the four plaintiffs and other blacks similarly affected. They asserted that college officials unconstitutionally denied blacks admission to the college "wholly and solely on account of their race and color," while at the same time, with "public funds," afforded white citizens the opportunity to attend the institution.[123] Thus the stage was set for the legal battle to come.

CHAPTER 3

Laying the Groundwork

The Challenge and the Backlash

Though the lawsuit filed by Barbara Hunt, Myra Dinsmore, Iris Welch, and Russell Roberts ultimately aimed to overturn segregation at Georgia State, the crux of the litigation centered on the alumni certification requirement. Chief counsel Moore and the NAACP counsels sought to build a case that proved the plaintiffs were denied admission solely because of their race.[1] The complaint claimed that the admissions policy requiring character certificates signed by two alumni was unreasonable and arbitrary and specifically intended to "hamper, restrain, and exclude the plaintiffs and other qualified Negroes of the privilege and right that is accorded to white students of attending said institution, on account of their race and color."[2] Moore alleged in the complaint that due to existing social patterns, the plaintiffs were not acquainted with any of the all-white alumni. He contended that opportunities for average persons of the two races to become acquainted were limited and that the prospects for blacks to form social relationships with white alumni were even more remote.

The complaint further alleged that by requiring certifications from white alumni as an element of the application process, Georgia State was allowing "private citizens" to determine the selection of students for admission.[3] Moore argued that granting alumni such "unreasonable and arbitrary power and authority to determine the qualifications of the plaintiffs for admission to said institution, with unlimited discretion to certify, or not to certify, the plaintiffs for admission" was discriminatory, denying his cli-

53

ents "due process of law in contravention and in violation of the Fourteenth Amendment to the Constitution of the United States."[4]

Because Georgia State had "no Negro alumni," the policy effectively gave white alumni the unfettered authority to certify or not certify the applications of the black applicants and thereby determine their qualifications for admission.[5] Moore concluded that this requirement imposed "unreasonable burdens, restrictions, and conditions" on black applicants and denied them equal protection under the law.[6] The plaintiffs brought the action against the members of the Board of Regents, Chancellor Harmon W. Caldwell, President Sparks, and admissions director Blair.

Attorney General Eugene Cook, attorneys E. Freeman Leverett and Robert H. Hall, and Deputy Assistant Attorney General B. D. Murphy represented the defendants. Like the regents, the chancellor, the university president, and the admissions director, the defendants' attorneys were all white men. Cook, who had served as attorney general since 1945, was renowned for his fight to preserve Georgia's segregation laws and statutes and led a formidable defense to sustain the all-white Georgia State College.[7]

Cook stood out among white supremacists through his willingness to publicly espouse his personal views in defense of the Jim Crow system. A few months before the six black students failed in their attempt to enroll at Georgia State, Cook had shared his views on segregation in an address before the Conservative Society at Yale Law School. Cook denounced the Supreme Court's declaration against segregation in the public schools as the "judicial usurpation of legislative power and abridgement of the rights of States and individual citizens."

The following excerpts from Cook's speech, titled "The Southern View of Segregation," bluntly convey his racial intolerance:

> The Brown et al. decision is held in utter contempt by most Georgians and it will not be respected or enforced in my State within the foreseeable future.... We in Georgia intend to circumvent this decision and Congress and the people have furnished many precedents for our action....
>
> At this point, it is in order for me to tell you in part how we in Georgia propose to do this. Our General Appropriations Act contains a provision requiring the withholding of State funds from any city or county school system in which the races are mixed and, since the State supplies 75 to 90 per cent of all public school funds, it is obvious that no system could continue to operate without State aid. In addition, last January the General Assembly enacted a law making it a felony for any public or school official to permit the spending

of State or local funds for mixed schools and holding such officials personally liable for any sums so spent. . . .

Segregation in the South is viewed by whites and negroes [sic] alike as a matter of practical human relations, inborn racial instinct and personal choice. The United States Supreme Court and the National Association for the Advancement of Colored People to the contrary notwithstanding, it is neither predicated upon hatred of either race for the other nor considered as a badge of superiority or inferiority by either.

In a society where from one-third to one-half of the citizens belong to a different race, the overwhelming majority of both white and colored citizens agree that segregation serves the best interests of both races and desire that it be continued.[8]

Cook, like most southern white political leaders of the 1950s, had no regard for the *Brown* decision (as evidenced by the Southern Manifesto). He and other political leaders therefore sought to undermine the ruling by enacting state legislative actions, including felonious behavior charges for officials who spent state or local funds on "racially mixed" schools. Subscribing to a widely held white supremacist view that supposedly justified racial separation, Cook lambasted the NAACP by contending that "amalgamation or intermarriage of the races" was "the ultimate goal of the NAACP" in its crusade for equal justice.[9]

In another public airing of his personal views about segregation, Cook rationalized his quest to destroy the NAACP in an address titled "The Ugly Truth about the NAACP." Cook delivered this speech before the Peace Officers Association of Georgia in 1955. He excoriated the NAACP and its leaders in the speech, characterizing the organization's founders as "descendants of the rabble-rousing abolitionists who fomented the strife which precipitated the War Between the States, a conflict which could have been avoided but for the activities of those abolitionists. . . . Through its activities, the NAACP is fomenting strife and discord between the white and Negro races in the South and is disrupting relations between these races which heretofore have been—and at present are—harmonious and friendly in every respect."[10]

Cook and his white supremacist contemporaries also sought to discredit the NAACP and halt its fight for equality by declaring that the organization and its leaders were influenced by Communists. In his speech, Cook attacked the NAACP for attempting to force the "Communist-inspired doctrine of racial integration . . . upon the South." Cook characterized the

NAACP crusade as among "the most ominous... threats to arise during [their] lifetime."¹¹

In his book *Black Struggle, Red Scare*, Jeff Woods explores the intersections of the black freedom struggle and Communism in depth. Woods observes that Cook's speech could more accurately have been titled "The Ugly Half-Truth about the NAACP," contending that Cook "widely exaggerated Communist influence over NAACP policies."¹² Although Cook used the fact that some NAACP founders were socialists and descendants of abolitionists to try to smear the organization as Communist-influenced, key NAACP leaders, including Thurgood Marshall and executive secretary Roy Wilkins, were in fact among "the group's most extreme anti-Communists."¹³ Marshall even worked with FBI director J. Edgar Hoover "to remove Communists from the NAACP."¹⁴

Despite Wilkins and Marshall publicly disavowing that the NAACP was a Communist or Communist-inspired organization, however, Cook's assertions about the NAACP and his opposition to civil rights gained popularity. On March 24, 1956, just one day after the black applicants sought to enter Georgia State, "before a packed crowd of eight thousand people at the New Orleans Municipal Auditorium, Cook and fellow Georgian Roy V. Harris shared the podium" with some of the "strongest advocates of segregation and anti-Communism in the South."¹⁵ Cook repeated his speech on "The Ugly Truth about the NAACP," labeling the organization and its leaders as Communists. As Woods notes, "for a conservative southern audience predisposed to accept a black and red conspiracy, the Georgia attorney general confirmed their worst fears."¹⁶

Cook claimed that his viewpoint represented the opinion of the majority of "whites and negroes [sic]," ludicrously contending that blacks preferred a system of segregation that relegated them to second-class citizenship. In reality, due to fear of lynching and other savagery of whites toward blacks, blacks often saw no choice but to tolerate the apartheid-like system in the interest of their own survival. Nonetheless, Cook, with his misguided and misleading perceptions of the NAACP and the black freedom struggle, was Georgia's elected state attorney general. His ingrained racial views thus provided the backdrop for the bitter opposition the plaintiffs and their attorneys confronted in their quest to open the doors of Georgia State to black students.

Cook's chief legal assistant, B. D. Murphy, was a brilliant trial lawyer and effective legal advocate for segregation who directed most of the state's arguments against civil rights during the 1950s and 1960s. Murphy also conducted most of the examinations and cross-examinations of witnesses in the *Hunt* trial. He had previously served as the personal attorney for Governor Herman Talmadge, who often selected him to represent the state in defense of the system of segregation. For example, when Talmadge deputized Murphy to represent the state in the *Ward* case, he issued a pointed order: "Keep that damned nigger out of the University of Georgia as long as I'm governor."[17]

Though Murphy was lauded by the segregationist establishment as an effective barrister for the proponents of segregation, Jesse Hill observed, "He used all the traditional tactics that you'd find throughout the South, and he tried to discredit witnesses. I found him very obnoxious."[18] Hollowell's objection to Murphy's pronunciation of the word "Negro" during the *Hunt* trial highlights one crude example of Murphy's offensiveness:

> MR. HOLLOWELL: Please the Court, I hear pretty well, and it appears to me that what I am hearing from counsel in his, I suppose, attempt to pronounce N-e-g-r-o is coming out as N-i-g-g-e-r, and I am certain that it would certainly be improper, if it is, and that is what I am hearing, and if what I think I am hearing is correct, I would certainly like to object to it.
>
> THE COURT: Well, I will instruct counsel to be respectful in the cross examination, and if you will be very careful to pronounce "Negro" properly.[19]

Murphy's response speaks volumes about the entrenched racial environment. "I thought I was, Your Honor. I had no intention to pronounce it other than the way I have been pronouncing it all my life."[20] *Atlanta Journal* writer Margaret Shannon, who covered the trial exhaustively, reported that after Hollowell's objection and Sloan's admonition, Murphy pronounced the word "Negro" henceforth.[21]

Hollowell was no stranger to such racial indignities before the bar. In 1952, Hollowell represented Willie Nash, a black defendant charged with the murder of a white man and the rape of a white woman in Atlanta.[22] Frank French, co-solicitor in the case, referred to one of his own witnesses as "that fat nigger."[23] Though Hollowell succeeded in winning Nash's acquittal, he had to contend with such shameful behavior in the courtroom by a solicitor.

French's and Murphy's behavior was not an anomaly. Judges and prosecutors often used racial slurs in reference to black lawyers and their clients and turned their backs on black attorneys when they addressed the bench. Vernon Jordan, who worked with Hollowell on a case involving a black defendant in Greene County, Georgia, recalled that the bailiff insisted that he and Hollowell represent their client from the segregated balcony section of the courtroom where the court relegated blacks to sit.[24]

Noting a commonplace experience in courtrooms of the 1960s, Howard Moore, Hollowell's law partner, recounted, "I appeared before judges who'd just as soon call me 'nigger' as look at me. One time in court, a prosecutor picked up a chair to hit me. When I called the judge's attention to it, he damn near put me in contempt."[25] In the era of Jim Crow, black attorneys pursuing civil rights for blacks through the bar of justice had to navigate racial obstacles within the bar itself.[26]

In addition to obstruction by state officials and the racial insults they confronted in the courtroom, the applicants faced an unwelcome environment from Georgia State students as well. As noted previously, Jesse Hill and other black leaders considered Georgia State more favorable than the University of Georgia for an attack on segregation, both due to its urban location and because its older student body was considered to be more mature and less likely "to react violently to integration efforts." Nevertheless, the *Georgia State Signal*, Georgia State's student newspaper, penned an editorial in virulent opposition to the admission of black students.[27]

Echoing the defiance expressed by state and regional public officials in the Interposition Resolution and Southern Manifesto, the editorial stated:

> The *Signal* gives unqualified support to segregation in the long battle ahead. Let us say now: we believe in segregation. We feel it is the only answer to the racial problem. We can see nothing in integration but racial strife. We realize no reason for mixing the races in schools and colleges now or in the years ahead.
>
> We must resist all attempts by federal courts to force integration upon us. We must maintain deep and intense opposition to United States Supreme court [sic] rulings. But this opposition cannot be carried on by the shrill cries of demagogic politicians.
>
> In the impending battle we must raise ourselves above the realm of demagogues. We must unite as a band of solid Georgians, abandon our old devices and cliches, and prepare to fight until doomsday with legal weapons to maintain segregation in our state schools.
>
> [The] United States Supreme Court opened this week on another year of handing down segregation decisions. A court which has laid down its program for ending segregation in public schools.
>
> In the same week four negroes [sic] sought admission to Georgia State through a suit filed in United States district court [sic] here.
>
> What can the State of Georgia do?

The Negroes have made their move.
Now it is our move.
We must realize that we have a legal fight ahead.
We are fighting a fourteenth amendment [sic] to the United States Constitution, the passage of which was forced on Georgia by military edict during Reconstruction.
... When the court proposes that its social revolution be imposed upon Georgia and Georgia State College "as soon as practicable." The Signal would respond that "as soon as practicable" means never at all.[28]

The racist views expressed in the editorial were not surprising in the 1950s social milieu. According to an intensive study of southerners by Princeton University researchers in 1950, "the image of the Negro held by the majority of whites pictured a basically inferior being."[29] Between "65 and 70 percent" of those interviewed in the study believed blacks were "lacking in morality and ambition," and almost 60 percent believed "Negroes [were] inferior to whites in intelligence."[30]

As the specter of "inferior Negroes" entering Georgia State loomed, a subsequent *Signal* editorial questioned the applicants' judgment. The editorial encouraged the applicants to attend an "all-colored" institution, asserting that they were pawns of the Communist-inspired NAACP. Repeating verbiage from Booker T. Washington's 1895 Cotton States and International Exposition address, the hostile editorial, titled "Four Negroes Acting Unwise," lambasted the applicants and sought to justify racial segregation:

Four Negroes are trying to enter Georgia State College of Business Administration as students. Why?

You four do not seek something that is being denied you—you have the opportunities and facilities to obtain the education offered here at Georgia State.

Within the surrounding area of Atlanta, there are more institutions of higher learning for Negroes than in any other city in the United States....

In light of this, the Signal objects violently to your attempts to enter Georgia State and the methods you are using.

Will you four be like Ward, another Negro who tried to enter the University of Georgia Law Schol [sic] while enrolled in the law school of Northwestern University and be a pawn for the National Association for the Advancement of Colored People?

Or will you be wise according to a distinguished scholarly member of your own race, Booker T. Washington?

According to Washington, in his famous speech at the Cotton Exposition in Atlanta in 1893, "The wisest among my race understand that the agitation of questions of social equality is the extremest [sic] folly, and that progress in the enjoyment of all the privileges that will come to us must be the result of severe and constant struggle rather than of artificial forcing."

The Signal agrees with Washington that the "agitation of questions of social equality is . . . folly." You four Negroes are now agitating, which by definition means to excite, perturb.

So, in the first place, you have set about to excite, perturb. You ask to equate socially across a color barrier not created by, but observed by the white race in Georgia.

Washington calls you unwise—the Signal can not [sic] disagree.

Secondly, you are attempting to "artificially force" your way into an institution that you have no need for, and you have not followed Washington's advice to "struggle constantly and severely" for your goals. . . .

In addition, many of the leaders of the NAACP have been cited by the House Un-American Activities Committee for Communist affiliations. These leaders are the people who lead your attempts to cross a social barrier by force. . . .

Attempting to obtain at an all-white institution an education easily available in Atlanta at an all-colored institution is not justifiable in the opinion of the Signal. . . .

Therefore, the Signal asks that you four Negroes reconsider your applications for admission to Georgia State and withdraw them. This would convince the Signal that you are actually seeking an education and not publicity or glory.[31]

Ominously, the editorial that "violently" objected to the black applicants' admission closed with a warning that urged the students to reconsider, with a reference to the risk to their safety. "The Signal recommends this action, for you will find no haven at Georgia State."[32]

Booker T. Washington, noted educator and founder of the Tuskegee Institute, was a dominant force on race issues at the turn of the twentieth century.[33] However, black leaders, including W. E. B. Du Bois, the towering intellectual and cofounder of the NAACP, rightly criticized Washington's famous Cotton States address. In Washington's speech, which became known as the Atlanta Compromise, Washington stated, "In all things that are purely social we can be as separate as the fingers, yet one as the hand in all things essential to mutual progress."[34] Washington argued, moreover, that "in exchange for black acceptance of restrictions on the franchise and no further demands for 'social equality,' the South's white rulers were to allow gradual progress in agriculture and business and to rein in the rednecks."[35] He espoused sacrificing social justice and the right to vote in exchange for white authorities allowing black economic advancement and restraining white terrorists.

James D. Anderson provides a cogent narrative on Washington's beliefs. Anderson correctly observes that a philosophy that expected black southerners to "eschew politics and concentrate on economic development, was not, as it has been hailed, a great compromise. It was the logical extension of an ideology that rejected black political power while recognizing that the South's agricultural economy rested on the backs of black agricultural workers."[36] Anderson explains that Washington's notion of interracial harmony and his emphasis on nonacademic industrial education for blacks, which essentially endorsed the racial hierarchy of the South, was predicated on a social foundation of political disenfranchisement, civil inequality, and racial subordination.[37]

Washington's views contrasted with those of Du Bois and a number of other prominent black leaders, who unequivocally demanded civil and human rights and an end to black disenfranchisement.[38] Du Bois maintained that Washington's doctrine disparaged blacks and relegated them to second-class citizenship. In his seminal narrative, *The Souls of Black Folk*, Du Bois contended: "But so far as Mr. Washington apologizes for injustice . . . does not rightly value the privilege and duty of voting, belittles the emasculating effects of caste distinctions, and opposes the higher training and ambition of our brighter minds—so far as he, the South, or the Nation, does this,—we must unceasingly and firmly oppose them."[39] Although Du Bois strongly criticized Washington's social and educational philosophy, which "advocated that African Americans forgo political power, civil rights, and higher education and focus on the accumulation of wealth," Du Bois also acknowledged that Washington sometimes "spoke out against lynchers and mob violence and at times used his influence to improve black conditions."[40]

A number of scholars have excoriated Washington for his Cotton States speech and for propagating a view that, according to Du Bois, "accepts the alleged inferiority of the Negro races."[41] However, historian Derrick Alridge and a number of other scholars, including Michael West and Louis Harlan, have argued for a more complicated understanding of Washington that looks beyond the "clichéd representations of the Washington versus Du Bois debate and vocational versus classical educational dichotomy too often used to describe Washington's educational philosophy."[42] Additionally, David Levering Lewis, in his work *W. E. B. Du Bois: Biography of a Race, 1868–1919*, observes that Washington had an "impressive record of secret civil rights maneuverings."[43] For example, Lewis notes that Washington worked behind the scenes to outlaw grandfather clauses, covertly lobbied and funneled monies for a legal assault on disenfranchisement clauses, and supported lawyers fighting racial exclusion from juries.

Despite the complexities of Washington's philosophy and his covert actions to resist racial injustice and improve the quality of black life, his public address that advocated forgoing civil rights played into the hands of whites who espoused white supremacy and racial inequality. For the *Signal* editors, his address aptly rationalized relegating the black applicants to an "all-colored" institution, despite the fact that Georgia State was a state institution supported by taxpayers, including a generous portion of blacks.

In lockstep with white political leaders, the editorial alleged that Communist-inspired NAACP leaders had brainwashed the applicants. It was commonplace to brand civil rights advocates as Communists, and segregationists used the ploy to help rouse opposition to the civil rights movement. The Communist label was frequently used to try to denigrate the character of Martin Luther King Jr. and the integrity of the black freedom struggle. From the onset of his prominence as a civil rights leader to the end of his life, King was "chased by allegations, especially from segregationists, that he was a Communist or was controlled by them."[44] In 1954, reacting to the *Brown* mandate for racial equality in schools, Governor Griffin had contended that "race baiters and communists" were attempting to destroy "every vestige of states' rights."[45] Vowing to discredit the NAACP leaders supporting the students in *Hunt*, the defendants' attorneys attempted to establish that these leaders were Communist or Communist-influenced with ulterior motives.[46]

Each of the defendants' attorneys in the Georgia State case had been involved in successfully defending the state against Ward's complaint. Predictably, they recycled their patent denial that the admissions procedures were discriminatory and averred that the regulations were equally applicable to both white and black applicants. The defendants also contended that the complainants had not complied with the Board of Regents' policy requiring the submission of a character certificate from the clerk of the Superior Court. Hoping to replicate the outcome in *Ward* and have the case dismissed on technical grounds, Cook argued that the court should dismiss the matter because the plaintiffs, as a group, had no right to bring the complaint. He asserted that their rights, if any, were individual, and a class action could not attack the admissions regulations.

Eager to forestall federal judicial review of the matter and uphold segregated education, Cook argued forcefully that the federal court should not rule on the matter in advance of the courts of Georgia. Cook also claimed that the complaint filed by the plaintiffs was "clearly within the power and authority of the Board of Regents" to resolve.[47] He chose not to view the plaintiffs' complaint within the context of the Fourteenth Amendment and pleaded with the judge to dismiss the case and thereby remand it to the state.

Cook's argument, based on "states' rights doctrine," had the fervent support of Governor Griffin and the Georgia legislators who had approved the doctrine. Despite Georgia officials' protestations that the state did not practice racial discrimination, they knew well that a federal court trial that reviewed the matter on constitutional grounds posed a significant threat to maintaining separate schools and colleges. As noted previously, prior to *Hunt v. Arnold*, a panoply of lower courts as well as the U.S. Supreme Court had declared segregated education unconstitutional in a number of southern and border states, including Alabama, Maryland, Missouri, Oklahoma, and Texas.[48]

From June 10, 1957, until the trial began, many pretrial motions, conferences, depositions, and other legal actions occurred, including numerous legal maneuvers by the defendants' attorneys seeking dismissal of the suit. On June 29, 1957, in Cook's motion for dismissal, he argued unabashedly that Georgia State's entrance requirements were "valid and lawful administrative regulations, adopted in good faith, and reasonably calculated to improve the quality of students admitted" to Georgia State.[49] Cook filed a subsequent motion in October 1958 claiming that the suit brought by the black applicants was "not being maintained in good faith" and that "it was brought at the insistence and urging of the NAACP," practically a carbon copy of his argument against Ward's lawsuit.[50]

In Cook's attempt to prove the NAACP's complicity in the case, he filed a motion before Sloan to compel local NAACP president John Calhoun to answer pretrial questions. Calhoun was subsequently subpoenaed to testify at a deposition on September 26, 1958. The indomitable Calhoun declined to respond to questions about the NAACP's participation in the suit.[51] Calhoun, a longtime Atlanta civil rights leader whose involvement in the fight for racial equality dated back to the 1940s, had openly refused to acquiesce to moderate civil rights leaders in Atlanta who urged him to tone down his activism.[52] In 1952, Gloster Current, the deputy executive director of the NAACP, observed that Calhoun's "activist leadership" was "too militant" for some of Atlanta's black leaders.[53]

Led by Moore, the attorneys for the four plaintiffs filed a response to Murphy's motion, seeking to resist the state's efforts to obtain information from Calhoun about support and assistance from the NAACP. The response asserted that "where a plaintiff alleges facts sufficient to bring him within the jurisdiction of the court which entitles him to relief," it was irrelevant whether other parties were financing that plaintiff or helping with the suit, and that therefore the defense attorneys had no right to this information. Moore and Hollowell also argued in their response that "[the] fact that others are paying the expenses of the litigation does not impair [the plaintiffs'] legal interest or standing to sue."[54] Sloan, however, granted Murphy's motion and ordered Calhoun to answer questions related to the NAACP's assistance to the plaintiffs.

Sloan held that information regarding the NAACP's assistance was relevant to the suit, compelling Calhoun to give pretrial testimony concerning the organization's involvement.[55] Yielding to Sloan's order, Calhoun subsequently acknowledged that the NAACP helped finance the litigation.[56] Similarly, when pressed by Murphy, McDaniel, who worked as a secretary for Calhoun, acknowledged that she had discussed with Calhoun the possibility of securing NAACP funds to help with the lawsuit. However, like her boss, McDaniel downplayed the influence of the NAACP. She contended that Calhoun was unaware of her involvement in writing a letter to Georgia State alumni, although the group of applicants had met at the NAACP office to write the letter, and McDaniel had made final edits and mimeographed it in the NAACP office before mailing it to the alumni.[57] McDaniel's close association with Calhoun, the applicants' use of the NAACP office as a meeting place, and their use of its facilities to prepare the letters raised questions about McDaniel's insistence that Calhoun was unaware of her involvement in preparing the letters.

Though Calhoun acknowledged that the NAACP helped the litigants by providing financial support, in response to Murphy's probing, and choosing his words very carefully, he insisted repeatedly that he had no records or documents in his custody or within the confines of his NAACP office pertaining to the Georgia State case. Calhoun had good reason to respond cautiously to Murphy's queries. Less than two years earlier, seeking to intimidate and harass the NAACP and its members into quietude, T. V. Williams, revenue commissioner of Georgia, demanded the NAACP's membership records. When Calhoun refused to turn over the records, local judge Durwood Pye, a diehard segregationist, held Calhoun guilty of contempt.[58]

Though Hollowell and Walden, Calhoun's attorneys, asked Pye to recuse himself due to racial prejudice against Negroes, Pye responded that he considered it insulting to be accused of racial bias against "nigras." However, openly showing his racial bias, he remarked, "The Court [referring to himself] also does not believe in mongrelization of the races."[59] In its coverage of Pye's judicial decision under the headline "NAACP Head Here Ordered Put in Jail," the *Atlanta Journal* reported, "Fulton Superior Court Judge Durwood Pye Friday ordered the Atlanta branch president of the National Association for the Advancement of Colored People be lodged in Fulton jail until he produces books of the organization."[60] Further penalizing Calhoun and the NAACP, on December 14, 1956, Pye fined the NAACP $25,000 and ordered the organization to turn over its records. Pye, however, suspended Calhoun's jail sentence, quipping, "so long as he behaves himself."[61]

In the meantime, Hollowell and Walden, with assistance from Robert Carter, quickly appealed Pye's ruling. The Supreme Court of Georgia eventually ruled in their favor two years later.[62] In addition to the importance of this high court victory for protecting NAACP records, the successful appeal served the useful purpose of keeping Calhoun out of jail.

At the time of the *Hunt v. Arnold* court proceeding, however, Pye's ruling had not yet been overturned. Pye's decree had had a chilling effect, for such a fine had the potential to cripple the NAACP's campaign for equity in Georgia. The local branch could hardly afford to pay the fine, yet in a letter to Hollowell, Carter bluntly stated, "We [the NAACP national office] are not going to be able to put up $25,000."[63] The prospect of going to jail and the threat of paying a $25,000 fine seemed to have tempered Calhoun. Though not submissive, the usually resolute Calhoun framed his responses to Murphy with care, even commenting during one telling exchange with Murphy, "I don't want to be in contempt again."[64]

On November 26, 1958, in a surprising move by the plaintiffs' attorneys, Moore notified the attorneys for the defendants of a motion filed with the court to strike the name of Russell T. Roberts as a plaintiff. On December 3, 1958, Sloan granted the request. A front-page article appeared in the *Atlanta Daily World* the following day with the blunt headline, "Plaintiff Quits Georgia College Entry Suit Here."[65] Moore said in the article that Roberts had been contemplating withdrawing from the lawsuit for some time, but he was not at liberty to reveal publicly the reason for Roberts's decision. The newspaper reported that Roberts was unavailable for comment, but the motion to strike his name indicated that his withdrawal was "on account of personal circumstances beyond [his] control."[66] Since the pending case had attracted widespread media coverage, Roberts's withdrawal was covered in national media outlets. *Jet Magazine*, the black-owned national publication, reported that Roberts withdrew from the "integration suit" for "personal reasons."[67]

Though the circumstances surrounding Roberts's withdrawal were not immediately made public, he had acknowledged during pretrial court proceedings that he possessed a criminal record, and he subsequently withdrew to avoid possibly jeopardizing the case and perhaps causing public embarrassment.[68] During a deposition given by Roberts on August 18, 1958, defense attorney B. D. Murphy posed a series of questions that resulted in Roberts divulging his criminal record. Under penetrating questioning by Murphy, which clearly showed that the defense had meticulously researched Roberts's personal background, Roberts revealed disturbing news that sealed his fate as a plaintiff in the case. He disclosed that he had been arrested and released under $10,000 bond to the Criminal Court of Fulton County in a lottery case.[69] According to the indictment, which Murphy read verbatim during the deposition, Roberts "in said County of Fulton on the 14th day of March 1958, did keep, maintain and operate a lottery known as the number game for the hazarding of money."[70]

Equally troubling, the defense attorneys had discovered that the Federal Income Tax Department had investigated Roberts for unreported income. In response to Murphy's questioning regarding this matter, Roberts stated that the Federal Income Tax Department had summoned him to bring his records for examination, which showed that his bank deposits exceeded his income for the year 1957.[71] Roberts contended that he had earned the money for the deposits that exceeded his 1957 income over a period of twenty years and had taken the money from his "strongbox" to make the deposits.[72] Though Hollowell and Moore objected vigorously to Murphy's line of questioning as "completely irrelevant and immaterial" to the *Hunt* case, Murphy repeatedly interrogated Roberts regarding his alleged unreported income and criminal indictment.

During one tense exchange, Murphy asked Roberts directly "whether or not [he was] guilty as charged" in the criminal indictment related to his alleged gambling. Moore strongly opposed the question, insisting, "We object to that on the ground that the question asks for a bald conclusion of law and it is a matter for the Court to decide and the jury to decide possibly upon the trial of that case as to whether or not this witness is guilty or not, and we accordingly shall instruct the witness not to answer the question on that ground."[73] Before Murphy completed his examination of Roberts, with a copy of Roberts's divorce proceeding in hand he inquired about yet another potential character issue he had uncovered in his background investigation.[74] Roberts's first wife, Marthenia Lockett, whom he married in 1946 and divorced in 1947, had had him arrested for nonsupport.[75]

In Murphy's exhaustive effort to discredit Roberts's character, he even questioned Roberts regarding traffic infractions. The extent of Murphy's unrelenting scrutiny of Roberts's personal background is revealed in a telling exchange:

> [MURPHY] Have you got an automobile driver's license?
> [ROBERTS] Yes, I do.
> [MURPHY] How many times has it been suspended?
> [ROBERTS] Once.
> [MURPHY] What was that for?
> [ROBERTS] Jumping a red light, I believe it was. No, it wasn't. I don't remember. It was, I believe it was I got two tickets in a six-months' period.
> [MURPHY] You were convicted twice in a six-months' period, weren't you?
> [ROBERTS] Beg pardon?
> [MURPHY] You were convicted twice in a six-month period of traffic violations?
> [ROBERTS] I paid two fines. I don't know whether you call that convicted or not.
> [MURPHY] Well, you didn't pay the fine just out of generosity to the City, did you?[76]

Though Roberts withdrew from the case in large measure due to the criminal indictment related to the illegal lottery, the other serious concerns Murphy had discovered, such as the alleged unreported income, raised questions about Roberts's character and moral suitability for admission to Georgia State. In Georgia's relentless campaign to sustain segregation, even the trivial misdemeanor traffic citation—let alone the lottery allegation and arrest for nonsupport—would have provided a basis sufficient to reject him on moral grounds and subsequently jeopardize the case.

In the *Holmes v. Danner* case, university officials attacked Hamilton Holmes for moral turpitude because he supposedly lied about a speeding ticket. Admissions counselor Morris O. Phelps testified during the *Holmes* trial that he "asked the boy . . . if he had ever been arrested, and he said no, he had never been arrested."[77] Phelps contended that he knew that Holmes's statement was untruthful because he was aware that Holmes had been arrested for speeding. Though Phelps, under intensive questioning by Donald Hollowell, acknowledged that the questions asked of Holmes were not customarily asked of white applicants, officials still used such information in their attempt to mar Holmes's reputation.[78] Clearly, in light of the more serious issues raised about Roberts, his desire to enter Georgia State was doomed.

Civil rights lawyers routinely screened complainants to identify potential weaknesses in their background that the defense might exploit. Constance Baker Motley noted in her autobiography, *Equal Justice under Law*, that shortly before the *Hunt* trial the legal team learned that "each woman had something in her past that would prove embarrassing."[79] However, the bombshell about Russell's gambling indictment and federal income tax problems seemed to come as a complete surprise to the plaintiffs' attorneys.

Since local attorneys and NAACP LDF attorneys had represented the plaintiffs for about two years and were keenly aware of the defendants' tactics in such cases, it is somewhat baffling that the attorneys did not do their due diligence in investigating Roberts's background. Though it is not conclusive, lack of time and resources were likely the culprits. The NAACP and local civil rights attorneys were litigating a number of civil rights cases at that time, seeking to undermine the laws that propped up state-sanctioned racial discrimination while also representing black defendants who were (often wrongly) charged with capital crimes in a racially hostile legal system.[80]

Moreover, the attorneys were litigating an immense number of civil rights cases on a shoestring budget. In a December 1956 report to the Georgia State Conference of NAACP Branches, Hollowell, in his role as chairman of Georgia's NAACP Legal Redress Committee, enumerated the large number of cases that the handful of civil rights lawyers were contesting at the same time they were involved with the *Hunt* case. Hollowell asserted that the Legal Redress Committee lacked the time, funds, and staff to "adequately cover [Georgia] with legal assistance."[81]

To convey the enormity of their task, Hollowell detailed for the state conference participants the major civil rights cases this small band of local lawyers was litigating across the state:

1. Valdosta Suit—Filed by Governor, through the Attorney General, four attorneys filed a suit to enjoin the Valdosta Board of Education from taking any action whatsoever toward integrating the public schools. . . .
2. Savannah Housing Case—This case was heard on appeal this Fall. Attorney Walden will report on the findings.
3. Holmes Golf Case—Supreme Court decision rendered enabling Negroes to play golf in Atlanta at all public golf courses. Attorneys E. E. Moore, Jr., R. E. Thomas, Jr., and S. S. Robinson were counsel in that case.

4. Georgia State College of Business Administration Case—filed last summer pursuant to obtaining entrance therein by Negroes. Atty. E. E. Moore, Jr. is counsel.
5. Ward Case—After nine different hearings since the return of plaintiff from the Armed Service, this case has now been set for trial December 17, 1956. Attys. A. T. Walden and D. L. Hollowell are counsel.
6. T. V. Williams, Tax Commissioner, vs. NAACP, a corporation, et al.— The NAACP and others are presently seeking to show cause why they did not produce certain records upon demand of agents of the Tax Commissioner and pursuant to a court order, and further why they should not be held in contempt for failing to comply therewith.[82]

To emphasize the magnitude of the litigation efforts, Hollowell added, "There have been several other cases investigated and some persons defended by your chairman and others."[83]

Moreover, Hollowell observed that there had been a surge of activity by Georgia officials bent on racial oppression, including direct attacks on the NAACP, which overwhelmed the Legal Redress Committee. "On the debit side has been the step-up of activities on the part of certain state officials and others who think like them, to inflame the minds of white people to an extent calculated to provoke violence against the NAACP, specifically, and our people generally. Yes, even now as I read this report, the very life of our organization in this State is being attacked."[84] Hollowell was referring to the state's legal actions to secure NAACP records and Attorney General Cook's request to the Georgia legislature to "declare the NAACP as a subversive organization."[85] Hollowell himself had been a defendant in the NAACP records case, but Cook dropped the charges against him after discovering that Hollowell was not an official of the NAACP at the time the revenue agents demanded the NAACP records.[86]

In yet another action designed to hamstring the NAACP as Moore and Hollowell were preparing for the *Hunt* trial, Georgia officials, led by Assistant Attorney General E. Freeman Leverett, sought to drive the NAACP out of Georgia by proclaiming that it was in violation of "barratry," whereby "a person or organization not directly involved caused the [legal] action to be brought."[87] Leverett, representing the attorney general's office, declared: "[The NAACP had] no legal foundation at all in a claim that the NAACP, by claiming to represent the Negro race, can escape any application of barratry laws.... The NAACP has no bona fide interest, under the law, in which students go to which schools, and cannot escape consequences of barratry if it, and not individuals directly concerned, actually instigate lawsuits."[88]

Troubled by a Georgia House-Senate committee's pending probe of the NAACP's alleged violation of barratry laws, in a March 7, 1958, letter to NAACP executive secretary Roy Wilkins, Calhoun pleaded with Wilkins to take proactive steps against the legislative committee "as an alternative to waiting for them to pick [the NAACP leaders] off... like 'sitting ducks.'"[89] Fearful of the possible dissolution of the Georgia NAACP and of adverse consequences for its officers, Calhoun also informed Wilkins that the Atlanta branch had retained Walden to represent branch officers and the Georgia State Conference had retained Hollowell to protect the interests of the state organization and its officers.[90] Calhoun had good reason to be fearful. In addition to the actions taken by Georgia officials to cripple the NAACP, by the end of 1956, Florida, Mississippi, North Carolina, South Carolina, and Virginia had instituted laws designed to harass the NAACP, and Alabama, Louisiana, and Texas had enacted laws banning the organization's actions outright.[91]

Wilkins was disturbed by the probe but insisted that the NAACP's legal actions representing the plaintiffs' efforts to end segregation were lawful. "Our blanket contention is that we are operating to defend the constitutional rights of Negro citizens and that we are doing so in a legal manner.... What they [the state officials] seek is harassment and there is little we can do to forestall a state from so acting. We can only refute after they act."[92]

Thus, in addition to the panoply of cases that the Legal Redress Committee was litigating, including the *Hunt* case, its attorneys were mired in a bitter fight with Georgia's leading public officials for the NAACP's very survival in Georgia. This may explain, in part, the NAACP lawyers' failure to devote adequate time and resources to vetting plaintiffs. In addition, the local civil rights lawyers were paid only a nominal fee for their services, forcing these already-overworked attorneys to practice a wide spectrum of law to pay their bills and support their families while working on civil rights cases.[93]

Notwithstanding the substantive issues raised concerning Roberts, dredging up extraneous and irrelevant issues in applicants' personal backgrounds was a stratagem favored by southern opposition lawyers seeking to disqualify black applicants. Motley noted that she could not recall a civil rights case in which the defendants did not go on a witch hunt, seeking grounds to disqualify the complainant on a basis other than race.[94] In this case, the defendants prevailed in disqualifying Roberts. With his dismissal, three plaintiffs remained at the center of the suit: Barbara Pace

Hunt, Myra Payne Dinsmore, and Iris Mae Welch. Following Roberts's withdrawal, Moore vowed that the remaining three plaintiffs would "not withdraw from the court action and [would] see the issue through until a final decision [was] made by the courts."[95]

Though disappointed with Roberts's withdrawal, Hunt, Dinsmore, and Welch were also resolute about continuing their lawsuit against segregation at Georgia State. Summing up her determination to persevere in the case and the frustration that led to her decision to become a plaintiff, Dinsmore described her resolve after Georgia State repeatedly rejected her application: "I encountered attorney Moore, and he asked me if I wanted to pursue it further. I said, 'I just think it is terrible that we pay taxes for that college or university and we can't go. I would like to pursue it.' And that's how the court case came about."[96]

In addition to their individual aspirations for higher education and personal quests for justice, Hunt, Dinsmore, and Welch worked for independent black entrepreneurs and businesses that were strong advocates for social justice. Hunt worked for the crusading *Pittsburgh Courier*, an activist newspaper; Dinsmore worked for NAACP stalwart Jesse Hill and the Atlanta Life Insurance Company, a major financial supporter of civil rights causes; and Welch worked for self-employed businessman and long-time civil rights activist J. E. Jordan. Hunt was also later employed at Atlanta University, where she undoubtedly was exposed to race leaders such as the intrepid William Madison Boyd, NAACP leader and Atlanta University Political Science Department chair, and Whitney Young, civil rights activist and Atlanta University dean of social work. Predictably, a number of Atlanta's activist-leaders and progressive black establishments, including the Atlanta branch of the NAACP, played key roles in supporting the plaintiffs throughout their protracted struggle to gain entrance to Georgia State.

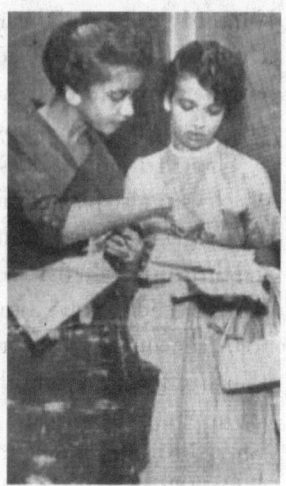

Applicants Myra Elliot Dinsmore and Barbara Hunt, two of the nine black applicants to the all-white Georgia State College of Business in 1956, talk over new entrance requirements after being denied the right to register at the Georgia State College of Business Administration, June 23, 1956. Courtesy of the *Pittsburgh Courier*

Plaintiffs Iris Mae Welch, Barbara Hunt, and Myra Elliot Dinsmore enter the Federal Court Building in Atlanta on the first day of hearings in their suit against Georgia State, December 9, 1958. Photograph by Harmon Perry, courtesy of Phyllis Perry

Donald L. Hollowell, Constance Baker Motley, and E. E. Moore Jr. hold discussion during a recess in the first day's hearing, December 9, 1958. Photograph by Harmon Perry, courtesy of Phyllis Perry

Austin Thomas Walden, dean of the handful of black attorneys in Georgia and one of the first African Americans to practice law in Georgia, n.d. Walden provided legal assistance to the black applicants and plaintiffs seeking to enter Georgia State. Courtesy of Kenan Research Center at the Atlanta History Center

Constance Baker Motley with Thurgood Marshall, NAACP LDF director-counsel, and Jack Greenberg, NAACP LDF attorney. Marshall and the NAACP joined local lawyers in filing the lawsuit against Georgia State on behalf of the plaintiffs. Courtesy of the NAACP Legal Defense and Educational Fund, Inc.

Atlanta civil rights leaders, including NAACP Atlanta branch president, pastor of Friendship Baptist Church, and Morehouse professor Rev. Samuel Williams (speaking to reporter); and Donald L. Hollowell (second row, center), Georgia's chief civil rights attorney, 1958. Courtesy of Archives Division, Auburn Avenue Research Library on African American Culture and History, Atlanta-Fulton Public Library System

John Calhoun, NAACP Atlanta branch president and community activist, n.d. Calhoun and the Atlanta NAACP provided support and assistance to the applicants and plaintiffs. Courtesy of John Calhoun Papers, Atlanta University Center Robert W. Woodruff Library

Jesse Hill Jr., Atlanta NAACP leader and president of Atlanta Life Insurance Company, n.d. Hill served as a key adviser to the applicants and plaintiffs. Courtesy of Archives Division, Auburn Avenue Research Library on African American Culture and History, Atlanta-Fulton Public Library System

Attorney General Eugene Cook of Georgia, lead attorney for the state in the *Hunt v. Arnold* case, confers with attorney Charles J. Bloch (right), representing Georgia's governor, before testifying in opposition to civil rights legislation at a House Judiciary Subcommittee hearing, February 7, 1957. In his testimony, Cook said enactment of civil rights proposals would result in the "creation of the federal gestapo" and upset social patterns the South was determined to maintain. Bloch served as a member of the Board of Regents and vice-president of the States' Rights Council of Georgia. Courtesy of AP Images

Marvin Griffin speaking at his gubernatorial inauguration, 1954. Courtesy of AP Images

George M. Sparks became director of the Georgia Tech Evening School of Commerce (now Georgia State University) in 1928. A former war correspondent and city editor for the *Macon Telegraph*, Sparks taught journalism at Mercer University and Georgia Tech, where he was put in charge of publicity and journalism before taking on the role of director. Courtesy of GSU Archives

Lead plaintiff Barbara Pace Hunt, high school graduation photograph, Beaver Falls High School, Beaver Falls, Pennsylvania, 1951. Courtesy of Crystal Freeman

Crystal Freeman holds a photo of her mother, Barbara Hunt. Photography by Meg Buscema, courtesy of Georgia State University

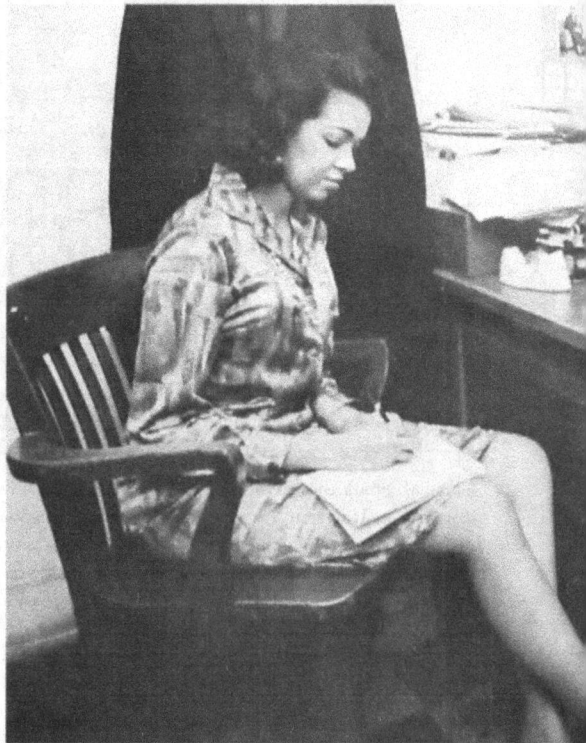

Barbara Pace Hunt, secretary, Southern Christian Leadership Conference public relations office, circa late 1950s. Courtesy of Crystal Freeman

Sylvia Hall Chapman, Wylma Long Blanding, Susan Cosby Freeman, and Ralph A. Long Jr. (top) fondly remember their relative, Annette Lucille Hall, Georgia State's first African American student. Photography by Meg Buscema, courtesy of Georgia State University

Marybelle Reynolds Warner, Georgia State's first full-time black student. Photography by Meg Buscema, courtesy of Georgia State University

CHAPTER 4

Hunt v. Arnold

The Trial Begins

From December 8 to December 12, 1958—more than two years after the suit was filed, and following vigorous efforts by the defendants to dismiss the case—*Hunt v. Arnold* was tried before Judge Boyd Sloan in the Atlanta Division of the U.S. District Court for the Northern District of Georgia.[1] In an article in the *Atlanta Journal*, Gene Britton summed up the principal issue in the case: whether Georgia State's admissions policies were "discriminatory against three Negro students who contend[ed] they applied for admission and were turned down because of their race."[2] Noting the impending legal skirmish between the state's segregationist leaders, led by Cook and Murphy, and "a corps of top Negro attorneys" led by Moore, Hollowell, and Motley, Britton wrote, "Big legal batteries will open fire here Monday morning in the bitter war over integration in public education."[3]

A front-page article in the *Atlanta Daily World*, the nation's first black-owned newspaper, reported in honorific tones that three Negro plaintiffs, "Mesdames Barbara Hunt, Iris Mae Welch and Myra Elliott Dinsmore, are attacking entrance requirements established by the State of Georgia and which they claim are contrary to the 14th Amendment to the United States Constitution."[4] Notably, the *ADW*'s identification of the women contrasted with the approach taken by a number of other newspapers, which impersonally referred to the plaintiffs as "the three Negro women." The *ADW* expressed the sentiments of the plaintiffs and the wider black community in contending that the black applicants were denied admission to Georgia

State due to racially biased requirements that "unlawfully exclude[d] Negroes" from entering the college.[5] In reporting on the civil rights advocacy by the three "Mesdames," the *ADW* cautioned its readers about the tremendous uphill battle that lay ahead to get rid of segregation. The paper underscored that if the litigants triumphed in the case and Georgia State admitted them, under Georgia law all state financial support to the institution would end.[6]

The trial began on Monday, December 8, at 10:00 a.m. before a standing-room-only crowd—including regents, university officials, and prominent black leaders—that was "evenly divided between whites and Negroes."[7] Moore and Hollowell centered their attack in the trial on the character certificates mandated by the regents, asserting that the requirement was simply a ploy to keep blacks out of Georgia State and other all-white institutions.[8] Hollowell homed in on the difficulty black applicants faced in securing recommendations from white alumni, asserting that the Board of Regents' certification requirement was "unreasonable and discriminatory."[9] In his cross-examination of regents officials, Hollowell elicited testimony confirming that the regents had adopted the certification requirements immediately following Horace T. Ward's application to the UGA law school in 1950.[10]

In response, and despite the hasty creation of the policy shortly after Ward's application, the defense sought to prove that state officials implemented the policy "in good faith" and that it did not discriminate against "Negroes." On the first day of the trial, Board of Regents officials repeatedly swore, *under oath*, that the board had "no segregation policy" and that they created the certification policy to improve the quality of students seeking entrance to university-system colleges.[11] Regent Howard Callaway testified that the regents were concerned about "the quality of education in the entire University System." He stated, "We felt very strongly that we needed all the safeguard [*sic*] we could have on the quality of applicants for admission to all units of the University System. We felt that one of the strongest ones was the fact that an alumnus, a man who would have enterest [*sic*] in that school and a man who would know about that school should certify the moral character of each of these people."[12] Despite the patently obvious motivation for the hastily devised certification requirement, Callaway insisted that the Board of Regents had no policy forbidding a white alumnus from providing a recommendation for a Negro applicant.[13]

In defense of the policy, Regent Everett Williams testified that he felt sure white alumni would certify a qualified Negro of good character.[14] In answer to a direct question from Hollowell, Williams surprisingly agreed that there were "Negroes of good character who possess[ed] the entrance qualifications" for admission to white colleges.[15] Though Board of Regents and Georgia State officials denied that race was a consideration in the policies that restricted blacks from white institutions of higher learning, they seldom acknowledged that blacks possessed the qualifications to enter white colleges or universities.

It was therefore a huge anomaly for Williams to make such an assertion, and the statement made newspaper headlines. Following his unexpected testimony about "qualified Negroes," the *ADW* featured a front-page article titled "Negroes Have Qualifications to Enter College, 1 Regent Admits."[16] Williams's statement was liberal in comparison to the views of his regents counterparts. Nonetheless, he refused to acknowledge that the regents had designed the racially discriminatory admissions policy to bar blacks from all-white colleges. His rationale for rejecting the plaintiffs and all other black applicants for admission was that "all previous Negro applicants failed to complete their application requirements."[17]

In the face of such a charade, Moore and Hollowell delved into questions that highlighted the bizarre and tragic nature of segregation. Their strategy, in part, was to show that Jim Crow laws, customs, and traditions made it extremely difficult for black applicants to secure recommendations from white alumni. Hunt, Dinsmore, and Welch testified that they had little social contact with white persons and confirmed that they did not know any Georgia State alumni. They also testified that they had visited Georgia State accompanied by two ministers in an effort to secure the alumni certificates. Hunt said she and the other plaintiffs had been refused recommendations by several white alumni because they did not know the applicants. She explained that although Reverend Williams had been present to vouch for her character, the alumni still refused to sign the certificate because they also did not know Williams.

During an interview with Dinsmore, she discussed the nature of social relationships between blacks and whites during the 1950s: "Well, back in the fifties, the chance of a black college-aged person knowing an alumnus well enough to request a character reference was almost out of the question, because your paths just didn't cross. You never were in a social or academic situation with whites. Those types of relationships were almost nonexistent."[18] Ironically, state officials, who strictly enforced laws maintaining the social order that obstructed relationships between blacks and whites, mounted a defense that downplayed the social distance between blacks and whites. Regents and university officials acknowledged the absence of social contact between white and black persons but at the same time attempted to disguise the fact that both law and custom thwarted such contact between the races.

Moore sought to educe testimony from Board of Regents chair Robert Arnold, a University of Georgia alumnus and prominent businessman who had served on the board since 1948, regarding whether there were any public institutions in which blacks and whites had social contact. Moore met with stiff resistance and absurd responses in his effort to get the board chair to acknowledge that existing social patterns in the South prevented Negroes from having social contact with whites, making it virtually impossible "for a Negro to know an alumnus well enough to acquire certification."[19]

In one tense exchange between Moore and Arnold concerning the extent of black and white social interaction, Arnold sardonically responded, "I have seen some in jails, chain gangs together."[20] In yet another ludicrous response, Arnold stated that he had seen "colored people" at barbecues. However, under relentless cross-examination, he admitted that he had never observed colored persons *seated* at a barbecue.

Further testimony by Arnold on this subject also tended toward the absurd, especially when Moore questioned him about his club membership:

MOORE: What clubs, if any, do you belong to, Mr. Arnold?
ARNOLD: Well, I belong to the Baptist Church, and that is—
MOORE: Are there any Negro members of your church?
ARNOLD: I don't think so. Not to my knowledge. I have never seen a list of the entire membership but—
MOORE: You have never known any yourself to be members, however, have you?
ARNOLD: I have seen them in the church, yes.
MOORE: You say of your own knowledge you have not known any to be members of your church?
ARNOLD: No, I haven't. No.
MOORE: What else do you belong to, sir? What other club or society that you are a member of?
ARNOLD: Well, I am a member of the Capital City Club in Atlanta.
MOORE: Are any Negroes a member of that club?
ARNOLD: I see lots of them around there but I don't know whether they are members or not. Some of them are mighty good friends of mine.[21]

Arnold, a life member of the Capital City Club, knew without a doubt that the most exclusively all-white private club in Atlanta had no black members.[22]

Arnold, who had served as the Board of Regents chair since 1952, when Horace Ward sought admission to the University of Georgia School of Law, had vividly conveyed his disdain for blacks in a February 25, 1952, letter to law school dean J. Alton Hosch. In response to a *Red and Black* student newspaper article written by a forward-thinking white student who expressed support for admitting Ward, Arnold made demeaning statements about the student and revealed his deplorable racist views: "I wonder what she could know about the personal traits of negroes [*sic*] and if B.O. could come under the head of traits with this young lady. Maybe her education is lacking somewhere, although she is a candidate for a major in education. With her thinking, she had best be careful to locate above the Mason & Dixon line."[23] Arnold's sentiments clearly displayed the bigotry underlying the tactics Georgia's leading officials employed to sustain segregation.[24]

To further bolster the claim that the regents had developed the alumni certification policy "in good faith" to improve the quality of students rather than to create barriers for blacks, Murphy called regent Charles Bloch to the stand. Bloch flatly denied that the regents adopted this admissions requirement to exclude blacks.[25] He testified about the inception of the requirement, which revealed that the timeline for creating the requirement closely paralleled the period in which Horace T. Ward was attempting to enter UGA.[26] Bloch was a regent from 1950 to 1957 and served as a member of the Board of Regents' Education Committee and chair of the state's Judiciary Council. Though Bloch lost in many of his efforts to sustain segregation before the federal courts, he was nevertheless a formidable segregationist lawyer whom the state of Georgia and local governments frequently retained in their fight to uphold segregation.[27]

A close ally of U.S. senator Richard Russell in his crusade against civil rights legislation, Bloch served as vice president of the segregationist States' Rights Council of Georgia and appeared before the House and Senate Judiciary Committees in 1957 to oppose the Civil Rights Bill.[28] In 1948, Bloch delivered the nomination speech for Russell when Russell was nominated for president of the United States at the Democratic National Convention. Bloch pledged that "with a Georgian in the White House," white southerners would not be "crucified on the cross of civil rights."[29] A decade later, in the year of the *Hunt* trial, while serving as vice president of the States' Rights Council he penned a defiant declaration titled "We Need

Not Integrate to Educate," which was widely embraced by the state's segregationist leaders. Bloch vowed, "No federal court can ever compel the Governor and the Legislature [of Georgia] to institute, maintain and operate a system of public schools in which the races are mixed."[30]

Though Bloch claimed to be "proud of [his] Jewish heritage" and faced anti-Semitism, he held the "conviction that there was no inherent contradiction in being both a Jew and a segregationist."[31] Though the "teachings of their faith and the historical experience of their people" led many Jews to support the black freedom struggle, Bloch observed, "I am frequently asked how a person of my religion—which is Jewish—can be a segregationist.... My answer is this.... I don't think the Jewish people have got anything in common with Negroes."[32]

Clive Webb, in his book *Fight against Fear: Southern Jews and Black Civil Rights*, asserted that it was in small towns and rural areas, "where entrenched racial prejudice and the pressures of political conformity were at their most severe, that southern Jews most readily adapted to the segregationist mores of the white Gentile majority."[33] Bloch had moved with his family from Baton Rouge, Louisiana, to Macon, Georgia, at an early age. After attending Mercer University in Macon and the University of Georgia in Athens, he established a law practice in the relatively small town of Macon, in the middle of rural Georgia. He was deeply ensconced in the "segregationist mores of the white Gentile majority" and often served as a national spokesman and staunch legal defender of the alleged virtues of their apartheid-like system.

In full accord with the white power structure and convinced that state officials could defeat Hunt, Dinsmore, and Welch as they had Ward, Bloch was absolute in his stance against the plaintiffs' arguments. He resoundingly defended the regents' adoption of the certification requirements as an authentic effort to recruit "better qualified students."[34] Bloch recounted that the regents initially adopted new admissions regulations in 1953, including aptitude tests for applicants to all schools in the university system, after the American Bar Association's committee investigating the University of Georgia School of Law criticized it for "no aptitude tests, and no other requirement for admission."[35] However, Hollowell's cross-examination of Bloch elicited confirmation that the regents had adopted the new regulations shortly after Ward applied for admission to the UGA law school and during the time his application was pending before the Board of Regents' Education Committee.

In its coverage of the first day of the trial, the *ADW* featured a front-page article written by John Britton with a photograph of Hunt, Dinsmore, and Welch entering the federal court building, as well as a photograph of Hollowell, Moore, and Motley holding a discussion during a court recess. Summing up its perception of a successful opening day for the plaintiffs, the article reported that "attorneys for three Atlanta women seeking to enter a Georgia business college established . . . that most of the strict entrance requirements in the university system were imposed after a Negro [Ward] attempted to enroll at a state school."[36] However, it noted, the "defendants were quick in declaring that race was not a factor which has allowed only white students to enter the Georgia State College of Business Administration."[37]

Hollowell continued to ask questions on the first day of the trial reiterating that the Regents' ex post facto action adversely affected Ward's pending application. Murphy adamantly objected, stating, "I don't think we can re-try the *Ward* case."[38] Judge Sloan, however, overruled the objection, ruling that Murphy had introduced questions about the regulation in his direct examination of witnesses. Sloan declared that the questions were relevant if Hollowell was trying to establish whether the new requirement was designed to thwart Ward's application for admission.[39]

On February 13, 1952, the regents had adopted a resolution asking the University of Georgia School of Law faculty to make recommendations concerning entrance examinations. Tellingly, *on the same day*, regents' executive secretary L. R. Siebert sent Ward a letter notifying him that his application would be delayed until the recommendations were submitted and approved.[40] Despite the incredible coincidence that adopting the new entrance criteria, which required "good moral character" certificates from law school alumni, made it essentially impossible for Ward to meet the requirements, Bloch unequivocally denied that the new requirements were imposed to make it difficult for blacks to gain admission.[41] Bloch, who had lived in Georgia since 1901, acknowledged that blacks and whites had practically no social interaction. Like Callaway, however, he did not concede that it would therefore be extremely difficult for blacks to comply with the regents' alumni certification requirement.[42]

When Chancellor Caldwell, chief executive officer of the Board of Regents, took the stand, he too unabashedly swore that there was no policy of segregation in state-supported colleges in Georgia.[43] He completely affirmed Bloch's testimony that the certification requirement had not been adopted for the purpose of "excluding Negroes from Georgia institutions."[44] Caldwell testified that the regents believed involving alumni in the selection process would lead to "better students" with regard to "character and ability."[45]

Caldwell audaciously claimed that "it would really be a discrimination in favor of the Negro applicants against the White [sic] applicants" to waive the alumni certification requirement. Although Caldwell acknowledged that "as a matter of practice . . . whenever a Negro file[d] an application with one of the colleges in the University System which [were] designated 'White' [sic]," those applications were forwarded to the regents' office for out-of-state aid, he expressed no concern about this blatant discrimination against black applicants.[46]

Caldwell had good reason to try to justify the requirement. Archival records reveal that he was a chief architect of the regents' resolution that blocked Ward's admission to the University of Georgia. In private correspondence with regent Bloch, Caldwell wrote that the resolution was "for the guidance of those who [were] considering the Horace Ward matter."[47] The resolution ultimately led to the alumni certification requirement supposedly imposed on all students seeking to enter the University of Georgia School of Law. The testimony in defense of the rigged system from regents' chair Arnold, the state's constitutional law expert Bloch, and the chief executive officer of the University System clearly illuminated that the segregationist policies the plaintiffs and their lawyers sought to surmount were propagated by the highest-level public officials in the state.

The plaintiffs also alleged in their complaint that they could not obtain a character certification from the clerk of the court of Fulton County because the Georgia State registrar's practice was to mail the certificates to the court in batches *after* the college processed them. However, the plaintiffs' applications were rejected by the college and therefore never mailed to the court. To validate this process, Moore elicited testimony from Judge Eugene Gunby affirming that he had sent Walden a letter on March 23, 1956, informing him that the applications for admission to Georgia State were provided to the court by the registrar's office in batches for the court to certify.[48] Yet Blair testified that the applications of Hunt, Dinsmore, and Welch were rejected not because of race but because they lacked the required certifications from white alumni and the court and were therefore incomplete.[49]

Though state law, regents' policies, and the rigid segregationist practices of white institutions unquestionably obstructed black students, Blair contended in his testimony that he did not know "that certain schools in Georgia [were] operated exclusively for white students."[50] Blair testified,

"I have never been instructed by the Board of Regents that Georgia State College is operated exclusively for the enrollment of white students."[51] Blair was unwavering in his insistence that Georgia State did not practice racial discrimination, even though Hollowell presented prima facie evidence that white colleges were listed in the 1955-56 Georgia State official bulletin under the heading "*white colleges*."[52]

However, despite Blair's claims that he was oblivious to segregated education and his insistence that racial equity characterized the admissions process, Moore succeeded in getting him to reveal to the court the obvious, hypocritical double standard in the treatment of applications from blacks. Blair admitted that he forwarded applications in batches to the Clerk of the Court for character certifications *after* his office processed them. Yet earlier he had testified that he refused to accept the applications from Negro applicants because they did not include the certification. Persisting in his effort to illustrate the disparate treatment of black applicants, Moore elicited testimony from Blair revealing that he could not recall any white applicant who had difficulty securing the certifications.[53]

President Sparks, Blair's superior, who with Blair played a key role in implementing the regents' certification policy and subsequently blocking the admission of the plaintiffs, ended his long tenure with Georgia State in 1957. Sparks passed away on October 29, 1958, shortly before the trial began.[54] To reaffirm the state's claim that it had implemented the certification requirement to improve the quality of students admitted to Georgia State, Murphy called Noah Langdale Jr., Sparks's successor, to reiterate Blair's contentions.[55]

Moore and Hollowell's pretrial work included a meticulous examination of the alumni certifications provided for the applications of white students. Their labor crystallized the inequitable treatment of white and black applicants in relation to the requirement. Hollowell presented evidence that Blair himself, who was *not* a Georgia State alumnus, had signed as an alumnus for a white applicant.

> [HOLLOWELL:] I will ask you to look on the last page and see who signed as the alumni?
> [BLAIR:] This is one that evidently I investigated myself, because I put my signature on it.
> [HOLLOWELL:] You signed as the alumni?
> [BLAIR:] Yes.
> [HOLLOWELL:] Are you a graduate of the Georgia State College of Business Administration?

[BLAIR:] I am not a graduate of the institution, and it is a common custom for the faculty members, so long as they are members there, it can be considered as alumni of the institution. That has been my understanding with the Alumni Association.[56]

In the next sequence of questions, which demonstrated extreme leniency in the way the policy was applied to prospective white students, Hollowell asked Blair whether it was true that whites could obtain certifications from "faculty members who [were] floating around in the halls."[57] Blair acknowledged that although it was not common practice, the alumni signatures for some white applicants had been provided by faculty members who were not alumni.[58] Hollowell also produced a number of applications from white students that were endorsed by employees in Blair's office.[59]

Building on the clear and mounting evidence of disparities in the treatment of black applicants as compared to their white counterparts, Hollowell's probing led Blair to admit that it would be a "rare matter" for a white student to experience difficulty obtaining signatures from alumni of the institution.[60] In what appeared to be yet another victory for the plaintiffs, under interrogation by Hollowell, Board of Regents secretary Siebert also admitted "that the certification ruling was initiated after Horace Ward attempted and failed to gain admission in the University of Georgia Law School in 1950."[61]

In response to these triumphs on behalf of the plaintiffs, the defendants met Moore and Hollowell's next line of questioning with attempts to disguise complicity and collusion as ignorance and innocence. Moore and Hollowell contended that segregation was in full force in public institutions in Georgia; that the discrimination against the plaintiffs was part of a pervasive system of laws, customs, and policies of the state; and that the regents had designed such practices purposely to exclude blacks.

According to testimony by Rev. Samuel Williams, on June 14, 1956, Barbara Hunt, Russell Roberts, Marian McDaniel, and Myra Dinsmore, accompanied by Williams and Reverend Searcy, visited Blair's office seeking admission. Williams "drew laughter from the spectators, mostly Negroes, in the crowded courtroom" when he recounted that he had asked Blair how the plaintiffs could obtain endorsements from Georgia State alumni "when the institution had just been made a college and had no graduates."[62] In deference to the regents and their policies regarding segregated education, Blair told Williams that he could not accept the applications until he had further instructions from the board.

Though Blair never departed from the white power structure's edicts and ploys to sustain segregation, he did appear to make efforts to help the applicants secure the certifications. For example, Blair directed the applicants to alumni present at the college who were approved by the alumni association to provide the certifications. Williams observed that although the applicants were unsuccessful in obtaining alumni certifications, "Mr. Blair's office was particularly kind to us on this visit, for not only did he point out to us that they must have the certifications by these alumni of the school, he also indicated that some such persons were at the school, and suggested we might see them and get them to sign them."[63]

Blair acknowledged in his testimony that after the applicants' failed attempt to secure the required signatures, he rejected their applications due to the absence of the alumni certifications. Blair then escorted the group to meet with President Sparks, who affirmed Blair's rejection of the applications on the same grounds. According to Williams, after he questioned Sparks about the rejections, Sparks asserted, "This is not our personal opinion, or our personal views at all, but we are simply servants of the Board. We are carrying out instructions, so you will have to see the Board of Regents."[64]

On the same day, Sparks called Siebert, executive secretary of the Board of Regents, and directed the parties to Siebert's office, which was located in a building adjacent to Sparks's office, to confer with him about their concerns. Citing the regents' policy that relegated blacks to receiving out-of-state aid, Siebert also refused to accept the applications. Siebert told the applicants and the ministers flat out that "our people usually go out of State to school." When asked by Reverend Williams, "Who are our people?" Siebert responded, "I guess I should have said Negroes receive out-of-state aid."[65]

Despite Siebert's rejection of the applications in accordance with regents' policy, in response to a series of pointed questions from Hollowell at the trial concerning the blatantly discriminatory regulation, the twenty-four-year veteran of the regents' office claimed under oath that he did not know that the purpose of the out-of-state aid policy was to sustain segregation.[66] Hollowell repeatedly grilled Siebert, who had served as executive secretary for the Board of Regents since 1934, regarding the regents' out-of-state aid policy. The policy stipulated that out-of-state aid could be granted to blacks "only in those fields of study which are provided white citizens of Georgia by the State of Georgia, but are not offered at any of the Negro state-supported schools."⁶⁷ For example, the regents provided aid to black students to attend Tuskegee Institute for training in veterinary medicine and to attend Meharry Medical College for training as physicians, to preserve the all-white veterinary college at the University of Georgia and the all-white Medical College of Georgia.⁶⁸

Siebert stubbornly refused to concede that officials had designed the program to shuttle blacks to other states to keep them out of Georgia's white colleges. In response to Hollowell's query regarding sending black students out of state, Siebert responded, "We don't send these students anywhere; out-of-state aid is offered to them, they take it, the Negro goes where they want to go [sic]."⁶⁹

Siebert's testimony starkly contradicted the Board of Regents' resolution that established the "scholarships for negroes," which stated clearly that the regents will provide aid "measured by the difference in cost to the applicant in the institution to which he *is sent* and the cost to white students obtaining similar work in the University System."⁷⁰ Siebert's responses also divulged that in addition to the out-of-state aid provided to black students, the regents had also provided "out-of-state" aid for blacks to take courses at Atlanta University that were offered a few blocks away at Georgia State.⁷¹

Caldwell defended the out-of-state aid program by resurrecting arguments presented in the *Ward* trial two years earlier, when he bragged about how the program provided benefits to blacks and how the regents allocated large sums of money each year for this aid.⁷² Under cross-examination by Hollowell during the *Ward* trial, Caldwell acknowledged the patently obvious purpose of the program: "We do wish in our institutions, and so far as possible, to preserve the segregation of the races."⁷³

In questioning Caldwell during the *Hunt* trial about the out-of-state aid program, Hollowell read Caldwell's testimony from the *Ward* trial. In response, Caldwell put forth a democratic principle to try to justify the racist policy. "The Board of Regents is a public body.... We know from practice that the vast majority of Negroes would rather have out of state aid." Caldwell then asserted that the majority of Georgia's "good Negro citizens" favored segregation."⁷⁴

Caldwell's reference to "good Negro citizens" alluded to the defendants' contention that blacks such as Ward, Hunt, Dinsmore, and Welch, who rejected white supremacy and demanded equal opportunity, were not "good Negro citizens" but instead NAACP pawns, influenced by outside agitators. State attorneys had asserted during the *Ward* trial that Ward was not interested in obtaining a legal education but was simply a tool of the NAACP, "a foot soldier for the integration efforts."[75] Regents and university officials made virtually the same arguments about Hunt, Dinsmore, and Welch.

In Caldwell's relentless effort to safeguard segregated education and justify the discriminatory out-of-state aid policy, he testified that the Board of Regents was a public institution and a servant of the people, and that the board sought "to be responsive to the will of the people whom they serve[d]."[76] It would have been despicable for any state official to try to defend the unconstitutional out-of-state aid program or to pretend, especially under oath, that the black plaintiffs had been treated fairly. However, it was especially despicable for Caldwell, a Harvard-trained lawyer and former president of the University of Georgia.

In an interview with the author, Hollowell observed: "There were some that I put greater responsibility upon than others. And yet I also recognized that if they had done other than what they did it could have been detrimental. At the same time, I say they had a responsibility to be truthful, and I don't think that some of them were really truthful."[77]

Commenting on the dishonest tactics of segregationist officials, Constance Baker Motley observed more bluntly:

> The [legal] system is based on people getting on the stand and telling the truth. But people who talk about their respect for tradition and integrity and the Constitution get involved in one lie after another. They're willing to break down the system to keep a Negro out. In Mississippi, university officials got up on the stand and said they had never discussed the Meredith case. They do the same kind of thing in voting cases. People are denied the right to vote, not because they are Negroes but because they didn't dot an "i" or they interpreted the Constitution incorrectly. This is one of the most serious byproducts of segregation. The people get a disregard for the law. They see supposedly important people get up day after day on the stand and lie.[78]

In his testimony, Board of Regents' chair Arnold proffered a similarly disingenuous response when Moore asked him whether the regents engineered discriminatory policies and operated schools on a segregated basis. Arnold audaciously insisted that the board had "no policy about any racial matters." Yet he conceded that all state-supported colleges were segregated "long before [he] came on the board."[79] Choosing his words carefully, Arnold testified, "Since I have been a Regent I have visited every one of those institutions [Georgia's public colleges] several times and I have never seen any White [sic] students at the colored schools and I have never seen any colored students at the White [sic] schools."[80] However, although it was common knowledge and well documented that "the Georgia legislature passed a long list of laws designed to thwart public school desegregation,"[81] Arnold refused to admit that Georgia officials had any hand in operating the schools on a segregated basis.

White officials also sought to refute the notion that the black applicants could be both serious students seeking an education and social activists who embraced the NAACP's campaign to end segregation. NAACP leaders actively pursued interested applicants who were willing to confront the segregated system. Though many students possessed the academic credentials to enter "white colleges," it was hard to find candidates who also possessed the interest and courage to become involved in an NAACP-supported federal court case against segregation. Benjamin Mays observed that plaintiffs involved in test cases were often "harassed and their lives threatened."[82] The plaintiffs in the Georgia State case possessed the academic ability and interest and, like Ward before them, the willingness to endure harassment and even jeopardize their personal safety.

Murphy characterized the NAACP's involvement with the plaintiffs as a sinister activity and made this involvement a major issue in the case. On the third day of the trial, the drama in the courtroom reached a fever pitch when Murphy, intent on discrediting NAACP leaders and the authenticity of the applicants' lawsuit, lashed out at NAACP leader and Morehouse College professor Rev. Samuel W. Williams. In accordance with Eugene Cook's crusade among white southern leaders to link high-ranking NAACP officials with Communism, Murphy asked Williams if he was "a member of the Communist Party."[83] An *Atlanta Journal* article bearing the headline "Red Query Stirs Row in School Suit: Witness, Attorney Trade Barbs as Tempers Flare" described how "emotions crackled" during the tense and heated exchange.[84]

Hollowell leapt to his feet to object to the question: "I would like to move to have stricken the last question as being irrelevant and immaterial, Your Honor."[85] In his objection, Hollowell contended that a "political party" had nothing to do with the complaint of racial discrimination.[86] Before Murphy could withdraw the question, the well-spoken and quick-witted Williams "wheeled around in his swivel chair to face Murphy" and indignantly retorted, "Do you hold membership in the Ku Klux Klan?"[87]

Williams's clash with Murphy made headlines in local and national print media outlets, including *Jet* magazine.[88] Williams told the court he considered the question an insult and that he had the right to "assume that [Murphy was] a member of the Ku Klux Klan as much as [Murphy had] a right to assume that [Williams was] a member of the Communist Party."[89] Sustaining Hollowell's objection, Sloan told Murphy that the question was improper and out of order.[90] However, Sloan also reprimanded Williams for his retaliatory answer and reminded him that he was a witness and that witnesses were not allowed to ask questions of attorneys.[91]

Undeterred by Sloan ruling him out of order, Murphy continued probing to establish a link between the plaintiffs and the NAACP, to demonstrate their lack of good faith in filing the suit. In response to Murphy's unyielding inquiry about Williams's NAACP affiliation, Williams responded with great aplomb, "I once said that any Negro in his right mind would be a member of the NAACP and I believe I am in my right mind."[92] Williams had expressed frustration previously in response to Murphy's line of questioning during his deposition a few months before the trial. When Murphy asked, "Did Barbara Hunt ever consult with you about whether or not she should file this application?" Williams responded, "I don't see how that would be a legitimate question under any circumstances. She is a citizen of this State and has a right to apply for an education. Why ask me should she apply? . . . It is pretty hard to me to see, sir, why it would be assumed a student seeking to enter a school would have to be advised to do so. An education is something anybody wants to get."[93]

Despite Williams minimizing his role in advising the plaintiffs, the eminent minister, scholar, and activist provided unswerving advice and support for many student activists in direct-action campaigns in Atlanta aimed at dismantling Jim Crow.[94] Williams served as professor and chairman of the Department of Philosophy and Religion at his alma mater, Morehouse College, from 1947 to 1970 and was a prominent leader in the fight for equal justice for blacks in Atlanta during the 1950s and 1960s. He taught and mentored Martin Luther King Jr. and a number of other notable civil rights leaders, including Maynard Holbrook Jackson. He embraced and collaborated with student activists, including the Georgia State black applicants and Hamilton Holmes and Charlayne Hunter. Civil rights leader and student activist Julian Bond recalled: "Williams was the one adult most trusted by Atlanta's fledgling student movement in the 1960s. We went to him for advice and he gave freely of his wisdom and experience. Wherever there was a struggle of black people in Atlanta he was there, offering his counsel, his philosophy and his energy."[95]

Williams's activism in the civil rights struggle was characteristic of a long line of Morehouse graduates and faculty who rebelled against racial injustice, including Bond, Morehouse president Mays, Atlanta Student

Movement cofounder Lonnie King, and Martin Luther King Jr.[96] Williams, who was elected president of the Atlanta branch of the NAACP in 1959 and served in this position until 1967, even openly advocated making the ultimate sacrifice for the cause of social justice. For example, in 1961, displaying solid support for incarcerated activists in the Atlanta Student Movement, Williams pledged, "We're going to stay with [the jailed students and pastors] and even die with them—if necessary. Some things are worse than dying; for instance, having your freedom denied permanently.[97]

In the *Hunt* trial, the state continued to center its defense on a blistering attack of the NAACP, leading John Britton of the *Atlanta Daily World* to pen that it was difficult to determine "whether the trial was one of ending segregation or a hearing on the membership and finances of the NAACP."[98] In his examination of Barbara Hunt, Murphy was unceasing in his efforts to link the applicants with the NAACP's civil rights activism. He bluntly told the court that he endeavored to show whether the application of Barbara Hunt was "in good faith" or whether Ms. Hunt had simply "loaned herself to a scheme or device of the NAACP" to bring a test case."[99] Hunt testified under cross-examination that she had discussed filing the suit with one of her friends, local NAACP secretary Marian McDaniel, who had also sought to enter Georgia State. She insisted, however, that she had not conferred with NAACP president John Calhoun prior to her attempt to enter the college.

Hollowell continually objected to the line of questioning regarding which persons or organizations assisted the plaintiffs. Hollowell argued, "Now if it please the Court, with whom the witness conferred with relative to bringing the lawsuit I don't see where that would have any relevancy to the issues in this particular case. It is within the prerogative to any person to bring a lawsuit if they see fit."[100] While Sloan said he agreed in principle with Hollowell's argument, he overruled Hollowell's objection in this instance, declaring that testimony on the NAACP's role was admissible "to illustrate whether the application was a real effort to enter the college or 'a gesture' preparatory to bringing the suit."[101]

Murphy seized the opportunity to continue trying to elicit testimony demonstrating that Hunt and her co-plaintiffs had no interest in higher learning but were mere NAACP stooges. He asked Hunt a long series of questions implying that she had colluded with the NAACP: "Has anybody in the NAACP agreed to pay you any money for being a party to this case? . . . Who if anybody from the NAACP, talked to you about going down there and making application?[102]

Despite the broad spectrum of questions aimed at showing that she was a tool of the NAACP, Hunt repeatedly stated that she sought financial help from Calhoun only *after* her meeting with Moore about filing the lawsuit. "We [Hunt, Elliot, Welch, and Roberts] knew Mr. Moore had to be paid and the group of us, well, we were working, we were not making enough money to just outright pay a lawyer full price so we had to get some assistance and we thought about Mr. Calhoun and that is when we talked with him."[103]

Similarly, in his cross-examination of Marian McDaniel, whom Moore had arranged to travel from Ohio to testify, Murphy repeated his assertions about the plaintiffs' ulterior motives. In response to Hollowell's objections to Murphy's belabored questioning of McDaniel about the sources of NAACP income to pay the lawyers, Murphy told the court: "I think it is admissible as a part of our overall contention that this case is not proceeding in good faith . . . that these people don't come into court with clean hands . . . and they are not bona fide applicants of that school. . . . I want to find out whether [funding to pay Hollowell and Moore] comes from New York, or whether it is raised locally, or where it comes from."[104] On this occasion Sloan sustained Hollowell's objection, ruling, "Where they get [the funds], I don't think has any relevance at all. I sustain the objection to that line of question."[105]

After incessantly pressing Dinsmore about the NAACP's link to the litigation, Murphy prevailed in finally eliciting testimony from Dinsmore that the NAACP provided assistance in the form of paying attorney fees for her and her fellow plaintiffs.[106] Murphy's pursuit of the plaintiffs' association with the NAACP in order to taint their sincerity, however, was ironically and sadly off base, as Myra Dinsmore later confirmed. In an interview with the Boggs Academy valedictorian, she affirmed that her desire for a college education was completely genuine:

> It was apparent that the defense attorney thought that we were stooges for the NAACP in an effort to break down segregation in the state of Georgia. . . . Well, I think he said that because that is what he wanted to believe. And from the way he cross-examined us, you could tell that is what he truly thought. . . . He never really seemed to have taken us seriously. However, he never could have known how badly I wanted a college education. . . . I can't speak for the other two plaintiffs, but everybody who knows me knows that I always wanted a college education.[107]

Similarly, Hunt, who had a fervent desire to enter Georgia State to take secretarial classes, "was devastated when turned away from the school."[108]

Although Sloan sustained Hollowell's objection to Murphy's questions about NAACP financial support, Murphy continued to focus heavily on Calhoun and the Atlanta branch of the NAACP. In seeking to demonstrate the plaintiffs' collusion with the NAACP, he focused particularly on Calhoun's involvement. In response to Murphy's query, Calhoun testified that he had explained to Roberts, Hunt, and other applicants who visited him requesting NAACP financial help with the lawsuit that the NAACP would provide assistance only under three conditions: One is that the person or a member of his family must request assistance from the NAACP; the second is that the branch must be convinced that it is a case that would involve his civil rights; and the third is that the branch must also be convinced that the successful prosecution of a case would affect the rights of others in the same class.[109]

Calhoun testified that "after consideration of all the facts," the Atlanta branch of the NAACP agreed to help with "financing the litigation."[110] The state concluded that Calhoun's testimony acknowledging the financing of the suit was a major win for the defense. Attorney General Cook announced in a press conference that he "wanted to get Calhoun's testimony in the record to show bad faith on the part of the plaintiffs." He contended that Calhoun's testimony affirmed one of the state's overriding claims: that "the plaintiffs were not actually interested in attending Georgia State College, but were only performing a function for the NAACP."[111]

Murphy also aggressively interrogated each plaintiff with personal questions, attempting to show that their character was unsuitable for admission to the college.[112] Looking for damaging evidence such as the "character flaws" that had led to Roberts's withdrawal from the suit, the defense attorneys focused zealously on the applicants' private lives. Under cross-examination, Hunt, a twenty-five-year-old mother of two, testified that her first child was born eight months before her marriage and her second was born four months after her wedding.[113] Moreover, determined to obtain a college degree, she revealed to the court that she had applied for admission and been accepted to Lincoln University in Missouri. Undoubtedly, more than two years after she initially sought to enter Georgia State, Hunt questioned whether the institution would ever admit her. She stated that she planned to go to Lincoln whenever she was "able, but first had to make arrangements for the care of her children."[114]

Under cross-examination, twenty-six-year-old Myra Dinsmore was compelled to reveal that she too had conceived a child before marrying the child's father. As noted earlier, in her autobiography *Equal Justice under Law*, Motley acknowledged that shortly before the trial she and the other plaintiffs' attorneys had discovered information about the plaintiffs' backgrounds "that would prove embarrassing." Though Motley did not specify the evidence that would prove embarrassing, undoubtedly she referred to the revelations concerning the private lives of Hunt and Dinsmore.

State investigators for the defense, on a witch hunt to find damaging information about the plaintiffs that could be used to disqualify them for admission on a basis other than race, discovered the evidence.[115] Since the plaintiffs' attorneys discovered the evidence shortly before the trial, yet went forward nevertheless, they clearly realized that the defendants' attorneys might discover the information about the women's private lives and were willing to take that chance, hopeful that this evidence would not jeopardize the case. Perhaps the difficulty civil rights lawyers encountered in finding plaintiffs with the academic credentials and willingness to legally challenge segregation, combined with the fact that Moore, Hollowell, and Motley discovered this evidence only shortly before the trial, convinced them to go forward despite the risks.

As the plaintiffs' attorneys likely anticipated, Murphy's vicious ad hominem tactics used the evidence to portray Hunt and Dinsmore as promiscuous. Though this kind of absurd investigation did not occur with white applicants, these revelations about the black applicants' private lives were especially damaging given the sexual mores of the time and the fact that the defense was looking for excuses to deny them admission.

Interestingly, on Thursday, December 11, shortly before the end of the trial, Hollowell called Edward Clemons as a witness for the plaintiffs. Clemons was a member of the initial group of black applicants who had attempted to enroll at Georgia State on March 23, 1956. Like Roberts, Clemons worked for the black-owned North Carolina Mutual Insurance Company. He had earned an undergraduate degree in business administration in 1955 from Clark College and desired to further his studies in that discipline to qualify as a certified life insurance underwriter.[116] Under examination by Hollowell, Clemons attested to his educational background and experience and described his unsuccessful attempt to enter Georgia State. He stated that he still aspired to attend Georgia State, and his testimony revealed that he had met most of the entrance requirements, including obtaining an endorsement from a white alumnus.[117]

The defense had had no reason to investigate Clemons to try to find information to smear his character, since he was not a party in the current lawsuit. As a result, Murphy's questions did not delve into Clemons's personal life. Unlike the attacks on the personal lives of Hunt and Dinsmore or the allegations of criminal activity with regard to Roberts, in the case of

Clemons, Murphy primarily sought to discredit his alumni certification, which had been signed by Reverend Welden.

Responding to a battery of questions from Murphy, Clemons's testimony raised questions about the appropriateness of the alumni certification provided by Welden. Clemons admitted that Welden had signed his application attesting to his good character before the two of them had ever met. In an attempt to discredit Welden's endorsement and perhaps the minister himself, Murphy hammered home the point that the clergyman signed the application although he did not personally know Clemons. Reading from the application form at one point during the exchange, Murphy questioned Clemons about how Welden could have certified that he was "personally acquainted with the applicant" and that "the applicant [was] of good character." Punctuating his line of questioning, Murphy asked, "You mean he signed yours in blank without ever seeing you?"[118] Clemons responded affirmatively.

Seeking to lessen any adverse effects of Clemons's revelation, under redirect examination Hollowell produced testimony from Clemons that Fulton County ordinary Eugene Gunby, who also did not know Clemons, promised to endorse his application if Clemons could obtain two alumni signatures.[119] Summarizing the exchange between Murphy and Clemons regarding Welden's support of Clemons's application, the *Atlanta Constitution* reported that the "white Decatur minister came under fire in the Georgia State College segregation trial when testimony revealed he attested to the good character of a Negro he had never met but who was trying to enroll in the college."[120]

In a surprising move, following Clemons's testimony Hollowell and Constance Baker Motley made a plea to Sloan to include Clemons as a plaintiff in the lawsuit.[121] The two attorneys argued in a motion to Sloan that the three women involved in the legal fight were not seeking only relief for themselves, but rather they were seeking "to establish the civil rights of every member of the class of which they [were] a part." They further contended that the three plaintiffs might not adequately represent the "Negro race seeking to end alleged discrimination."[122]

In light of a previous declaration by former governor Talmadge that "every Negro seeking admittance to a school listed as 'all-white' would have to file suit individually," if Sloan ruled favorably on behalf of the "class" it would be a far broader victory and undermine Talmadge's declaration. In addition to eliminating an enormous barrier for blacks beyond the three plaintiffs, a class-action victory would be a major triumph for the NAACP in its campaign for educational equity and would reduce the need for the organization to sponsor similar suits in the future.

However, vocal sympathizers to the state's case maintained that Hollowell sought to insert Clemons as a plaintiff because he believed he and his co-counsels had presented a weak case and "were likely to lose on the basis of existing evidence."[123] As the plaintiffs' case seemed to unravel, the *Atlanta Constitution* reported that "the motion made by Hollowell appeared to be a desperation move to snatch the case away from B. D. (Buck) Murphy" and reminded its readers that Murphy had "produced testimony against the good character of two of the three plaintiffs."[124] *Atlanta Journal* writer Margaret Shannon observed that Hollowell's effort "to add another plaintiff was generally interpreted as a virtual concession of defeat in the present case."[125] The *Atlanta Journal* and the *Atlanta Constitution* speculated that the plaintiffs' case had "crumbled," and the *Journal* pointed out to its readers that Georgia's University System had already "withstood one integration move" in 1957, "when Negro Horace Ward lost a suit for admission to the University of Georgia Law School at Athens."[126]

Some of the language in Hollowell and Motley's motion to insert Clemons as a plaintiff was perplexing and likely added to speculation that the case was doomed. For example, the attorneys seemed to acknowledge a possible ruling in favor of the defense when they contended in their motion that if Sloan declared "that university system admissions regulations on their face [were] not discriminatory," this ruling "would be binding on Mr. Clemons."[127] Hollowell and Motley also argued in the motion that the case was a class-action suit, and therefore "if the three women lost the case, Clemons as a Negro would in effect lose it too."[128]

The last-minute motion to include Clemons and the language in Hollowell and Motley's pleading seemed to indicate that they had some doubt about a favorable ruling for the three women. In fact, years later in her autobiography, Motley acknowledged, "We believed we had lost the case because of the personal indiscretion defense."[129] Clearly, the move to add Clemons as a plaintiff represented an effort to avoid defeat based on evidence the defendants' attorneys had presented regarding the private lives of Hunt and Dinsmore.

Murphy vigorously objected to Hollowell's motion to insert Clemons as a plaintiff, on the grounds that the request was untimely and no brief had been filed with the court or the defendants to support Clemons's inclusion. Sloan subsequently questioned the timeliness of Hollowell's action and overruled the motion to insert Clemons as a plaintiff. Sloan opined that granting the motion "in all probability" would have resulted "in the Court having to grant a continuance of the case in order to give the defendants time to make further investigation."[130]

Sloan also declared that the plaintiffs' attorneys had not conclusively shown that the suit could be considered a "class action."[131] It is curious that Clemons was not one of the plaintiffs initially, since he possessed an excellent academic background and good character, according to information presented during the trial, as well as having obtained a good character certificate from Reverend Welden. Whatever the reason that Clemons did not originally participate in filing the suit, Hollowell and his fellow counsels later concluded that he would be an asset to the case, but Sloan rejected their last-ditch effort to involve him as a plaintiff.

Sloan adjourned the nonjury trial of the major case against segregation in Georgia's colleges and universities on Friday morning, December 12, 1958, without issuing a decision. Though attorneys on both sides had the right to present oral arguments, Sloan recommended that they submit written briefs of their closing arguments to afford him a better chance to review the full spectrum of the case. Sloan instructed the lawyers to present the briefs to him before January 12, 1959, and to include in their respective written arguments a statement of what they believed the court's ruling should be based on the evidence presented in court.[132]

In their written arguments, counsels on both sides, in large measure, recycled contentions and evidence presented during the trial. On December 31, 1958, the *ADW* summarized the written brief that the plaintiffs' attorneys had submitted to the court and made public. The *ADW* reported that "Negro plaintiffs in the Georgia State College desegregation suit . . . asked Federal Judge Boyd Sloan to forbid use of Georgia State College admission requirements . . . designed to keep Negroes out of the all-white school."[133] The plaintiffs' attorneys argued in their closing statement that the certification requirement was invalid because the college had no Negro alumni, making it "difficult if not impossible for Negroes" to obtain the required signatures.[134]

In their closing brief, Moore, Hollowell, and Motley asked for an injunction that would prevent the college from requiring Negroes to comply with the alumni certification requirement, which they characterized as "an ingenious device for discriminating against Negroes."[135] They also recapped the plaintiffs' persistent and repeated efforts to obtain signatures from white alumni, even sending letters to alumni asking for a "get acquainted" meeting.[136] As argued in the complaint, they contended that "it was the policy, custom, practice, and usage of the Board of Regents to operate colleges on a racially segregated basis in violation of the rights secured to Negro students of Georgia by the due process and equal protection clauses of the 14th Amendment."[137]

The plaintiffs' attorneys also enumerated a phalanx of state laws devised to maintain segregation in schools and colleges. Given that the state had elicited testimony revealing that the NAACP had financed the suit, Hollowell, Moore, and Motley acknowledged in their closing argument that the NAACP had helped finance the case. However, they argued that the plaintiffs had sought to enter the college in good faith.[138]

In the closing briefs for the defendants, the attorneys relied heavily on the fact that the plaintiffs failed to comply with the Board of Regents' policy requiring applicants to obtain alumni signatures. The attorneys also hammered home the moral-character issues related to the two plaintiffs who admitted during the trial that they had conceived children out of wedlock. At the end of the five-day trial, Cook, Murphy, and other white officials—relying in part on the state's previous defeat of Ward in federal court and their attacks on the plaintiffs' moral and academic records—confidently predicted that Sloan's ruling would favor the state and suggested that the court action might even be dismissed.[139]

In a prepared statement released to the press, Cook and Murphy speculated that Sloan would dismiss the case based on three major premises:

I feel we successfully demonstrated the fact that:

1. The regulation adopted by the Board of Regents requiring endorsement of applicants by two alumni and the ordinary or clerk of the superior court, or three alumni in lieu of the ordinary or clerk . . . is reasonable, fair and non-discriminatory as applied to the Negro race, and
2. That the moral and scholastic background of the applicants cannot stand the test ordinarily required for admission, and
3. That the suit was not initiated in good faith by the complainants but is simply an effort on their part to perform a function for the National Association for the Advancement of Colored People—that is to say, that the complainants came into court without clean hands and without an honest motive to pursue a college education at the State College of Business Administration.[140]

Moore, Hollowell, and Motley were less vocal about the expected outcome for the case. Hollowell said he believed it would be "improper" for him to predict the outcome while the lawsuit was "in the breast of the court."[141] The plaintiffs, defendants, and attorneys on both sides, along with Georgia's leading public officials, the NAACP, and other interested parties, all eagerly awaited Sloan's decision.

CHAPTER 5

"The Higher Dictates of Justice and Equity"

Judge Sloan's Verdict

In his "Letter from a Birmingham Jail," Martin Luther King Jr. wrote, "Freedom is never voluntarily given by the oppressor; it must be demanded by the oppressed."[1] On January 9, 1959, despite the defense attorneys' predictions and their unequivocal insistence that Georgia State's admissions practices were administered "in good faith," Hunt, Dinsmore, Welch, and their attorneys prevailed in a legal victory against the oppressive conditions that banned blacks from so-called white public institutions of higher education. The plaintiffs and their legal team won a federal injunction that declared segregation at Georgia State unconstitutional and forbade the centuries-old racial discrimination in Georgia's colleges and universities.

In issuing his unprecedented ruling overturning segregation in higher education in Georgia, Judge Sloan accepted the plaintiffs' argument that "the policy, custom, practice and usage of the defendants in maintaining and operating Georgia State College of Business Administration on a racially segregated basis [was] violative of the rights secured to plaintiffs, and of rights secured to other Negro students of Georgia, who [were] similarly situated."[2] Sloan declared that the racially discriminatory policy and practices violated the due process and equal protection clauses of the Fourteenth Amendment.

Repudiating the state's claim that the admissions process was not racially discriminatory, Sloan agreed with the plaintiffs' argument that the policies demonstrated preferential treatment for white students. Sloan enjoined the regents "from continuing to limit the college to white students only" and admonished the defendants for some of their ludicrous tactics.[3] He declared that the entrance requirement created by the Board of Regents and implemented by Georgia State officials requiring blacks to obtain character recommendations from white alumni was unconstitutional.

Using language that was practically identical to Moore, Hollowell, and Motley's argument, Sloan struck down the requirement, noting, "It is not customary for Negroes and whites to mix socially or to attend the same public or private educational institutions in the state of Georgia, and . . . by reason of this presently existing social pattern, the opportunities for the average Negro to become personally acquainted with the average white person, and particularly with the alumni of a white educational institution, are necessarily limited."[4]

Sloan ruled that the effect of the alumni certificate requirement, simply put, was to prevent blacks from gaining admission to all-white state colleges and universities. Accordingly, and in precise accordance with the plaintiffs' contention, Sloan declared: "The alumni certificate requirement is invalid as applied to Negroes because there are no Negro alumni of any of the white institutions of the University System of Georgia, and consequently this requirement operates to make it difficult, if not impossible, for Negroes to comply with the requirement, whereas white applicants do not face similar difficulties."[5] He consequently ordered the college to end the policy and practice of requiring black applicants to furnish character certificates endorsed by white alumni.

Moreover, Sloan declared that the scholarship program that shunted black students out of state to attend college did not meet the requirement of equal protection.[6] Sloan's seventeen-page ruling thoroughly examined the background of Georgia State's admissions policy and the context of school segregation court precedents. Reflecting on his ruling, Sloan said he was bound by the decisions of the U.S. Supreme Court, noting that "to express disagreement with such decisions would not only be futile but improper."[7]

Responding to Murphy's claim that the applicants were not bona fide candidates but rather tools of the NAACP, Sloan found "not significant" the contention that "the motive of the Negroes in seeking admission had been to lay the groundwork for the suit."[8] He ordered that the three plaintiffs and other similarly situated blacks were entitled to an injunction prohibiting the defendants from continuing to operate Georgia State as a college for white students only. Sloan's decision to legally bar Georgia officials from refusing admission to blacks solely on the ground of race or color constituted the first federal court action against segregated education in Georgia.[9]

Sloan's ruling also contained a partial victory for the plaintiffs related to their academic qualifications. Sloan noted that each of the applicants had completed high school and some college work. Therefore, while their scholastic qualifications could rightly be subject to review under valid admissions requirements, nonetheless, each candidate possessed "scholastic credits sufficient to qualify them to make application for admission to the college."[10]

However, in a damaging and ultimately crippling blow to Hunt, Dinsmore, and Welch, Sloan expressly acknowledged the college's right to develop admissions requirements based on such qualifications as applicants' moral character. Sloan subsequently declined to order Georgia State to admit any of the plaintiffs. Even more ominously for the plaintiffs, the defendants' ad hominem tactics "aimed at showing that the moral . . . records of the plaintiffs (three Negro women) would not meet entrance requirements at the college" did indeed influence Sloan's decision.[11] Sloan declared that according to the evidence presented, "Barbara Hunt and Myra Elliott Dinsmore Holland, may not be of good moral character and for that reason may not be qualified for admission to the college."[12]

In the state's intrusive examination of the plaintiffs' private lives—a practice seldom, if ever, employed in the screening of white applicants—Murphy had presented evidence from birth and marriage records to raise concerns about the plaintiffs' character. In the contemporary court of opinion, Murphy's invasiveness represents an egregious offense against civil rights, but at the time it was unfortunately a "common indignity for blacks seeking legal redress."[13] Dinsmore's purported "moral character" issues related to her testimony that her oldest child, born on August 4, 1954, was conceived prior to her marriage to Adolphus Dinsmore Jr. on May 1, 1954.

As previously noted, Murphy's investigation into and invasive questioning regarding Hunt's private life led to her admission that she had given birth to her oldest child on March 4, 1953, eight months prior to her marriage to Eldridge Hunt Jr. on November 7, 1953, and to her second child on March 19, 1954, four months after her marriage.[14] In the social context of the 1950s, children born prior to marriage or conceived out of wedlock were labeled "illegitimate." In a January 1, 1959, *ADW* article, the paper reported that "two of the applicants . . . according to trial testimony, had illegitimate children."[15] Given the 1950s sexual mores, the state's invasion into the plaintiffs' personal backgrounds proved persuasive in Sloan's decision regarding the character of Hunt and Dinsmore.[16]

In view of the string of NAACP triumphs against segregation in higher education, the state could no longer keep the students out due to their race. In addition, Moore, Hollowell, and Motley had done an exquisite job of presenting compelling evidence about the plaintiffs' academic qualifications. The state thus turned to the plaintiffs' personal backgrounds to find reasons to disqualify them for admission.

Labeling the women as "sexually deviant" because of children born out of wedlock fit the common practice of stereotyping blacks as "sexual fiends," regardless of their good character or stature.[17] Four years later, for example, state officials commissioned a secret police investigation of the personal background of Mary Frances Early after she sought admission to the University of Georgia. At the time, Early was a graduate student at the University of Michigan and had been employed as an educator with the Atlanta Public Schools. Irrespective of Early's stellar reputation, professional standing, and enrollment at the University of Michigan, state officials, relying on unsubstantiated information from spies deputized by state officials, questioned her about alleged promiscuity, accused her of visiting houses of ill repute, and asserted that she was a prostitute.[18]

Despite the broad victory contained in Sloan's decision, including nullifying Georgia State's use of the alumni certificate requirement and out-of-state-aid program, the litigants "left the trial with a lingering sense of shame and indignity because of the defense's attacks upon their moral characters."[19] Dinsmore recalled the enormous mental anguish she experienced: "It hurt, it sort of deflated you. It was a very unpleasant experience. . . . It was one of the most challenging things that I've ever done. . . . Despite the fact that we won, it was obvious that we had not won [Judge Sloan] over. It dampened the victory."[20] Sloan's declaration regarding the character of two of the plaintiffs not only disheartened them personally but also provided the state with a convenient way to use "questionable character" instead of race as a guise for rejecting the applicants.

It is important to underscore, however, that the *Hunt v. Arnold* ruling, which broadly outlawed the regents' racially discriminatory policies, applied to every all-white college and university in the University System of Georgia. It also gained important legal ground for the civil rights movement in Georgia in at least three key ways. First, as Sloan declared, "the effect of the alumni certificate requirement upon Negroes ha[d] been, [was], and [would] be, to prevent Negroes from meeting this admission requirement."[21] Importantly, Sloan's order applied not only to Georgia State but also struck down the racially biased regulation throughout the entire University System of Georgia.[22] Prohibiting the Board of Regents and all of the state's white institutions from using the alumni certification requirement to stymie black applicants represented a significant victory in the struggle to overturn racial segregation.

In addition, although Horace T. Ward had lost his court battle with the University of Georgia, Sloan's final order in the *Hunt* case vindicated Ward in his contention that the regents adopted the post hoc requirements to keep him and other blacks out of so-called white colleges. More importantly, Sloan's judicial precedent in issuing an injunction against the regents' arbitrary "certificates of good moral character" requirement removed a major obstacle from the paths of future black applicants seeking to enroll in Georgia's white public colleges. Constance Baker Motley, who was renowned for her own well-reasoned, lucid arguments, observed that Sloan, who was considered a liberal judge, "was clear sighted enough to hold that the certification requirement violated black people's right to equal protection and struck it down."[23]

Second, the Board of Regents had adopted the out-of-state aid scholarship program in 1943 to safeguard segregation in Georgia's colleges and universities.[24] Although Georgia State and regents officials adamantly denied that they had designed this program to keep blacks out of Georgia's white institutions, Sloan clearly recognized the program as the deceptive device it was. In accordance with the 1936 U.S. Supreme Court victory by Lloyd Gaines, Sloan affirmed that the out-of-state scholarship program for blacks was not an appropriate or legal substitute for affording blacks educational opportunities in the state and therefore failed to meet the requirement of equal protection.

Third, a major contention by the plaintiffs was that the regents, in complicity with Georgia State officials, were refusing to admit blacks while at the same time granting whites the opportunities of attending said institutions. Affirming the plaintiffs' contentions in a victory for equal access, Sloan declared that the "policy, custom, practice and usage of the defendants in maintaining and operating the Georgia State College of Business" on a racially segregated basis violated the Fourteenth Amendment.[25] Since Ward had lost his bid to enter the University of Georgia School of Law, *Hunt* represented the inaugural victory against Georgia's snub of the

Brown decision and its legal stand to preserve segregation in its schools and colleges.[26]

Black and white print media in Atlanta and across the nation prominently reported the ruling. Margaret Shannon of the *Atlanta Journal*, who had speculated that the plaintiffs might lose, published a front-page article with the headline, "Negroes Win Right to Seek Admission." Shannon surmised that although the present decision focused on Georgia State, the ruling could eventually "crumble racial barriers" in all of Georgia's colleges and universities.[27] In a front-page article in the *New York Times*, under the headline "U.S. Judge Orders Georgia College to End Negro Ban," Claude Sitton reported even more decisively that "the decision had set a precedent affecting all public institutions of higher education in Georgia."[28]

In a thrilling and moderately radical tone, the black-owned *Chicago Tribune*'s headline read, "Judge Kills Racial Bar of Georgia School," and the black-owned *Pittsburgh Courier*'s caption similarly observed, "Ga.'s School Laws Ripped by Rulings."[29] Hailing the triumph as a major setback for segregation in Georgia, the *Courier* observed, "A gaping hole has been blasted in the armor surrounding Georgia's Jim Crow institutions of higher learning by a decision handed down here in U.S. District Court."[30] Even the *Georgia State Signal*, which had run editorials opposing an end to segregation, published a front-page article covering Sloan's ruling under the headline "Judge Sloan Rules Entrance Regulation at Ga. State Invalid." However, to calm any concerns about the state law requiring closure of the college in the event of court-ordered desegregation, the article emphasized that Sloan's decision did not "order admission of any of the three Negroes bringing the suit."[31]

Beyond the widespread public coverage of Sloan's decision, Phil Davis, a reporter for WSB television in Atlanta, sent a personal letter to Barbara Hunt commending her for the victory as well as offering "sympathy" for the abuse she had endured during the court fight. In his letter, Davis summed up how Hunt, Dinsmore, and Welch had won a fight for racial justice that would benefit all Americans:

> May I offer you my own "congratulations." You of course, don't know who I am, but I covered some of the preliminary hearings for WSB-TV.... It must seem strange, this letter, but under the circumstances (being in Georgia) it appears to me to be the best way I can express my interest and sympathy. Your cause is just, and is not only yours or that of the American Negro, but the cause of all of us, regardless of racial background. A poor, uneducated

class for any reason is NOT an advantage to any state, better education for all will eventually mean a better life for all.[32]

It is not definitively known what Davis meant by the phrase "being in Georgia," but one can speculate that the white newsman was not comfortable publicly expressing his congratulations and sympathy to the black women in the racial environment of the 1950s.

Sloan's ruling to protect the civil rights of blacks "shocked and disheartened the white public" and its segregationist political leaders.[33] Georgia's two U.S. senators, Herman Talmadge and Richard Russell, expressed dismay at the court decree and vowed to sustain segregation in Georgia's educational institutions. Talmadge observed:

> I deeply regret the ruling of the federal district court of the Northern District of Georgia striking down the right of a sovereign state to prescribe requirements for admission to its colleges and universities.
>
> I am confident that the members of the Board of Regents, state officials and the people of Georgia will utilize every resource at their command to maintain segregation in Georgia colleges and public schools.[34]

In stark contrast to the response of Georgia's segregationist leaders, black leaders celebrated the victory as a significant step in the struggle to end segregation in schools and colleges. The *ADW* reported that the Third Annual Freedom Dinner of the NAACP Atlanta branch honored Hunt, Dinsmore, and Welch with certificates of merit for their triumph. Walden, a member of the National Legal Committee of the NAACP, presented the awards at a formal affair held in the ballroom of the black-owned Waluhaje Hotel in northwest Atlanta. Wiley Branton, a prominent civil rights attorney in Arkansas and the principal lawyer for the nine children in the Little Rock public school case, served as the keynote speaker.[35] The NAACP also honored Moore, Hollowell, and Motley for their triumphant representation of the three plaintiffs.[36] It should be noted that although the "black Atlanta community was ecstatic," Hunt and Dinsmore were "mortified by the disclosures" about their private lives that were publicly revealed in the courtroom and covered on the front pages of newspapers.[37]

Despite widespread speculation that the plaintiffs' attorneys anticipated a decision against them and that this motivated their "desperate" last-minute attempt to add Clemons as a plaintiff, Hollowell said he "wasn't too surprised" by the victory. He observed, "I had great hopes, of course. . . . As I see the case, this decision will apply to all branches of the

University System." An optimistic Hollowell expressed hope that the suit would result in "Negroes and public officials getting together and discussing proper means of ending college segregation."[38]

Though relentlessly hammered by Murphy during the trial for allegedly colluding with the plaintiffs in bad faith, Calhoun voiced a similar hope that the ruling would bring "responsible leaders" of both races together to find solutions to racial problems. Surprisingly, the militant Calhoun sought to work collaboratively with white officials even though his federal contempt charge for withholding NAACP records was still pending. He observed, "Negroes want their rights, but we in Atlanta are not crying for immediate changes. We are willing to work in harmony with whites to lessen tension and make the transition amicably."[39] The older and wiser Walden, however, expressed less confidence in the potential for abolishing segregation through collaborative efforts between blacks and whites. He praised Sloan's ruling but cautioned that further litigation would be necessary to compel "Georgia State and other all-white institutions to accept Negroes."[40]

Protestations by political leaders, legal wrangling, and the case's impact on social change aside, the authentic voice of Iris Mae Welch highlighted the importance of the ruling with regard to her aspirations for higher learning and enrollment at Georgia State. Welch planned to coordinate her work schedule to allow her to enroll at Georgia State. She said, "I hope to study typing and shorthand, and other business courses. . . . I think I can handle the subject matter, and I need the education in my work."[41]

Hollowell, Moore, and Walden posited that Sloan's judgment represented a prelude to the end of blatant racial barriers in Georgia's colleges and universities.[42] Conveying the bitter irony and injustice of the race-based policies and customs, the plaintiffs' attorneys observed in a press release: "It is equally as inexplicable as it is indefensible that the youth of every other race under the sun are not only permitted, but bidden to enter Georgia State College of Business Administration, as well as the University of Georgia, while the Negro youth of Georgia whose forebears have lived here more than 300 years are excluded from entrance solely on account of race."[43] Jubilant over the decision, Hollowell, Moore, and Walden concluded, "The judgment of the United States District Court declaring as unconstitutional the exclusion of Negroes from that institution solely on the basis of race is naturally gratifying to us, our clients, and to all fair-minded citizens, particularly since counsel are of the opinion that the court's decree is supported not only by the law and evidence, but also by the higher dictates of justice and equity."[44]

Yet despite Sloan's decree and its victory for justice and equity, as Attorney General Cook was quick to point out, Sloan did not order the admission of the plaintiffs, who had labored for nearly three years to enter Georgia State. In granting the injunction against continuing to operate Georgia State for white students only, Sloan declared, "It is to be kept in mind that the authorities in control of the operation of the Georgia State College of Business Administration have the primary right and responsibility of fixing and passing upon the qualifications for admission."[45] Minimizing the impact of the federal injunction, Cook seized on this aspect of Sloan's ruling, publicly proclaiming, "The court has stated in no uncertain terms that the authority and responsibility for passing upon the moral and scholastic qualifications of applicants for admission are vested in school officials."[46] A defiant Cook declared that Sloan did not rule that the three women were "entitled to admission, and the decision would not have the effect of admitting them."[47]

The applicants were disappointed that Sloan did not order the college to admit them and also disheartened by the questions raised concerning their moral character. In her closing argument, Motley had contended that Georgia State had denied the applicants not on the ground of personal indiscretion but in accordance with "the state's policy, custom, and usage of excluding all blacks from white public institutions of higher learning in Georgia."[48] Even though Sloan accepted Motley's argument and expressly forbade the college from excluding blacks through means such as the alumni certificate requirement and other forms of racial discrimination, he left it to the college's discretion to determine whether the applicants met all other valid requirements.[49] Abusing this discretion, officials would find other pretexts for denying black applicants admission.

Despite the hopes expressed by NAACP officials of working amicably with white officials to end segregation, Georgia's leading white political figures were determined to uphold white supremacy. Instead of working collaboratively to desegregate colleges and universities, officials opted to "utilize every resource at their command to maintain segregation in Georgia colleges and public schools," as advocated by U.S. senator Talmadge. They created new obstacles to make admission to Georgia State a painstakingly gradual and arduous process for black applicants. In a vivid example of defiance by state and Board of Regents officials, on April 22, 1959, less than four months after Sloan declared the practice unconstitutional in accordance with a decades-old U.S. Supreme Court decision, the regents allocated nearly $300,000 for out-of-state "Scholarships for Negroes" to maintain all-white colleges and universities.[50]

Not surprisingly, none of the plaintiffs in *Hunt v. Arnold* were ever admitted to Georgia State. This explains, in part, why the case has been ignored as a milestone in the black freedom struggle, despite its historic civil rights victory against segregated education in Georgia. Though "legal and legislative victories" generally fit well into the narrative of the civil rights movement, the victory in this case was largely undercut by the fact that the applicants did not gain admission.[51] This also helps explain why the victory has been virtually unrecognized as "a significant step toward the failure of massive resistance [to desegregation in education] in the Southern states and more locally in the state of Georgia."[52]

In contrast, the injunction issued by Judge Bootle in the *Holmes v. Danner* case, which culminated in the admission of Hamilton Holmes and Charlayne Hunter to the University of Georgia, has been celebrated nationally and chronicled as historically significant.[53] The desegregation of Georgia's flagship and most-cherished university and the admission of Holmes and Hunter are indisputably historically significant events. Moreover, the Georgia State case played a prominent role in laying the legal groundwork that ultimately opened the doors of the University of Georgia to black students and forced the state to abandon its stalwart resistance to desegregation. Nevertheless, a number of historians and scholars have ignored the importance of the federal court order against racial discrimination at Georgia State.[54] By striking down the regents' arbitrary character certification requirement aimed at black applicants, Sloan removed the most substantial impediment confronted by Ward and the Georgia State applicants.[55]

Donald Hollowell and Jesse Hill, two of the principal leaders in the Georgia State and UGA desegregation efforts, highlighted the significance of the Georgia State case as well as the earlier Horace Ward case in the desegregation of UGA. Hill observed:

> The Horace Ward case, as well as the efforts we had at Georgia State, laid the foundation, taught us a lot of good lessons and things we had to prepare for.... They helped to lay the foundation, helped us to avoid obvious, easy mistakes to make in this process.... The Horace Ward and the Georgia State cases ... were very instructive. They ... gave us a lot of dos and don'ts as far as going forward. Those two cases were a very vital foundation.[56]

Despite the valuable lessons learned and vital progress made toward desegregating higher education in Georgia, Georgia State would continue to deny applications from blacks for several more years. Although Sloan's injunction had forbidden racial bias, because he did not issue a court order admitting the plaintiffs, "the state subsequently found administrative means with which to subvert the judge's findings." Chief among them was a focus on the "moral character" of black applicants.[57] Hollowell observed, "The moral issue was to become a favorite ploy of the attorney general's office and other lawyers of the state during the years to come. As a result local Negro attorneys and lawyers from the Inc. Fund [NAACP Legal Defense Fund, Inc.] began to take even greater pains to scrutinize the backgrounds of the plaintiffs they represented."[58]

On the national front there were several judicial decisions, including rulings from the Supreme Court, affirming the rights of blacks guaranteed by the Fourteenth Amendment in cases where officials had found ways to circumvent, delay, or simply ignore court orders. This practice was abundantly evident following the historic *Brown v. Board of Education* decision. "On May 17, 1954, the Constitution of the United States was destroyed because of the Supreme Court decision," said Mississippi senator James Eastland. "You are not obliged to obey the decisions of any court which are plainly fraudulent [and based on] sociological considerations."[59] Georgia governor Herman Talmadge declared the *Brown* ruling "a mere scrap of paper."[60]

Shortly after the *Hunt* trial, Dinsmore went back to work at the Atlanta Life Insurance Company. She and her husband subsequently had two additional children, continuing to work and raise their family, and she abandoned her efforts to attain a college degree for several years. Although later in her life she attended Atlanta-area DeKalb Community College and Atlanta Junior College, she did not complete a four-year college degree.

Despite Georgia State's refusal to admit her and the fact that she did not earn a college degree, in retrospect, Dinsmore accurately sees herself and her fellow plaintiffs as trailblazers. In an interview with the author, she passionately conveyed the vicarious satisfaction she experiences from seeing other black students, including her own niece, attend Georgia State decades after her legal case.

> Well, it makes me feel extremely proud to know that [black students] can apply with ease and if they are qualified they can attend and won't be treated the way I was treated. Sort of ignored and [officials] tried to keep my application from even getting into the system. So I'm extremely proud to have been a part of that case and to see my children and children in my family and black

children in general, to be able to at least come, and be accepted if they qualify.... Even though I was never able to take advantage of the opportunity myself, so many young people have been able to take advantage of it. I have always been proud that I was one of the ones who helped enable [blacks] to be able to attend [Georgia State] in Atlanta, and the University of Georgia in Athens. I didn't say anything to anybody, but the day I went down and saw my niece graduate from the Georgia State University School of Accounting, the school that I had always wanted to graduate from, I cried. I was so happy. I said, "Well, we finally did it!"[61]

Lead plaintiff Barbara Hunt also never earned a degree from Georgia State. However, this grassroots activist, who played a key role in the struggle against segregated education in Georgia, later earned a bachelor's degree from the University of Texas at Arlington. Tellingly, this alleged "pawn of the NAACP," who was accused of seeking "publicity and glory" and having no real interest in higher education, subsequently earned two master's degrees—one from the University of Texas at Arlington and the other from North Texas State University in Denton.[62] Hunt's personal papers and other documents, including a Georgia House of Representatives resolution honoring Hunt for her civil rights activism, reveal that Hunt later worked as a part-time secretary for the Southern Christian Leadership Conference (SCLC), led by Martin Luther King Jr.[63] Hunt also "knew all of the principals involved in the civil rights movement" and continued to engage in grassroots activism throughout her life.[64]

Hunt recounted receiving death threats from the Ku Klux Klan and encounters with the White Citizens' Council stemming from her role as a plaintiff in the Georgia State case. The potential risk to her personal safety and the safety of her family led her to change her name and eventually move to Texas.[65] Hunt continued her activism in Texas and later returned to journalism, her lifelong passion, and worked as managing editor for *La Vida News*, an African American weekly newspaper serving the Fort Worth–Arlington area. She also worked as an urban planner and community affairs manager for the city of Fort Worth.[66] Hunt's achievements in higher education and involvement in the cause of civil rights clearly debunk Murphy's myopic contention that Hunt and her colleagues' efforts to enter Georgia State were made in "bad faith" and that they were mere pawns of the NAACP.

Recognizing Hunt's unheralded, trailblazing work, civil rights icon Rosa Parks and Southern Poverty Law Center cofounder Morris Dees presented Hunt with the "Wall of Tolerance" award on February 17, 2003. On

March 7, 2014, the Georgia House of Representatives also approved a resolution recognizing Hunt, in part, for helping to pave the way for the desegregation of Georgia's institutions of higher education and declaring that "her courage resulted in Georgia State University having one of the highest graduation rates for African Americans in the United States of America."[67]

Though it would be understandable for Crystal Freeman, daughter of Barbara Hunt, to express bitterness about the manner in which the state unfairly characterized and mistreated her mother, she has chosen to take the high road. She observed that although her mother was not a direct beneficiary of the court's ruling, she is grateful that her mother played a central role in advancing Georgia State's progress with regard to diversity and inclusion: "I'm glad she lived long enough to see all nationalities attend Georgia State. Georgia State has one of the highest graduation rates for African Americans. Where it was a sad story in the 1950s, it is such a success story today, and she lived long enough to see that."[68]

In an interview, Dinsmore recounted how the black applicants' efforts to enter Georgia State began and reflected on the organic nature of their journey:

> One day, a group of us, when we got off work. We had learned that you could attend school at night and work in the daytime. So that suited us just fine....
>
> We came over to [Georgia State to] pick up some applications, a group of us from work. And they gave us the applications, but not readily. When we walked in, they ignored us for a while. And finally one lady asked us, "what did we want? We explained to her what we wanted. So she went in the back and stayed for a while and then came out and gave each one of us an application.... We brought them back with the money order for the application fee.... We were told that they were incomplete because we did not have the signatures of two alumni, nor the signature of the clerk of the Superior Court.[69]

It is also important to underscore the impact of the local lawyers—Moore, Walden, and Hollowell—in the NAACP's victory. The local lawyers advised the black applicants and ushered them through the protracted process from the "ground up," commencing with their initial attempts to gain admission to the college and secure character certifications from white alumni and culminating with the federal court victory that prohibited Board of Regents officials from implementing subterfuges to stymie black applicants. Dinsmore described the trial process as "discouraging" for the plaintiffs but reported that Moore, Hollowell, and Walden had a profound impact on the women during this time, uplifting and inspiring them with the message, "Don't give up."

Dinsmore also fondly remembered the unique role and invaluable contributions of New York–based LDF attorney Constance Baker Motley, which she considered even more impactful. She recalled, "We were all women and we found a bond with her, being a woman in such a high position. Somehow I felt more comfortable with her there, comfortable in that I could get up there on that stand and answer those questions. She was just a source of comfort and advice, many times, many days."[70]

Though often overlooked or portrayed as supporting cast members for their male counterparts, black women played leading and vital roles in the civil rights movement. Motley exemplifies a black woman whose brilliant work has been largely overshadowed in civil rights narratives by the work of Thurgood Marshall, Robert Carter, Jack Greenberg, and other male lawyers. Yet in *Hunt* and numerous other precedent-setting civil rights cases, although Marshall, Carter, and Motley collectively represented the NAACP and the LDF, Motley provided most of the expert assistance to the local lawyers and laid the crucial groundwork at the trial.

In his book *Beyond Atlanta: The Struggle for Racial Equality in Georgia, 1940–1980*, Stephen Tuck posits, "In both urban and rural Georgia, women played crucial, albeit often unheralded, roles."[71] Though there were a number of effective women leaders in the civil rights struggle, civil rights leaders themselves often relegated women to obscure roles. Ella Baker, cofounder of SNCC, who led a number of civil rights campaigns in Georgia and other states, observed that the predominantly black clergy at the helm of the civil rights movement were accustomed to seeing women only in subservient roles.[72]

Despite the barriers and condescending perceptions women confronted in the movement, Motley's excellence propelled her to the ranks of the highest echelon of civil rights lawyers. Thurgood Marshall hired her as a law clerk for the LDF in 1946, before she graduated from Columbia Law School. Motley worked in partnership with Marshall and other NAACP leaders on a number of groundbreaking civil rights cases and helped craft strategies to defeat segregation in the late 1940s and throughout the 1950s and 1960s.

Motley helped write the briefs for the historic *Brown* case and was the principal NAACP LDF lawyer in the cases that led to the desegregation of the University of Georgia, the University of Mississippi, and the University of Alabama. She argued ten cases before the U.S. Supreme Court and won nine.⁷³ Tomiko Brown-Nagin has observed that beyond her extraordinary legal acumen and courtroom skills, Motley "shattered race, gender, and class norms and offended many simply by appearing in the courtroom and claiming to be a lawyer."⁷⁴ In 1966 she became the first African American woman appointed to the federal bench.

A number of grassroots activists and community-based organizations, including the black and white ministers who tried to help the applicants circumvent barriers to their admission, also provided vital support in the battle to end segregation at Georgia State. Local NAACP activists were foremost among the advocates in the struggle. For example, local NAACP president John Calhoun effectively resisted the state's claims that the applicants were not interested in higher education but instead were part of a sinister ploy to undermine segregation.

Even so, Calhoun's trial testimony downplayed his leadership role and the extensive involvement of the Atlanta branch of the NAACP in supporting the black students seeking admission to Georgia State. For example, Calhoun testified that he did not recall an agreement between the counsels for the litigants and the Atlanta branch of the NAACP, nor did he recall any payment to the attorneys.⁷⁵ However, NAACP archival records show that Calhoun was directly involved in matters related to determining legal fees and subsequent payments to counsels.

The records include correspondence between Calhoun, Thurgood Marshall, and Robert Carter. In a "Personal and Confidential" letter from Calhoun to Marshall dated May 12, 1956, Calhoun reported on the progress of "several cases being sponsored by the Atlanta Branch," including the Georgia State case.⁷⁶ The report designated the attorneys working on the case and their estimated fees:

Georgia State College of Business Administration Case
D. L. Hollowell, Chief Counsel, S. S. Robinson, Romae Turner,
    R. E. Thomas, Jr., A. T. Walden
Estimated cost $4500.00⁷⁷

Interestingly, Calhoun expressed serious concern about the lawyers' estimated fees. In his letter to Marshall, Calhoun observed: "I am very much concerned about the case of the Georgia State College of Business Administration. There has been growing opposition to the fees being charged by our lawyers. . . . Opposition to the $4500.00 fee developed a serious controversy, which threatens to divide the Executive Committee."⁷⁸ Calhoun noted that the controversy stemmed, in part, from the fact that other branches of the NAACP paid much lower fees. Notwithstanding the concerns about fees, Calhoun observed that the attorneys on the case were "a fine group of lawyers."[79]

It appears that Calhoun inadvertently omitted E. E. Moore Jr. from the list of attorneys in his May 12, 1956, correspondence to Marshall. A series of letters and other documents found in the NAACP Papers, as well as court records related to the Georgia State case, show that Moore and Walden were the first local lawyers involved in the case, and Moore emerged as chief local counsel. In addition to Hollowell and Walden, who were intimately involved with the case, Calhoun's letter revealed that S. S. Robinson, R. E. Thomas Jr., and Romae Powell also served as local counsels during the formative stages of the case. It should also be noted that although Robinson, Thomas, and Powell did not devote their practice primarily to civil rights as did Hollowell and Walden, they also joined Hollowell and Walden in the critical 1956 legal fight to defend Calhoun and the NAACP's existence in Georgia, in which the state demanded that Calhoun and the organization turn over its membership records. Their collaboration on such litigation illustrates the camaraderie among the small cadre of black attorneys and shows how they banded together for important civil rights cases.[80]

Moore had also assisted Thomas and Robinson in the *Holmes v. City of Atlanta* triumph that opened Atlanta's public golf courses. Powell, a Howard University law school graduate, stood out as an able, local African American female lawyer determined to win civil rights for blacks. Appointed to the Fulton County Juvenile Court in 1973, Powell became the first black person to preside over a state court in Georgia.[81] Notably, with the involvement of Moore, Hollowell, Walden, Robinson, Thomas, and Powell, nearly the entire population of black lawyers in Georgia at the time had some hand in the Georgia State case.

Though Thurgood Marshall, Constance Baker Motley, and other national civil rights leaders provided brilliant legal strategy and expert assistance, records and other documents in the NAACP papers clearly reveal that the nine black applicants (Mae Boone, Edward Clemons, Myra Dinsmore, Barbara Hunt, Charlie Mae Knight, Marian McDaniel, Rosalyn McGhee, Russell Roberts, and Iris Mae Welch) who sought admission to Georgia State in March and June 1956 also received an abundance of support from the Atlanta branch of the NAACP, of which most of them were members. The NAACP was the dominant protest organization in Georgia during the 1950s, and its Atlanta branch spearheaded support for the black applicants in their quest for racial equality at Georgia State.[82]

The applicants also received enormous grassroots support from Atlanta's progressive black community. Most of the nine black applicants were employed by black-owned businesses, organizations, or institutions of higher education, including the Atlanta Life Insurance Company, the Atlanta office of the *Pittsburgh Courier*, Atlanta University, Clark College, and the SCLC. In addition, Russell Roberts and Edward Clemons were employed by the black-owned North Carolina Mutual Life Insurance Company; Marian McDaniel, one of the applicants who was not involved in the lawsuit, worked for the Atlanta branch of the NAACP; and plaintiff Welch was employed by local civil rights activist and entrepreneur J. E. Jordan, an active member of the Atlanta branch of the NAACP.[83]

In her August 22, 1958 deposition preceding the trial, Welch stated that Jordan encouraged his employees to join the NAACP and that she became a member after she moved to Atlanta to work for him.[84] Affirming the ground-up nature of the case, Welch stated that Jordan had approved of and advised her in her decision to seek admission to Georgia State and furnished her with an application for the college.[85] Following admissions director Blair's declaration that Welch's application was incomplete and he therefore would not consider it, Jordan advised Welch to seek legal assistance from Moore, who in turn involved Thurgood Marshall and the LDF.[86]

Although Welch insisted that the NAACP did not influence her decision to apply to Georgia State and that she and her co-plaintiffs retained Moore's services on their own, she displayed extreme nervousness during her deposition and trial testimony.[87] Notwithstanding the anxiety expected of a first-time plaintiff in federal court being intensely scrutinized by a highly skilled defense lawyer, Welch appeared completely rattled, leading Hollowell to try to calm her nerves: "Ms. Welch you seem just a little nervous. There is nothing to be nervous about here and nobody is going to harm you, so just take your time."[88]

Hollowell seemed to suggest that Welch might have been fearful of possible reprisal for her testimony or participation in the case. It is not inconceivable that Welch may have also received personal threats, in light of the death threats from the Ku Klux Klan reported by Hunt. Moreover, just a few months before the trial, in a *Georgia State Signal* editorial, the editors had warned Welch and the other plaintiffs that they would not find a safe place at Georgia State.[89] In addition, the governor and attorney general had made inflammatory statements regarding their determination to sustain Jim Crow.

Even more ominously, just over twelve years earlier, the Malcoms and Dorseys had been lynched less than forty-five miles away at Moore's Ford, and in 1942, even the supposedly moderately racist Governor Arnall had forecast calamitous consequences for "any nigger who tried . . . to enter the [University of Georgia]."[90] Such atrocities and ongoing threats of violence lingered in the individual and collective memories of black people and no doubt remained in the minds of Hunt, Dinsmore, and Welch. Civil rights history records an abundance of incidents during this time in which whites threatened or sought to intimidate black students seeking to apply to or entering white schools or colleges.[91] Just three years later, in 1961, Hamilton Holmes's and Charlayne Hunter's entrance to the University of Georgia sparked a riot, with hostile students burning effigies of Holmes and even federal judge William Bootle.[92] Historian Robert Cohen provides extensive documentation, including notes from FBI files, revealing the potential danger of this incident and the rioters' complicity with the Ku Klux Klan.[93]

Whatever the basis for Welch's anxiety, she made a number of contradictory statements about her employment history, address, and even the date and year of her birth. Hollowell and Moore coaxed her to speak up throughout her testimony. In an effort to minimize the adverse impact of the inconsistencies in her deposition and testimony at the trial, Hollowell queried Welch about her nervousness: "I will ask you whether or not you were pretty nervous on the day the deposition was taken?" Welch replied, "I was."[94]

Clemons also revealed during the trial that local officials in the North Carolina Mutual Insurance Company encouraged him to apply to Georgia State and had made Georgia State admission applications available at the insurance office.[95] Affirming the significance of the grassroots support that emerged, in an interview with Jesse Hill, he observed that a number of community-based individuals and groups assisted the legal efforts to dismantle segregation in Atlanta during this time, including black physicians and dentists, black commercial businesses, and the leaders of Atlanta's historically black colleges and universities.[96]

Local NAACP president and self-employed business leader J. H. Calhoun, who owned a real estate company and a furniture business on Auburn Avenue, also played a crucial role in advising the black applicants and coordinating support for the case.[97] Calhoun actively resisted Jim Crow in his business pursuits. For example, in his real estate business, he accepted listings from white sellers in areas that had not been approved by the segregationist establishment for interracial sales. His violation of the status quo "did not go unpunished"; the "Georgia Real Estate Commission revoked Calhoun's license to sell real estate because of his failure to abide by the color line."[98] Unabashed in his fight for civil rights and with support from the Empire Real Estate Board, a black realty board, Calhoun, who had been the target of a lawsuit filed by the state to secure NAACP records, filed a suit of his own against the real estate commission. Calhoun ultimately prevailed in the suit, which resulted in the reinstatement of his license.[99]

Calhoun, like Hill and other black business activist-leaders who were self-employed and/or generated their income largely from the black community, could advance the black freedom struggle without intimidation from the white power structure. Even when whites sought to impose economic reprisals against blacks who resisted the Jim Crow order, such as revoking Calhoun's license, the largely autonomous and self-sufficient black businesses were free to use resources generated primarily from black patrons to legally challenge such actions. Jesse Hill also emphasized that "the black church is, always has been, and always will be the key bastion of support and help in these causes."[100]

However, despite the large measure of solidarity within Atlanta's black community that supported efforts to desegregate Georgia State and advance the black freedom struggle, some blacks favored a more gradual approach to change. Political scientist and social change activist Robert Brisbane, who founded the Morehouse College Department of Political Science in the 1950s, has challenged the "erroneous assumption" that "all blacks were unified in support" of the efforts of social-change activists in the 1950s and 1960s.[101] For example, Brisbane observed that when Horace Ward sought admission to the University of Georgia, "there were some [blacks] who felt he was doing too much too fast and that he should be content and take the out-of-state aid and be satisfied. They just felt he was just making too many waves."[102]

A number of blacks feared adverse or even violent consequences for challenging white oppression; others feared for their families' economic survival, as many blacks depended solely on whites for employment. In the view of Rev. Samuel Williams, however, blacks who did not support students' civil rights activism were either "victims of brain washing or profiting from the system."[103] Despite the existence of blacks who did not embrace social change, a generous portion of both well-known and lesser-known blacks cast their lot with the black freedom struggle and helped to advance its cause.

Interestingly, on the very same day that Sloan issued the injunction against racial discrimination at Georgia State, Williams and Rev. John Thomas Porter, another largely unremembered Atlanta civil rights trailblazer and Morehouse activist, won yet another significant victory in the black freedom struggle in Georgia. Georgia and Atlanta officials suffered a major defeat when federal judge Frank Hooper declared segregated seating in Atlanta's buses and trolleys invalid. The case stemmed from a bus operator confronting Williams and Porter in an attempt to enforce segregated seating, and the previous arrest and indictment of six courageous local black ministers (William Holmes Borders, Joseph Johnson, Howard Bussey, Robert Shorts, Ray H. Williams, and Albert Franklin Fisher) for violating a Georgia statute and City of Atlanta ordinance requiring segregated seating on buses and trolleys.

On January 9, 1957, led by Reverend Borders, the six churchmen occupied seats reserved for whites on an Atlanta trolley. Police officials arrested the ministers and hauled them to jail in a police paddy wagon. Tellingly, two years after he characterized Atlanta as "the city too busy to hate," Mayor Hartsfield instructed Atlanta police chief Herbert Jenkins to swear out warrants charging the ministers with breaking segregation laws.[104] The segregation ordinance stipulated the following:

> Passengers on trackless trolleys operated in the limits of the city, and in territory outside the city limits which has been incorporated as a part of the city for police purposes, must observe and obey the requirements of the penal laws of the state as to the separate seating of the races in such cars; and any passenger failing to obey the directions of the conductor or person in charge of the car in this respect in so far as it is practicable to do so, shall be guilty of an offense and punishable as provided.[105]

Citing the *Browder v. Gayle* case, affirmed by a unanimous vote of the U.S. Supreme Court, Hooper declared the ordinances and statutes unconstitutional, thereby abolishing segregation on the buses in Atlanta.[106] In the *Browder* case, the court ruled that the statutes and ordinances requiring "segregation of the white and colored races on the motor busses of a common carrier of passengers in the City of Montgomery . . . violated the due process and equal protection of the law clauses of the Fourteenth Amendment to the Constitution of the United States."[107] Atlanta, purportedly the "city too busy to hate," in reality lagged behind a number of other southern cities—including Montgomery, Alabama; Richmond and Norfolk, Virginia; and Charleston and Columbia, South Carolina—that preceded it in desegregating city buses and trolleys.[108] Outlawing segregation and opening the way for mixed seating in Atlanta's public transportation represented another triumph for the voices of protest in Atlanta's black community.[109]

Despite the federal injunction against racial discrimination at Georgia State and the federal court-ordered bus desegregation, it would take a mass movement in Atlanta, initiated by largely unremembered student demonstrators, as well as a number of additional court edicts to achieve a more significant break in the rigid wall of segregation in Atlanta. In March 1960, shortly after the historic Greensboro, North Carolina, student sit-ins, Morehouse College students Lonnie King, Julian Bond, and Joe Pierce initiated efforts to challenge Atlanta's segregated restaurants and other businesses.[110] Roslyn Pope, president of Spelman College's student government association, collaborated with King, Bond, Pierce, and other student leaders to pen a petition titled "An Appeal for Human Rights," which appeared in major local and national press outlets.[111] The *Atlanta Daily World*, the *Atlanta Constitution*, and the *Atlanta Journal* originally published the appeal as a paid advertisement, but it was eventually printed in national outlets, including the *Congressional Record* and the *New York Times*. Their efforts rallied hundreds of student protesters and resulted in mass arrests, including the incarceration of Martin Luther King Jr.

The direct-action campaign, which became known as the Atlanta student sit-ins, set the stage for a number of lawsuits in the 1960s attacking segregation at Atlanta's Grady Hospital, the city's erection of a barricade between black and white neighborhoods to sanction Jim Crow housing practices, and white restaurateurs' refusal to serve black citizens.[112] Even Atlanta's emerging international airport relegated black patrons to eating in a corner of the restaurant in its airport terminal. H. D. Coke, a Delta Airlines passenger, rejected the second-class treatment and filed a federal lawsuit to end the practice.[113] Notably, Atlanta's small band of black lawyers, including Hollowell, Walden, and Ward, with assistance from Thurgood Marshall and the LDF, prevailed in court victories against racial discrimination in health care, housing, and public accommodations on behalf of largely overlooked local activists.

In his book *Representing the Race: The Creation of the Civil Rights Lawyer*, Kenneth Mack observes that the push for agency has impelled civil rights historians to lessen their focus on well-known figures like Martin Luther King Jr., NAACP leaders, and liberal Supreme Court justices and "embark on their own search for the true representatives of the race."[114] Mack argues that historical accounts of well-known civil rights figures, "admirable as they are," have given way to a drive to discover "the authentic voice of protest among the masses of African Americans themselves" and to illuminate the organizing traditions of local southern black communities "that developed their own organic forms of protest."[115] The 1956 Georgia State black applicants, like other unsung activists such as H. D. Coke and the local NAACP lawyers, businesses, and community-based activists who supported them, are among the authentic voices that developed their own organic forms of protest, albeit strongly supported and at times directed by well-known civil rights leaders such as Thurgood Marshall.

Martin Luther King Jr. himself highlighted the significance of unheralded grassroots activists in the civil rights movement, referencing them as "the ground crew." In King's December 10, 1964, acceptance speech for the Nobel Peace Prize, he proclaimed:

> From the depths of my heart I am aware that this prize is much more than an honor to me personally.
>
> Every time I take a flight, I am always mindful of the many people who make a successful journey possible—the known pilots and the unknown ground crew.
>
> So you honor the dedicated pilots of our struggle who have sat at the controls as the freedom movement soared into orbit. . . .
>
> You honor the ground crew without whose labor and sacrifices the jet flights to freedom could never have left the earth.
>
> Most of these people will never make the headlines and their names will not appear in *Who's Who*. Yet when years have rolled past and when the blazing light of truth is focused on this marvelous age in which we live—men and women will know and children will be taught that we have a finer land, a better people, a more noble civilization—because these humble children of God were willing to suffer for righteousness' sake.[116]

The bold Georgia State applicants and their supporters, the black ministers in the bus and trolley desegregation case, and the other community activists who stepped up to try to overcome white supremacy are all members of the "unknown ground crew." Their labor and sacrifices, which ultimately led to two federal injunctions against racial discrimination in Atlanta on the same day, unquestionably helped propel the black freedom movement forward.

CHAPTER 6
The Struggle Continues

Following the *Hunt* trial, several new black applicants were emboldened to seek admission to Georgia State. The applicants received the fervent support of Jesse Hill Jr., Donald Hollowell, Rev. Samuel Williams, and other community leaders. Yet despite the historic civil rights victory *Hunt* represented, state officials devised other arbitrary and capricious tactics to evade Sloan's ruling and continue to block the admission of black applicants.

Only a few months after the *Hunt* decision, Georgia State rejected the applications of Ernestine Brown, Mary Rogers, and Alice Wyche, three black women over the age of twenty-one. Georgia State declared that the applications were inadequate based on the women's academic credits and their ages.[1] Shamefully, because the plaintiffs and other black applicants seeking to enter white institutions of higher education had been exclusively older students, Georgia officials had deviously adopted an act requiring that applicants must be *under twenty-one years old* to pursue undergraduate study.

State representative J. Roy McCracken "justified the bill on grounds that the NAACP had difficulty finding young blacks willing to get involved in litigation and that, for various reasons, blacks tended to start college later." McCracken observed that some black applicants to Georgia State were in their forties.[2] The act stipulated: "No person shall be admitted initially to any college or undergraduate school of the University of Georgia or any of its branches after such person has reached twenty-one (21) years of age."[3]

Following the trial, Georgia State officials, "finding no grounds to deny admission to the third plaintiff, Iris Mae Welch, a woman in her forties," used this newly enacted criterion to deny her enrollment.[4] The requirement doomed the chances of admission for any of the three plaintiffs. Georgia State had used "moral grounds" to exclude Hunt and Dinsmore from enrolling; now Welch, whom Sloan had explicitly declared "to be of good character and not lacking in qualification for admission," was also declared ineligible for admission due to her age.[5]

The hastily enacted bill, which was a desperate overreach by state officials to maintain segregation, would potentially also affect white applicants over twenty-one years old. However, Speaker pro Tempore George T. Bagby made it clear that the legislative act would not adversely impact white students when he assured members of the House "that the bill would not discriminate against a single white." Bagby crudely stated that the bill was "designed to keep the nigger out!"[6] He recommended, "If that's what you want to do, then vote for it!"[7] The bill overwhelmingly passed the legislature. Nonetheless, the bill often proved to be a nuisance to whites over twenty-one and disrupted "the plans of white adults who simply wanted to go to college in Georgia."[8] To accommodate white applicants affected by the act, the legislature approved a provision in the bill that granted institutions the authority to make exceptions for persons found to possess sufficient ability and fitness.[9] The age requirement ploy was only one of numerous actions by the Georgia legislature intended to sidestep judicial decisions banning racial segregation.[10]

In *Hunt*, the plaintiffs and their attorneys had taken an important legal step toward ending segregation in higher education in Georgia. However, Georgia was still a segregationist state, and its white political leadership mounted sweeping actions to guarantee that blacks would not enter white schools. As Walden had predicted, more litigation would be required to break the chains of segregation.

In another direct attack on segregation in education in Georgia, immediately after the *Hunt* decision, Hollowell, Moore, and NAACP LDF lawyers filed a lawsuit on behalf of black children in Atlanta against the Atlanta Public Schools. One year later, in another legal blow to Jim Crow, Federal District Court judge Frank Hooper ruled that the Atlanta Board of Education unlawfully operated a racially discriminatory school system. Hooper ordered the board to present a plan to the court for desegregating its public schools. Though Hooper's ruling created another crack in the wall of segregation, because Hooper did not order the immediate admission of black students to white schools, desegregation of the school system would proceed at a glacial pace.[11]

In response to the court order in the *Hunt* case and subsequent black students seeking admission to Georgia State, the state scrambled to sustain segregation. Newly elected governor Ernest Vandiver warned that the state was prepared to shut down colleges if the federal courts forced Georgia colleges to integrate. He quickly suggested to Board of Regents chairman Arnold that the regents order institutions to cease accepting applications until members of the Board of Regents had an opportunity to thoroughly review Sloan's ruling.[12]

In a move to counter Sloan's order, Arnold complied and immediately suspended any new applications to each of the nineteen state colleges and universities. According to an article by Claude Sitton in the *New York Times*, Vandiver proposed the action based on the assumption, "confirmed in Negro circles," that blacks would seek to enter other all-white institutions in addition to Georgia State.[13] Despite Vandiver's hurried actions, he ironically urged that "the people of Georgia and all of the officials concerned not be stampeded into hasty action." In a prepared statement, he defiantly vowed, "The incoming Governor and incoming administration will exhaust every resource of the State to sustain and to uphold Georgia's way of life and her sacred traditions."[14] Vandiver asserted, "We want to have in our arsenal all possible weapons."[15]

Vandiver threatened to implement the state law that required officials to automatically cut off funds if a court ordered a black person admitted to a white college. He also proposed to the 1959 Georgia General Assembly legislation "to streamline the private school plan," which provided "state income tax credits to pay for private school tuition."[16] The general assembly also passed "a provision forbidding the creation or use of an ad valorem tax to fund integrated education" and other measures to sustain segregation.[17] Other legislative acts to evade the court order included a bill that allowed Vandiver to close any public school under federal court order to desegregate and laws that "prohibited cities with independent school systems from levying property taxes to support desegregated schools" and even "permitted the state to pay legal counsel to defend segregated schools."[18]

Vandiver, desperate to fulfill the centerpiece of his racially derogatory campaign promise that "no, not one" black would be admitted to a white school during his tenure as governor, even hatched a plan to shut down black schools "if any of the state's white schools were ordered integrated."[19] Reiterating the state's line of defense from the *Hunt* trial, Vandiver labeled the efforts of black students to gain admission to white schools "another conspiracy on the part of the NAACP to shut down [Georgia's] schools."[20] Vandiver forewarned that he would take no action to repeal Georgia laws requiring the closing of schools in the event of court-ordered desegregation. Instead, shifting the onus to the NAACP and even black parents, he said, "Let us hope . . . that the NAACP will not force the closing of a single school in Georgia"[21] and urged "Negro parents not to press desegregation suits."[22]

In a strongly worded statement, on January 14, 1960, NAACP executive director Roy Wilkins denounced Vandiver's attempt to blame the NAACP for his plan to close schools, asserting: "The NAACP will not act to close any school. We have neither the desire, intent, or power to do so. . . . If any school is closed in Georgia . . . it will be because Georgia officials and members of the Georgia State Legislature choose to penalize the children of Georgia in order to defy the Constitution and to try to maintain a dead way of life. Use of the NAACP as a whipping boy will not conceal what Georgians are doing to Georgians."[23] Ardently supporting Vandiver's defiance, Bloch, Georgia's constitutional expert on segregation, declared, "No Federal Court can ever compel the Governor and the Legislature [of Georgia] to institute, maintain and operate a system of public schools in which the races are mixed."[24]

Nonetheless, though not a complete victory, Sloan's edict helped Georgia civil rights legal strategists begin to chip away at the Jim Crow system in public higher education, as white political leaders scrambled to circumvent the court order. Although the Georgia State applicants themselves were left in limbo, their efforts secured historic legal ground by overturning significant legal barriers concocted by the state to sustain segregation. Sloan's decisions became a precedent that others could draw on in the challenge to desegregate institutions of higher education in Georgia.

Beginning with Ward's quest to enter the all-white University of Georgia, aspiring students and black community activists had been involved for nearly a decade in legal efforts to win the admission of blacks to a white public institution of higher education in Georgia. Yet the struggle to overcome racial segregation in higher education would continue, requiring yet another fierce legal battle against the white segregationist power structure. After the state had successfully used the moral issue and the age issue to block the Georgia State applicants, in *Holmes v. Danner*, the subsequent case to achieve desegregation in higher education, Hollowell, Hill, and other Atlanta black community leaders meticulously canvassed black high schools in Atlanta "to identify students with superior ability and character who could withstand the intense scrutiny they would encounter if they applied to predominantly white colleges."[25]

Following a thorough examination of a number of potential candidates, the black leaders selected Hamilton Holmes and Charlayne Hunter as the top male and female candidates to apply to a white college or university. In July 1959, only six months after Sloan's decree in the Georgia State case, Holmes and Hunter submitted their applications to the University of Georgia. UGA officials summarily rejected their applications, purportedly due to limited dormitory space and, in the case of Hamilton Holmes, moral character issues. Following the rejection of their applications and a series of failed appeals to university and Board of Regents officials, with the help of chief counsel Donald Hollowell and the NAACP they filed the *Holmes v. Danner* case.

Despite the extensive vetting of these two exceptional candidates, white officials unsurprisingly recycled some of the same tactics used in the Georgia State case, in a sinister effort to attack their characters and mar their records. Hoping to discover some moral ground on which to forestall the applicants, University of Georgia officials hired secret informants to spy on Holmes and Hunter as well as their families, seeking to uncover something illicit in their backgrounds that could justify denying them admission.

A report from the investigator who spied on Holmes observed:

> Confidential Informant of known reliability advised that Hamilton Holmes and Charlayne Alberta Hunter dated during their senior year at Turner High School. The night of graduation, Hamilton Holmes, Charlayne Hunter, and another boy and girl, after the graduation dance stayed out together until about 4:00 A.M.
>
> Reportedly Hamilton Holmes has bragged that he intends to be in the University of Georgia next September. Information has also been developed indicating that the college group is frequenting a House of Ill Repute believed to be on Sunset somewhere near Magnolia. The spot reportedly has "Pot parties, tea parties, beatnik parties." . . . Reportedly this house has white girls as well as colored girls for the proper price. There were approximately twenty-five white boys and girls ranging from the ages of 18 to 25 also at this dance. Hamilton and his friends were drinking beer, scotch, and Thunderbird wine. Informant is of the opinion that possibly some form of narcotic was being smoked.[26]

A confidential informant also issued a report on Charlayne Hunter. The report revealed that the undercover investigator had inspected files from "governmental agencies" to determine whether Hunter was a member of the "Communist Party" and if "any child ha[d] been born to Charlayne Alberta Hunter."²⁷

Despite state and university officials' efforts to vitiate the characters and qualifications of Holmes and Hunter, their investigations did not yield any credible adverse information. After a protracted court battle, Holmes and Hunter won their case, and federal judge Bootle ordered their admission to the University of Georgia in 1961. As previously noted, Federal Appeals Court judge Elbert Tuttle and the U.S. Supreme Court subsequently affirmed Bootle's declaration. The historic U.S. Supreme Court victory relied heavily on the foundation laid by the ground crew of Hunt, Dinsmore, Welch, and other black applicants to Georgia State.

Hollowell and activist Jesse Hill Jr. characterized the *Hunt* and *Ward* cases as the bedrock that fortified the *Holmes* triumph.²⁸ As Sloan had before him, Bootle, who presided over *Holmes*, ruled that denying blacks admission to Georgia's colleges and universities solely on the basis of color blatantly violated the Fourteenth Amendment. However, expanding on the *Hunt* precedent, Bootle went further than Sloan. On Friday, January 6, 1961, he ordered the *immediate admission* of Holmes and Hunter to the all-white University of Georgia just three days later.²⁹

On January 9, 1961, Holmes and Hunter broke the color barrier in higher education at the University of Georgia. In scaling the walls of segregation in Georgia, they unquestionably stood on the broad shoulders of Georgia State's black applicants and plaintiffs.³⁰ On the same day, Vandiver, who had risen to gubernatorial success on his "no, not one" slogan, contradicted his own hardline segregationist stance. Vandiver abandoned massive resistance and proposed several new school bills that included repealing mandatory school closings. Although the proposals included a measure that provided tuition grants to allow white students to attend white private schools, in effect, Vandiver's proposals conceded to court-ordered desegregation and "no longer defended absolute segregation."³¹

Having been lured into taking an extreme position against racial equality to outpace a gubernatorial opponent who characterized him as weak on segregation, Vandiver now retreated. Explaining this turnaround, in an interview with the author, Vandiver passionately recounted:

> I knew that we had to make a change and to make a radical change in our political system. So I called over fifty people who are my political friends, who helped me get elected governor. I called them out to the executive mansion. . . . I went around the room, doctor, and of those fifty people who were

there, forty-eight said, "Let's close the schools." There were two people in that group that said, "We cannot close the schools." One of them was Carl Sanders, who later succeeded me as governor. The other was Frank Twitty, a man from deep South Georgia who was my floor leader.[32]

Vandiver's decision to follow the recommendation of Sanders and Twitty and his proposals stemming from federal court-ordered desegregation helped bring an end to state-sanctioned massive resistance in Georgia. Vandiver later apologized for his "no, not one" declaration: "I made a major statement, 'neither my child or your child will ever go to an integrated school, no, not one.' That was a statement I should not have made.... My friends and I sat up all night working out a campaign speech on what I should say and what I should not say. About half my friends told me I should not make that statement. The others said, 'Well, you got to counteract the fellow [opponent] over here who is giving you hell.' I made the wrong decision."[33]

Two years after the *Hunt* triumph and less than a month after Bootle ordered the admission of Holmes and Hunter to the University of Georgia, James Meredith began his efforts to enter the all-white University of Mississippi. With the help of the NAACP LDF and local lawyer R. Jess Brown, Meredith won the historic *Meredith v. Fair* case in 1962. Constance Baker Motley, in her book *Equal Justice under Law*, contends that "the *Meredith* case effectively put an end to massive resistance in the Deep South."[34] As discussed earlier, the Fifth Circuit Court of Appeals noted that the University of Mississippi's requirement of certifications from white alumni, ruled unconstitutional in the *Hunt* case, violated Meredith's rights under the provisions of the Fourteenth Amendment. The federal appeals court opined that the university's insistence on white alumni recommendations was evidence of racial segregation and that Meredith was unlawfully denied admission. To the extent that the ruling in the *Hunt* case, as explicitly noted by the Fifth Circuit, contributed to Meredith's legal victory and admission to the University of Mississippi, it is important to underscore that the *Hunt* ruling played a crucial role in the historic case that essentially ended massive resistance in the Deep South.

In his chronicle *Simple Justice: The History of* Brown v. Board of Education *and Black America's Struggle for Equality*, Richard Kluger explains, "Many unheralded people persevering in widespread communities over long, hard decades contributed to what the Supreme Court decided on the seventeenth day of May 1954."[35] Likewise, many unheralded people, including the litigants in the fight to end segregation at Georgia State, contributed to the *Holmes* triumph, the *Meredith* triumph, and subsequent victories leading to the desegregation of institutions of higher learning and the end of massive resistance. Hunt, Dinsmore, and Welch, buttressed by many unremembered local activists, lawyers, and black business and educational leaders in Atlanta's thriving black mecca, laid important groundwork for these subsequent cases through their activism and the judicial precedents established in their own case.

Three years after Hunt, Dinsmore, and Welch won their case, and one year after the triumph of Holmes and Hunter, two black women, building on the activism and momentum created by the desegregation of the University of Georgia, successfully enrolled at Georgia State. On June 12, 1962, Annette Lucille Hall, who earned a bachelor's degree from historically black Spelman College in 1939 and a master's degree from Atlanta University in 1953, broke the color line at the Georgia State College of Business Administration, becoming the first African American student to enroll at the institution.[36] Unlike the disorderly environment encountered by Holmes and Hunter at the University of Georgia in January 1961, no protest or riotous mobs emerged to try to thwart Hall's admission.

The state had repealed the age limit requirement following the historic *Holmes* decision, making it possible for Hall, a history and social studies teacher at J. P. Carr High School in the Rockdale County Public Schools, to enter Georgia State at the age of fifty-three. Hall entered the college to "take continuing education courses in the Institute on Americanism and Communism, a course required of all social studies teachers by the 1962 Georgia Legislature."[37] After completing her registration on June 12, 1962, Hall attended her first class without fanfare the following day.[38]

Like Hunt, Dinsmore, and Welch, Hall was a quiet, unassuming trailblazer who did not seek adulation. David Smith Jr., author of *Georgia State University: An Institutional History, 1913–2002*, describes Hall as "a quiet warrior, so humble that she didn't even tell her family that she was the first African American student." Nevertheless, Hall's influence looms large. Her inspiration influenced her nephew, Ralph Long Jr., who helped desegregate Georgia Tech in Atlanta, and her niece, Carolyn Long Banks, the first African American city council member in the city of Atlanta.[39]

A few months after Hall's admission, Marybelle Reynolds Warner enrolled as Georgia State's first full-time black student. Warner, who held a bachelor's degree from St. Louis University and a master of social work degree from Washington University in St. Louis, desired to become a music teacher and majored in music education.[40] Marybelle Warner was the wife of black physician, U.S. Army veteran, and civil rights activist Clinton Warner, who was active in the group of Atlanta black leaders who encouraged and supported Hamilton Holmes and Charlayne Hunter in their quest to enter the University of Georgia.[41] Three years after the enrollment of Hall and Warner, Joseph Howard McClure earned a bachelor of business administration degree at Georgia State, becoming the university's inaugural black graduate.[42]

Since the epic struggle to break the shackles of segregation at Georgia State initiated by Russell T. Roberts, Myra E. Dinsmore, Mae Thelma Boone, Edward Jacob Clemons, Rosalyn Virginia McGhee, Charlie Mae Knight, Marian McDaniel, Barbara Pace Hunt, and Iris Mae Welch in 1956; the court victory of Hunt, Dinsmore, and Welch; and the enrollment of Hall and Warner in 1962, the urban university has become the most racially diverse institution in the University System of Georgia. In the spring of 2018, Georgia State University—the former Georgia State College of Business Administration—had the highest percentage (41.5 percent) and number (20,357) of African American students among research universities in the University System of Georgia.[43] It also has one of the largest populations of African American students in the nation among traditionally white institutions. In addition, for the last five years, Georgia State "has awarded more bachelor's degrees to African Americans . . . than any other nonprofit college or university in the country."[44]

In his compelling narrative *Born to Rebel*, Benjamin Elijah Mays observes, "It is to Atlanta's credit that her colleges and universities are now wide open to black students. But it should be remembered that black people had go to federal court to break the color bar in higher education."[45] It is therefore fitting to record and honor the history of the fight by black people who had to go to federal court to break the color barrier at Georgia State University and to recognize and document the contributions of the courageous local activists who fought for equity and social justice in a hostile environment. Georgia State owes a tremendous debt of gratitude to Hunt, Dinsmore, Welch, and their comrades for its progress and its evolution as an open and diverse research institution that embraces African Americans.

Fannie Lou Hamer, the quintessential grassroots civil rights activist, admonished that we must "never forget from whence we came and always praise the bridges that carried us over." We must not allow the bold, selfless grassroots activists who helped to make real the promise of democracy at Georgia State, and subsequently all of Georgia's colleges and universities, to be forgotten. We must praise and celebrate the legacies of all those who sacrificed enormously to make it possible for Georgia State to embrace diversity and equity to the extent that today the institution prides itself on its large African American student population.

The struggle for equity and justice is not over. For example, although Georgia State now awards a remarkable, even laudable, number of degrees to African American students, its percentages of African American senior administrators and faculty are dismal in comparison to the percentage of African Americans in the state. Nonetheless, the grassroots activists' remarkable achievements in the fight to end segregation at Georgia State have tremendously advanced the cause of social justice. In the continuing struggle for equity, the record of the activists and lawyers who won the historic victory against segregation at Georgia State serves as a blueprint for personal courage, perseverance, and civil rights from the ground up.

NOTES

Introduction

1. *Holmes v. Danner*, 195 F. Supp. 394 (M.D. Ga. 1961).
2. Maurice C. Daniels, *Saving the Soul of Georgia: Donald L. Hollowell and the Struggle for Civil Rights* (Athens: University of Georgia Press, 2013). Atlanta attorney Donald L. Hollowell emerged as Georgia's chief civil rights lawyer during the 1950s and 1960s. In this role he defended African American men accused or convicted of capital crimes in a racially hostile legal system, represented movement activists arrested for their civil rights work, and fought to undermine the laws that maintained state-sanctioned racial discrimination. Hollowell represented civil rights leaders Martin Luther King Jr. and Ralph David Abernathy and Atlanta student sit-in and Albany Movement protesters. He played a central role in the *Hunt v. Arnold* case and served as chief counsel in *Ward v. Regents* and *Holmes v. Danner*, the historic cases that ultimately led to the desegregation of higher education in Georgia.
3. Maurice C. Daniels and Cameron Van Patterson, "(Re)considering Race in the Desegregation of Higher Education," *Georgia Law Review* 46, no. 3 (Spring 2012): 543.
4. *Holmes v. Danner*, trial transcript, 191 F. Supp. 394 (No. 450) (on file with Federal Records Ctr., East Point, Ga.).
5. Daniels, *Saving the Soul of Georgia*, 76.
6. Ibid.
7. *Holmes v. Danner*, 191 F. Supp. 394, 407 (M.D. Ga. 1961).
8. See Maurice C. Daniels, *Horace T. Ward: Desegregation of the University of Georgia, Civil Rights Advocacy, and Jurisprudence* (Atlanta: Clark Atlanta University Press, 2001); Daniels, *Saving the Soul of Georgia*; Maurice C. Daniels, executive producer, *Foot Soldier for Equal Justice: Horace T. Ward and the Desegregation of the University of Georgia*, Georgia Public Television Broadcast (Athens: University of Georgia Cen-

ter for Continuing Education, 2000); Charlayne Hunter-Gault, *In My Place* (New York: Vintage, 1993); Robert Pratt, *We Shall Not Be Moved: The Desegregation of the University of Georgia* (Athens: University of Georgia Press, 2002); Calvin Trillin, *An Education in Georgia: Charlayne Hunter, Hamilton Holmes, and the Integration of the University of Georgia* (New York: Viking Press, 1964).

9. *Meredith v. Fair*, 306 F.2d. 374 (1962). For a study of the struggle to desegregate the University of Mississippi, see Charles W. Eagles, *The Price of Defiance: James Meredith and the Integration of Ole Miss* (Chapel Hill: University of North Carolina Press, 2009).

10. *Meredith v. Fair*, 298 F.2d. 696 (1962).

11. *Meredith v. Fair*, 305 F.2d. 343 (1962).

12. Eagles, *Price of Defiance*, 221.

13. Constance Baker Motley, *Equal Justice under Law: An Autobiography* (New York: Farrar, Strauss & Giroux, 1998), 166. Local counsel R. Jess Brown and NAACP LDF counsels Jack Greenberg and Derrick Bell worked with Motley on the *Meredith* case.

14. Because the NAACP did not qualify under its original charter as a tax-exempt organization, some donors, including major benefactors such as John D. Rockefeller Jr., refused to renew their contributions. In 1940, the NAACP established the NAACP Legal Defense and Educational Fund, Inc. as a separate charitable, tax-exempt organization to do the legal work of the association. On March 20, 1940, the LDF charter was approved by the Supreme Court of New York County. Motley, *Equal Justice under Law*, 99; Daniels, *Horace T. Ward*, 12.

15. Kenneth Mack, *Representing the Race: The Creation of the Civil Rights Lawyer* (Cambridge, Mass.: Harvard University Press, 2012), 2.

16. Tomiko Brown-Nagin, *Courage to Dissent: Atlanta and the Long History of the Civil Rights Movement* (New York: Oxford University Press, 2011), 22.

17. Daniels, *Saving the Soul of Georgia*, 56.

18. Mack, *Representing the Race*, 8; Myra Elliott Dinsmore, interview with author, Atlanta, February 19, 1997.

19. "Reconstructing Civil Rights Legal History from the Bottom Up," *Virginia Journal* 13 (2010): 8.

20. Daniels, *Saving the Soul of Georgia*, 7.

21. Emilye Crosby, *Civil Rights History from the Ground Up: Local Struggles, a National Movement* (Athens: University of Georgia Press, 2012), 19.

22. Mack, *Representing the Race*, 7.

23. Maurice J. Hobson, *The Legend of the Black Mecca: Politics and Class in the Making of Modern Atlanta* (Chapel Hill: University of North Carolina Press, 2017), 2.

24. Crosby, *Civil Rights History*, 5.

Chapter 1. Breaking the Color Line

1. See Thomas Dyer, *The University of Georgia: A Bicentennial History, 1785–1985* (Athens: University of Georgia Press, 1985), 290–93; David Smith Jr., *Georgia State University: An Institutional History, 1913–2002* (self-pub., CreateSpace, 2010), 198; *Hunt v. Arnold*, 172 F. Supp. 847, U.S. Dist., 1959, 3–4.

2. Smith, *Georgia State University*, 198; *Hunt v. Arnold*, 172 F. Supp. 847, U.S. Dist., 1959, 3–4.

3. Kevin Michael Kruse, *White Flight: Atlanta and the Making of Modern Conservatism* (Princeton, N.J.: Princeton University Press, 2005), 3, 40. For a review of William Hartsfield's political career, see Harold H. Martin, *William Berry Hartsfield: Mayor of Atlanta* (Athens: University of Georgia Press, 1978).

4. John N. Popham, "'Breathing Spell' for Adjustment Tempers Region's Feelings," *New York Times*, May 18, 1954, 1, 20.

5. James F. Cook, *The Governors of Georgia, 1754-1995* (Macon, Ga.: Mercer University Press, 1995), 274.

6. Albert Riley, "Georgians Stiffen Resistance to Pressure for Integration," *Atlanta Journal*, January 15, 1956, 1.

7. Gordon Roberts, "Griffin Gives Race Stand; Sanders Raps 'Inheritance,'" *Atlanta Journal*, August 15, 1962.

8. Roberts, "Griffin Gives Race Stand."

9. Stephen G. N. Tuck, *Beyond Atlanta: The Struggle for Racial Equality in Georgia, 1940-1980* (Athens: University of Georgia Press, 2001), 19.

10. Frederick Allen, *Atlanta Rising: The Invention of an International City, 1946-1996* (Atlanta: Longstreet Press, 1996), 3.

11. Allen, *Atlanta Rising*, 9.

12. Ibid., 5; Laura Wexler, *Fire in a Canebrake: The Last Mass Lynching in America* (New York: Scribner, 2003), 35. Also see Stetson Kennedy, *The Klan Unmasked* (Boca Raton: Florida Atlantic University Press, 1954), 22.

13. See Wexler, *Fire in a Canebrake*.

14. Ibid., 38.

15. Ibid., 125.

16. Ibid.

17. W. Fitzhugh Brundage, *Lynching in the New South: Georgia and Virginia, 1880-1930* (Urbana: University of Illinois Press, 2011), 253-54.

18. Charles S. Bullock, Scott E. Buchanan, and Ronald K. Gaddie, *The Three Governors Controversy: Skullduggery, Machinations, and the Decline of Georgia's Progressive Politics* (Athens: University of Georgia Press, 2015), 86.

19. Harold H. Martin, *Georgia: A Bicentennial History* (New York: W. W. Norton, 1977), 191; Harold Paulk Henderson, *The Politics of Change in Georgia: A Political Biography of Ellis Arnall* (Athens: University of Georgia Press, 1991), 138-39, 246. Henderson provides a comprehensive narrative of Arnall's political career, illuminating the complexities and contradictions of racial politics during the Jim Crow era. On the one hand, Arnall engaged in vicious rhetoric demeaning blacks. On the other hand, he "complied with the federal judiciary's mandate to allow blacks to vote in the state's white primaries . . . and admitted that the South had not lived up to the equal requirement of the *Plessy v. Ferguson* decision." During Arnall's 1942 gubernatorial campaign against Talmadge, noted writer Lillian Smith observed that "Arnall had defended segregation and repudiated racial equality just as vehemently as Talmadge."

20. Benjamin Elijah Mays, *Born to Rebel* (New York: Charles Scribner & Sons, 1971), 221; Henderson, *Politics of Change in Georgia*, 49; William Anderson, *The Wild Man from Sugar Creek: The Political Career of Eugene Talmadge* (Baton Rouge: Louisiana State University Press, 1975), 210.

21. Henderson, *Politics of Change in Georgia*, 139; Anderson, *Wild Man from Sugar Creek*, 210.

22. Charles H. Martin, "Racial Change and 'Big Time' College Football in Georgia: The Age of Segregation, 1892–1957," *Georgia Historical Quarterly* 80, no. 3 (1996): 532–62, here 552. Based on a "gentlemen's agreement" that was "widely accepted by the early 1920's and which lasted until the 1950's," northern schools with black student-athletes were expected to disallow them to play when competing against a southern white school, "even if the game site were located in the North" (537–38). Martin's article covers the history of the University of Georgia's and Georgia Tech's racial policies related to sports. In the early 1900s, both schools subscribed to Jim Crow policies and refused to compete against any team that included a black student-athlete. During the early 1950s, the schools reluctantly began to schedule contests with teams that included black players if the competition was held outside the South (534).

23. Martin, "Racial Change," 552. See also Kenneth Coleman, *A History of Georgia* (Athens: University of Georgia Press, 1991), 365.

24. Martin, "Racial Change," 553–54.

25. Maurice C. Daniels, *Horace T. Ward: Desegregation of the University of Georgia, Civil Rights Advocacy, and Jurisprudence* (Atlanta: Clark Atlanta University Press, 2001), 50.

26. Roy Harris, "Strictly Personal," *Augusta Courier*, October 2, 1950.

27. Martin, "Racial Change," 556.

28. Martin, "Racial Change," 554.

29. Ibid., 532, 554.

30. Ibid., 556.

31. Dyer, *University of Georgia*, 315.

32. Bullock, Buchanan, and Gaddie, *Three Governors Controversy*, 220.

33. Allen, *Atlanta Rising*, 60.

34. Albert Pickett, interview with author, Augusta, Ga., January 13, 1977; Edward McIntyre, interview with author, Augusta, Ga., January 13, 1997.

35. William McCracken, interview with author, Augusta, Ga., January 13, 1997.

36. McIntyre, interview.

37. Numan V. Bartley, *The Rise of Massive Resistance: Race and Politics in the South during the 1950's* (Baton Rouge: Louisiana State University Press, 1969), vii.

38. Walter White, *A Man Called White: The Autobiography of Walter White* (New York: Viking Press, 1948), 143. For a study of Charles Hamilton Houston's civil rights work, see Genna Rae McNeil, *Groundwork: Charles Hamilton Houston and the Struggle for Civil Rights* (Philadelphia: University of Pennsylvania Press, 1983).

39. *Smith v. Allwright*, 321 U.S. 665 (1944); *King v. Chapman*, 154 F.2d. 460 (5th Cir. 1946).

40. Darlene Clark Hine, *The Rise and Fall of the White Primary in Texas* (Columbia: University of Missouri Press, 1979), 2.

41. Ibid. With the help of Texas branches of the NAACP and the national office, Texas resident Lonnie Smith, a dentist in Harris County, Texas, filed the historic *Smith v. Allwright* case. Thurgood Marshall and fellow LDF attorney William Hastie won the unanimous decision on April 3, 1944.

42. *Gaines v. Canada*, 305 U.S. 337, 352, 59 S. Ct. 232, 238 (1938); *Sipuel v. Board of Regents of University of Oklahoma*, 332 U.S. 631, 68 S. Ct. 299 (1948); *McLaurin v. Oklahoma*, 339 U.S. 637–42 (1950); *Sweatt v. Painter*, 339 U.S. 629 (1950).

43. James W. Endersby and William T. Horner, *Lloyd Gaines and the Fight to End Segregation* (Columbia: University of Missouri Press, 2016), 16–17.

44. Ibid., 1; Daniels, *Horace T. Ward*, 10; *Gaines v. Canada*, 305 U.S. 337, 59 S. Ct. 232, 238 (1938).

45. Constance Baker Motley, *Equal Justice under Law: An Autobiography* (New York: Farrar, Strauss & Giroux, 1998), 64–65; Maurice C. Daniels and Cameron Van Patterson, "(Re)considering Race in the Desegregation of Higher Education," *Georgia Law Review* 46, no. 3 (Spring 2012): 539. See also Ada Lois Sipuel Fisher and Danney Goble, *A Matter of Black and White: The Autobiography of Ada Lois Sipuel Fisher* (Norman: University of Oklahoma Press, 1996).

46. Daniels and Van Patterson, "(Re)considering Race," 539.

47. Ibid.; White, *Man Called White*, 149.

48. Jack Greenberg, *Crusaders in the Courts: How a Dedicated Band of Lawyers Fought for the Civil Rights Revolution* (New York: Basic Books, 1994), 64; Motley, *Equal Justice under Law*, 61.

49. Patricia Sullivan, *Lift Every Voice: The NAACP and the Making of the Civil Rights Movement* (New York: New Press, 2009), 380–81; *Sweatt v. Painter*, 339 U.S. 629 (1950). For a comprehensive account of Heman Marion Sweatt's struggle to enter the University of Texas School of Law, see Gary M. Lavergne, *Before Brown: Heman Marion Sweatt, Thurgood Marshall, and the Long Road to Justice* (Austin: University of Texas Press, 2010).

50. Daniels, *Horace T. Ward*, 16. See *McLaurin v. Oklahoma*, 339 U.S. 637–42 (1950).

51. White, *Man Called White*, 89; Bartley, *Rise of Massive Resistance*, 46.

52. White, *Man Called White*, 90.

53. "Harris Likens NAACP Acts to 'Carpetbaggers,'" *Atlanta Journal*, February 19, 1956.

54. Ibid.

55. "Text of Address of Roy V. Harris at Savannah State College Dedication," *Savannah Evening Press*, February 19, 1956; "Harris Likens NAACP."

56. "Text of Address"; "Harris Likens NAACP."

57. "Text of Address"; "Harris Likens NAACP."

58. For information and documentation on terror and lynching, see the National Association for the Advancement of Colored People, *Thirty Years of Lynching in the United States 1889–1918* (New York: NAACP, 1919); Gregory Mixon, *The Atlanta Riot: Race, Class, and Violence in a New South City* (Gainesville: University Press of Florida, 2005); Mark Bauerlein, *Negrophobia: A Race Riot at Atlanta, 1906* (San Francisco: Encounter Books, 2001); Leon F. Litwack, *Trouble in Mind: Black Southerners in the Age of Jim Crow* (New York: Knopf, 1998).

59. Joy Ann Williamson, *Radicalizing the Ebony Tower: Black Colleges and the Black Freedom Struggle in Mississippi* (New York: Teachers College Press, Columbia University, 2008), 24.

60. Ibid.

61. R. O. Johnson, "Desegregation of Public Education in Georgia—One Year Afterward," *Journal of Negro Education* 24, no. 3, 228.

62. Molly O'Brien, "Discriminatory Effects: Desegregation Litigation in Higher Education in Georgia," *William & Mary Bill of Rights Journal* 8, no. 1/2, 15.

63. James D. Anderson, *The Education of Blacks in the South, 1860-1935* (Chapel Hill: University of North Carolina Press, 2008), 248.

64. Marybeth Gasman and Christopher L. Tudico, eds., *Historically Black Colleges and Universities: Triumphs, Troubles, and Taboos* (New York: Palgrave Macmillan, 2008), 2. See also O'Brien, "Discriminatory Effects."

65. O'Brien, "Discriminatory Effects," 10.

66. Johnson, "Desegregation of Public Education," 230.

67. Annual Report of University System Board of Regents for the Fiscal Year 1958-1959, Atlanta, Georgia, July 1, 1959.

68. Mark V. Tushnet, *The NAACP's Legal Strategy against Segregated Education, 1925-1950* (Chapel Hill: University of North Carolina Press, 1987), 9, 36. For a comprehensive study of the disparities in educational funding and resources allocated to blacks as compared to whites in the South, see Anderson, *Education of Blacks*.

69. "Roy Harris Makes Blast at 'Modern Carpetbaggers,'" *Savannah Tribune*, February 23, 1956; "Harris Warns against Efforts to Divide South: Racial Progress Is Reviewed in Speech at Negro College," *Savannah Evening Press*, February 19, 1956. W. W. Law served as the Georgia NAACP state president from 1955 to 1966 and as president of the NAACP Savannah branch for twenty-six years. Law was a prominent figure among the national NAACP's board of directors and an effective advocate who guided mass demonstrations and protests on the local level, which led to defeating Jim Crow in Savannah. See Tuck, *Beyond Atlanta*.

70. "Roy Harris Makes Blast."

71. "Harris Warns against Efforts."

72. "Harris Likens NAACP."

73. "Roy Harris Makes Blast."

74. Ibid.

75. Ibid.

76. Ibid.

77. Janie Culbreath Rambeau, "Ripe for the Picking," in *Hands on the Freedom Plow: Personal Accounts by Women in SNCC*, ed. Faith S. Holsaert, Martha Prescod Norman Noonan, Judy Richardson, Betty Garman Robinson, Jean Smith Young, and Dorothy M. Zellner (Urbana: University of Illinois Press, 2010), 95.

78. Williamson, *Radicalizing the Ebony Tower*, 1.

79. Ibid., 4-6.

80. Ibid., 129.

81. Anderson, *Education of Blacks*, 276-77.

82. Ibid., 277.

83. Maurice C. Daniels, *Saving the Soul of Georgia: Donald L. Hollowell and the Struggle for Civil Rights* (Athens: University of Georgia Press, 2013), 140-41.

84. Williamson, *Radicalizing the Ebony Tower*, 4.

85. Daniels, *Saving the Soul of Georgia*, 99–100.

86. See Erik Gellman, *Death Blow to Jim Crow: The National Negro Congress and the Rise of Militant Civil Rights* (Chapel Hill: University of North Carolina Press, 2012). For information on SNYC, see also James Jackson and Esther Cooper Jackson Papers, Wagner Archives, Taminet Library, New York University, New York.

87. Gellman, *Death Blow to Jim Crow*, 213–14.

88. Daniels, *Saving the Soul of Georgia*, 26.

89. Ibid., 25.

90. Williamson, *Radicalizing the Ebony Tower*, 28. Williamson provides an in-depth analysis of black colleges against the backdrop of the black freedom struggle.

91. Letter from Roy Wilkins to Robert O. Arnold, Chairman, Board of Regents of the University System of Georgia, February 20, 1956, Papers of the NAACP, Georgia State University Special Collections, Atlanta, Ga.

92. *Lucy v. Adams*, 134 F. Supp. 235 (D.C. N.D. Ala. 1955), 5; also see *Lucy v. Adams*, 350 U.S. 1, 76 S. Ct. 33 (1955).

93. *Lucy v. Adams*, 134 F. Supp. 235 (D.C. N.D. Ala. 1955), 4.

94. Ibid., 5.

95. Bartley, *Rise of Massive Resistance*, vii.

96. Martin, "Racial Change," 553.

97. Paul E. Mertz, "'Mind Changing Time All over Georgia': HOPE, Inc. and School Desegregation, 1958–1961," *Georgia Historical Quarterly* 77, no. 1 (Spring 1993): 42.

98. Coleman, *History of Georgia*, 365.

99. Marvin Griffin, "Interposition Is an Appeal to Reason" (interposition address to the Georgia Commission on Education, Atlanta, Georgia, February 6, 1956), 2, 3.

100. General Acts and Resolutions, vol. 1, no. 97, House Resolution 232-743r, December 10, 1953.

101. Griffin, "Interposition."

102. *The Southern Manifesto*, 102nd Congressional Record 4515–16, 1956.

103. Jason Morgan Ward, *Defending White Democracy: The Making of a Segregationist Movement and the Remaking of Racial Politics, 1936–1965* (Chapel Hill: University of North Carolina Press, 2011), 145.

104. Ibid., 16.

105. Julian Bond, interview with author and Derrick P. Alridge, Charlottesville, Va., October 21, 2004.

106. Mary Frances Early, interview with Greg Morrison, Athens, Ga., January 17, 2017.

107. Quoted in Frederick Allen, *Atlanta Rising: The Invention of an International City, 1946–1996* (Atlanta: Longstreet Press, 1996), 93.

108. Daniels, *Saving the Soul of Georgia*, 65.

109. Calvin Trillin, *An Education in Georgia: Charlayne Hunter, Hamilton Holmes, and the Integration of the University of Georgia* (New York: Viking Press, 1963), 8.

110. For a study of Horace T. Ward's battle to enter the University of Georgia, see Daniels, *Horace T. Ward*.

111. Mays, *Born to Rebel*, 206.

NOTES TO CHAPTER ONE

112. Tuck, *Beyond Atlanta*, 19; Dyer, *University of Georgia*, 226. For a review of events leading to the firing of Walter Dewey Cocking and the subsequent turmoil, including the Southern Association of Colleges and Schools withdrawing accreditation from the white colleges of the University System of Georgia, see Charles S. Gurr, *The Personal Equation: A Biography of Steadman Vincent Sanford* (Athens: University of Georgia Press, 1999); "Georgia Students 'Burn' Their Governor in Protest of His Academic Meddling," *Life*, October 27, 1941, 43. Also see Martin, *Georgia: A Bicentennial History*, 175–76.

113. Dyer, *University of Georgia*, 229.

114. Ibid. For a review of Talmadge's interference with the University System of Georgia's Board of Regents that led to the system losing accreditation, see Calvin McLeod Logue, *Eugene Talmadge: Rhetoric and Response* (New York: Greenwood Press, 1989).

115. Daniels, *Horace T. Ward*, ix–xi.

116. Motley, *Equal Justice under Law*, 141.

117. Jesse Hill Jr., interview with author, Atlanta, December 17, 1996.

118. Daniels, *Saving the Soul of Georgia*, 45; Ernest Vandiver, interview with author, Sky Valley, Ga., August 14, 1996.

119. Hill, interview.

120. Letter from John Calhoun to Thurgood Marshall, January 15, 1956, Papers of the NAACP, Part 3: *The Campaign for Educational Equality: Legal Department and Central Office Records, 1913–1950*, series D: 1956–1965. The Papers of the NAACP Collection, hereafter referenced as NAACP Papers, are located at the Library of Congress, Washington, D.C. Reproduced copies of the 1913–1950 and 1951–1955 records are located in the University of Georgia Libraries. Reproduced copies of the 1956–1965 records are located at the Emory University Robert Woodruff Library.

121. *Hunt v. Arnold*, 172 F. Supp. 847, U. S. Dist., 1959, 4; *Hunt v. Arnold*, Civil Action No. 5781, trial transcript, December 1958, 115.

122. For a review of the alumni certification requirements, see University System of Georgia, Board of Regents minutes, June 11, 1952, p. 2; "Negroes Seek to Enter Ga. College, Unused Printed Technicalities Stymie Six School Applicants," *Atlanta Daily World*, March 24, 1956, 1; "Negroes Fail in Attempt at Enrolling in Atlanta College; Fight Promised," *Macon Telegraph*, March 24, 1956, 1.

123. "Only Three Negroes Ask to Enter State: Other Applicants Rejected on Grounds Regents Rules Not Complied With," *Atlanta Journal*, June 15, 1956; "State College to Reject 6 Negro Applications," *Atlanta Constitution*, March 28, 1956.

124. "Fed Court Action Looms as Next Step," *Atlanta Daily World*, March 26, 1956.

125. "Negroes Seek to Enter"; University System of Georgia, Board of Regents minutes, June 11, 1952, 2; Deposition of Honorable Eugene Gunby, Judge, Court of Ordinary, *Hunt v. Arnold*, Atlanta, December 5, 1957, 3.

126. David Wayne Nunnery, "The Attempted Integration of Georgia State College of Business Administration in 1956: A Significant Step toward the Withdrawal of Georgia from the Massive Resistance Stance" (honors thesis, College of Arts and Sciences, Georgia State University, 1995), 7; Deposition of Honorable Eugene Gunby, *Hunt v. Arnold*; Deposition of Russell T. Roberts, *Hunt v. Arnold*, Atlanta,, August 18, 1958, 26; *Hunt v. Arnold*, trial transcript, 662.

127. Howard Moore Jr. "The Tenth Black Lawyer in Georgia," *Widener Law Journal* 13 (2003): 210–16.

128. Tomiko Brown-Nagin, *Courage to Dissent: Atlanta and the Long History of the Civil Rights Movement* (New York: Oxford University Press, 2011), 29.

129. *King v. Chapman*, 62 F. Supp. 639 (M.D. Ga. 1945); *King v. Chapman*, 154 F.2d. 460 (5th Cir. 1946).

130. Daniels, *Horace T. Ward*, 25; Brown-Nagin, *Courage to Dissent*, 18, 29. In 1949, Walden and the prominent statesman and civil rights activist John Wesley Dobbs founded the Atlanta Negro Voters League, which "served as a broker for the black political agenda until the early 1960s." See Maurice J. Hobson, *The Legend of the Black Mecca: Politics and Class in the Making of Modern Atlanta* (Chapel Hill: University of North Carolina Press, 2017), 19.

131. Constance Baker Motley, interview with author, New York City, March 30, 1995.

132. Tuck, *Beyond Atlanta*, 105.

133. *Hunt v. Arnold*, Civil Action No. 5781, trial transcript, December 1958, 34–35; J. Pennington, "6 Negroes Try to Enroll Here at Georgia State," *Atlanta Journal*, March 23, 1956; Deposition of Myra Elliott Dinsmore, September 26, 1958, Atlanta, Georgia, 34–35.

134. "Fed Court Action Looms as Next Step," *Atlanta Daily World*, March 26, 1956.

135. Ibid.

136. Albert Riley, "Regents Tighten Entry as Negroes Eye Classes Here," *Atlanta Constitution*, June 14, 1956.

137. The Board of Regents adopted a resolution on August 11, 1943, to establish "scholarships for negroes." According to the November 8, 1944, minutes, the board had granted out-of-state scholarships totaling $2,398.26 to twelve Negro students.

138. University System of Georgia Board of Regents' minutes, August 11, 1943, June 4 and 5, 1944, January 11, 1956, Archives, Office of the Board of Regents, Atlanta; see Roger M. Williams, *The Bonds: An American Family* (New York: Atheneum, 1971), 139.

139. University System of Georgia Board of Regents' minutes, January 11, 1956, and May 9, 1956, Archives, Office of the Board of Regents, Atlanta.

140. See University System of Georgia Board of Regents' minutes, June 4–5, 1944, and July 12, 1950, for discussion of the regents' out-of-state scholarship aid policy. Chief Justice Hughes expressly stated that it was the duty of the state to provide for all its citizens within the state. See *Gaines v. Canada*, 305 U.S. 337, 59 S. Ct. 232, 238 (1938).

141. Myra Elliott Dinsmore, interview with author, Atlanta, February 19, 1997.

142. "Negroes Fail in Attempt," 1.

Chapter 2. Renewing the Struggle

1. Regarding threatening phone calls, see Samuel Adams, "3 Negroes Denied Entry to College," *Atlanta Daily World*, June 15, 1956.

2. *Hunt v. Arnold*, 172 F. Supp. 847, 854 (N.D. Ga. 1959); Deposition of Iris Mae Welch, *Hunt v. Arnold*, Civil Action No. 5781, Atlanta, August 22, 1958, 21, 40.

3. Thomas Dyer, *The University of Georgia: A Bicentennial History, 1785–1985* (Athens: University of Georgia Press, 1985), 290.

4. Robert Cohen, "Two, Four, Six, Eight, We Don't Want to Integrate: White Student Attitudes toward the University of Georgia's Desegregation," *Georgia Historical Quarterly* 80 (1996): 617–18.

5. Robert Cohen and David J. Snyder, eds., *Rebellion in Black and White: Southern Student Activism in the 1960s* (Baltimore: John Hopkins University Press, 2013), 17.

6. Letter from J. A. Williams to Hamilton Holmes, January 12, 1961, Hargrett Rare Book and Manuscript Library / University of Georgia Libraries, O. C. Aderhold Papers, folder: Integration at UGA; Maurice C. Daniels, *Horace T. Ward: Desegregation of the University of Georgia, Civil Rights Advocacy, and Jurisprudence* (Atlanta: Clark Atlanta University Press, 2001), 154.

7. Daniels, *Horace T. Ward*, 154.

8. Charlayne Hunter-Gault, *In My Place* (New York: Vintage Books, 1993), quote from caption in illustrations.

9. Hamilton Earl Holmes, interview with author, Atlanta, February 24, 1995; Isabella Holmes, interview with author, Atlanta, June 15, 2001. Also see Daniels, *Saving the Soul of Georgia: Donald L. Hollowell and the Struggle for Civil Rights* (Athens: University of Georgia Press, 2013).

10. Jesse Hill Jr., interview with author, Atlanta, December 17, 1996.

11. Calvin Trillin, *An Education in Georgia: Charlayne Hunter, Hamilton Holmes, and the Integration of the University of Georgia* (New York: Viking Press, 1964), 10.

12. Myra Elliott Dinsmore, interview with author, Atlanta, February 19, 1997.

13. Tomiko Brown-Nagin, *Courage to Dissent: Atlanta and the Long History of the Civil Rights Movement* (New York: Oxford University Press, 2011), 31.

14. Ibid., 31.

15. Hill, interview.

16. Maurice. J. Hobson, *The Legend of the Black Mecca: Politics and Class in the Making of Modern Atlanta* (Chapel Hill: University of North Carolina Press, 2017), 12.

17. Hobson, *Legend of the Black Mecca*, 2.

18. Ibid.

19. See Mark Bauerlein, *Negrophobia: A Race Riot in Atlanta, 1906* (San Francisco: Encounter Books, 2001); Gregory Mixon, *The Atlanta Riot: Race, Class, and Violence in a New South City* (Gainesville: University Press of Florida, 2005).

20. Allison Dorsey, *To Build Our Lives Together: Community Formation in Black Atlanta, 1875–1906* (Athens: University of Georgia Press, 2004), 3.

21. Hobson, *Legend of the Black Mecca*, 17.

22. Brown-Nagin, *Courage to Dissent*, 34.

23. Derrick Alridge, *The Educational Thought of W. E. B. Du Bois: An Intellectual History* (New York: Teachers College Press, 2008), 45–46; "Victim Sees Negro Shot: Relatives Do Not Wait for Trial When She Identifies Him," *Washington Post*, August 1, 1906; "Woman Sees Negro Assailant Shot," *New York Times*, August 1, 1906.

24. Hobson, *Legend of the Black Mecca*, 3.

25. James D. Anderson, *The Education of Blacks in the South, 1860–1935* (Chapel Hill: University of North Carolina Press, 2008), 2–3. Anderson provides a definitive history of the evolution of black education in the South after the Civil War, including the role of the Freedmen's Bureau, missionary societies, industrialists, and philanthropists.

26. Daniels, *Horace T. Ward*, 28–30.

27. Anne S. Emanuel, *Elbert Parr Tuttle: Chief Jurist of the Civil Rights Revolution* (Athens: University of Georgia Press, 2011), 175; Hill, interview.

28. Daniels, *Saving the Soul of Georgia*, 227, 233–34. Other activist leaders associated with the group included M. Carl Holman, professor of English at Clark College and editor of the *Atlanta Inquirer*; Whitney M. Young Jr., dean of the Atlanta University School of Social Work and later director of the National Urban League; Leroy Johnson, Georgia's first black state senator; Donald Hollowell; and Samuel Williams. See also Stephen G. N. Tuck, *Beyond Atlanta: The Struggle for Racial Equality in Georgia, 1940–1980* (Athens: University of Georgia Press, 2001), and Jack Lamar Walker, *Sit-Ins in Atlanta* (New York: McGraw Hill, 1964).

29. The New Yorker Magazine, *The 60s: The Story of a Decade*, ed. Henry Finder (New York: Random House, 2016), 128.

30. Dinsmore, interview.

31. Trillin, *Education in Georgia*, 10.

32. *Hunt v. Arnold*, trial transcript, 496, 573. Margaret Shannon, "Red Query Stirs Row in School Suit: Witness, Attorney Trade Barbs as Tempers Flare," *Atlanta Journal*, December 10, 1958.

33. *Hunt v. Arnold*, Civil Action No. 5781, trial transcript, 574, 589.

34. Hill, interview.

35. Daniels, *Horace T. Ward*, 36; University System of Georgia, Board of Regents minutes, June 11, 1952, 2.

36. *Hunt v. Arnold*, Civil Action No. 5781, trial transcript, December 1958, 199.

37. *Hunt v. Arnold*, Civil Action No. 5781, trial transcript, December 1958, 203; Deposition of Russell T. Roberts, *Hunt v. Arnold*, Atlanta, August 18, 1958, 27.

38. *Hunt v. Arnold*, Trial Transcript, 511–15; Gene Britton, "3 in State College Suit Deny Aid by NAACP," *Atlanta Constitution*, December 10, 1958; *Hunt v. Arnold*, 172 F. Supp. 847, 854 (N.D. Ga. 1959), 5.

39. *Hunt v. Arnold*, trial transcript, 383–84.

40. *Hunt v. Arnold*, 172 F. Supp. 847, 854 (N.D. Ga. 1959), 5; Deposition of Russell T. Roberts, *Hunt v. Arnold*, Atlanta, August 18, 1958, 28–29.

41. *Hunt v. Arnold*, Civil Action No. 5781, trial transcript, December 1958, 198; *Hunt v. Arnold*, 172 F. Supp. 847 (N.D. Ga. 1959), 5.

42. Deposition of Myra Elliott Dinsmore, September 26, 1958, Atlanta, 48–49.

43. Deposition of Rev. Dr. Samuel Williams, *Hunt v. Arnold*, Atlanta, September 26, 1958, 90; *Hunt v. Arnold*, trial transcript, 452.

44. *Hunt v. Arnold*, trial transcript, 422, 466, 478; Shannon, "Red Query Stirs Row"; G. Britton, "3 in State College Suit."

45. Samuel Adams, "3 Negroes Denied Entry to College," *Atlanta Daily World*, June 15, 1956.

46. *Hunt v. Arnold*, trial transcript, 364.

47. Ibid., 378, 453.

48. Adams, "3 Negroes Denied Entry."

49. Ibid.

50. Deposition of Rev. Dr. Samuel Williams, *Hunt v. Arnold*, 94–95. In his Septem-

ber 26, 1958, deposition, Reverend Searcy stated that Rosalyn McGhee, who had been a member of his church, asked him to accompany her to "testify as to her character." Deposition of Rev. E. R. Searcy, *Hunt v. Arnold*, Atlanta, September 26, 1958, 104–5.

51. Deposition of Russell T. Roberts, *Hunt v. Arnold*, Atlanta, August 18, 1958, 44–45.

52. Adams, "3 Negroes Denied Entry."

53. Ibid.

54. J. Pennington, "Registrar Declines to See Negroes at State College Here," *Atlanta Journal*, June 14, 1956.

55. Ibid.

56. Thelma Boone was a graduate of Tennessee State College and secretary at Clark College in Atlanta; Edward J. Clemons was an insurance agent with North Carolina Mutual Insurance Company. See J. Pennington, "Negroes Hint College Case Court Action: Attorney Walden Says Two Really Want to Get in Here," *Atlanta Journal*, March 24, 1956; *Hunt v. Arnold*, Civil Action No. 5781, trial transcript, December 1958, 185.

57. Pennington, "Negroes Hint College Case Court Action."

58. Clarence Jordan, *The Substance of Faith and Other Cotton Patch Sermons*, ed. Dallas Lee (New York: Association Press, 1972), 3.

59. Jeff Woods, *Black Struggle, Red Scare: Segregation and Anti-Communism in the South, 1948–1968* (Baton Rouge: Louisiana State University Press, 2004), 29.

60. Daniels, *Saving the Soul of Georgia*, 134. Southwest Georgia was one of the most notoriously racist parts of the state of Georgia.

61. Tuck, *Beyond Atlanta*, 12; *Screws v. United States* at 135; Judge Herbert Phipps, interview with author, Atlanta, June 22, 2004.

62. Tuck, *Beyond Atlanta*, 12.

63. For more information on Jordan and the Koinonia community, see Jordan, *Substance of Faith*, and other writings by Jordan.

64. "Negroes Seek to Enter Ga. College, Unused Printed Technicalities Stymie Six School Applicants," *Atlanta Daily World*, March 24, 1956; 1; "Negroes Fail in Attempt at Enrolling in Atlanta College; Fight Promised," *Macon Telegraph*, March 24, 1956, 1.

65. J. Britton, "Witness Asks If Lawyer in School Case Is Klansman," *Atlanta Daily World*, December 11, 1958.

66. Ibid.

67. Regarding Georgia State's history, see Dyer, *University of Georgia*, 290–93. For the status of the institution's graduates, see Testimony of Harmon Caldwell, *Hunt v. Arnold*, Civil Action No. 5781, trial transcript, 793–94. Caldwell testified that students who graduated from Georgia State when it was associated with the University of Georgia or Georgia Tech could elect to be alumni of one of those schools or Georgia State. According to his testimony, alumni would have been eligible to provide a certification only for the institution they had selected.

68. *Hunt v. Arnold*, Civil Action, trial transcript, 472.

69. J. Britton, "Witness Asks."

70. *Hunt v. Arnold*, Civil Action, trial transcript, 472, 476.

71. J. Britton, "Witness Asks."

72. Hill, interview, 310.

73. Lauren Holmes, interview with Derrick P. Alridge, New York City, May 8, 2002; Gary Holmes, interview with Maurice Daniels and Derrick P. Alridge, Atlanta, June 15, 2001; *Holmes v. City of Atlanta*, 124 F. Supp. 290 (N.D. Ga. 1954); Nagin, *Courage to Dissent*, 117.

74. Benjamin Elijah Mays, *Born to Rebel* (New York: Charles Scribner & Sons, 1971), 286; *Holmes v. City of Atlanta*, 879 (1955).

75. *Holmes v. City of Atlanta*, 879 (1955); *Holmes v. Atlanta: Changing the Game*, exhibit, Bobby Jones Golf Course, Atlanta, 2015. On November 7, 1955, the U.S. Supreme Court issued a ruling in *Holmes v. City of Atlanta* calling for the racial desegregation of Atlanta's public golf courses. The exhibit, presented by the family of Alfred "Tup" Holmes and the Friends of the Bobby Jones Golf Course, commemorates the sixtieth anniversary of that decision.

76. Nagin, *Courage to Dissent*, 119–20; Daniels, *Saving the Soul of Georgia*, 69.

77. Hobson, *Legend of the Black Mecca*, 13.

78. Letter from E. E. Moore to George M. Sparks, June 15, 1956, box 28, folder 357, George M. Sparks Collection, Georgia State University Special Collections.

79. "Regents Reject Request, Block Negro Entries," *Georgia State Signal*, July 13, 1956.

80. Letter from George M. Sparks to E. E. Moore, June 22, 1956, box 28, folder 357, George M. Sparks Collection, Georgia State University Special Collections.

81. George Manners, interview with Lee Hough, director of Special Collections, and Joe Constance, university archivist, Georgia State University, 1985, Georgia State University Special Collections.

82. General Appropriations Act, Secs. 8–9, Ga. Laws (1951), 425. Similar provisions appear in the General Appropriations Act, Secs. 8–9, Ga. Laws Jan.–Feb. Session (1953), 154, and General Appropriations Act, Secs. 8–9, Ga. Laws (1956), 762.

83. Daniels, *Horace T. Ward*, 143.

84. Paul E. Mertz, "Mind Changing Time All over Georgia: HOPE, Inc. and School Desegregation, 1958–1961," *Georgia Historical Quarterly* 77, 1 (Spring 1993): 42.

85. Manners, interview.

86. "Negroes Filed Late, College Prexy Says," *Atlanta Daily World*, March 27, 1956.

87. "GSU's First President," *Georgia State University Magazine*, July 28, 2017.

88. Ibid.

89. Letter from George M. Sparks to attorney E. E. Moore, June 22, 1956, box 28, folder 357, George M. Sparks Collection, Georgia State University Special Collections; letter from Sparks to Attorney General Eugene Cook, June 18, 1956, box 28, folder 357, Sparks Collection; *Hunt v. Arnold*, 172 F. Supp. 847 (N.D. Ga. 1959).

90. *Hunt v. Arnold*, 172 F. Supp. 847 (N.D. Ga. 1959), 6.

91. Deposition of Russell T. Roberts, *Hunt v. Arnold*, Atlanta, August 18, 1958, 36.

92. Ibid., 38, 40.

93. Deposition of Barbara Hunt, *Hunt v. Arnold*, Atlanta, August 18, 1958, 19–20.

94. Ibid., 22.

95. Ibid., 25.

96. *Hunt v. Arnold*, Trial Transcript, 506, 539, 543.

97. Deposition of Barbara Hunt, *Hunt v. Arnold*, 11-13.

98. *Hunt v. Arnold*, Civil Action No. 5781, trial transcript, December 1958, 191-95, 207-12; *Hunt v. Arnold*, 172 F. Supp. 847, 854 (N.D. Ga. 1959), 2; Deposition of Barbara Hunt, *Hunt v. Arnold*, 6-12.

99. Deposition of Barbara Hunt, *Hunt v. Arnold*, 7, 9.

100. For a study on the origin and history of the *Pittsburgh Courier*, see Andrew Bunie, *Robert L. Vann of the Pittsburg Courier: Politics and Black Journalism* (Pittsburgh: University of Pittsburgh Press, 1974). In 1907, Edwin Nathaniel Harleston started the newspaper primarily as an outlet for his personal writings. In 1910, Harleston, Robert L. Vann, and a small group of blacks incorporated the newspaper as the *Pittsburgh Courier*. The paper became the "nation's leading black weekly" during the first half of the twentieth century, with a circulation of "a quarter million and an influence that touched every black community in the country," x-xi, 41-43.

101. "Desegregation," *Pittsburgh Courier*, June 23, 1956.

102. Deposition of Barbara Hunt, *Hunt v. Arnold*, 16.

103. Deposition of Myra Elliott Dinsmore, *Hunt v. Arnold*, Atlanta, September 26, 1958, 7, 8.

104. Ibid., 11-12.

105. *Hunt v. Arnold*, 172 F. Supp. 847, 854 (N.D. Ga. 1959), 2; Dinsmore, interview; Deposition of Myra Elliott Dinsmore, 3, 4.

106. Deposition of Myra Elliott Dinsmore, 19; *Hunt v. Arnold*, trial transcript, 556.

107. Deposition of Myra Elliott Dinsmore, 15, 17-18.

108. Ibid., 17.

109. *Hunt v. Arnold*, trial transcript, 294-95.

110. *Hunt v. Arnold*, 172 F. Supp. 847, 854 (N.D. Ga. 1959); Deposition of Iris Mae Welch, *Hunt v. Arnold*, Civil Action No. 5781, Atlanta, August 22, 1958, 3-7, 10, 14.

111. *Hunt v. Arnold*, 172 F. Supp. 847, 854 (N.D. Ga. 1959); Deposition of Iris Mae Welch, *Hunt v. Arnold*, 22-23.

112. Deposition of Russell T. Roberts, *Hunt v. Arnold*, Atlanta, August 18, 1958, 12, 16.

113. Daniels, *Saving the Soul of Georgia*, 58-60.

114. Letter from William Madison Boyd to Thurgood Marshall, August 19, 1949, in Papers of the NAACP, The Campaign for Educational Equality: Legal Department and Central Office Records, Supplement to Part 1, 1940-1955. Legal File: Schools-Irwin County, Georgia, NAACP Archives, Library of Congress, Washington, D.C.; Tuck, *Beyond Atlanta*, 98.

115. Letter from Boyd to Marshall, August 19, 1949.

116. Daniels, *Horace T. Ward*, 77-78.

117. Brown-Nagin, *Courage to Dissent*, 21; Daniels, *Saving the Soul of Georgia*, 128.

118. Brown-Nagin, *Courage to Dissent*, 21.

119. Hal Gulliver, "Walden to Keep Busy at 78—Office Will Give Free Advice," *Atlanta Constitution*, September 30, 1963.

120. Ibid.

121. Eugene Patterson, "A. T. Walden: A Great Southerner," *Atlanta Constitution*, July 5, 1965.

122. See A. T. (Austin Thomas) Walden Papers, 1885-1965, Atlanta History Center, Atlanta. Born in 1885 in Fort Valley, Georgia, Walden earned an AB degree from Atlanta University in 1907 and an LLB degree from the University of Michigan School of Law in 1911. He joined the army during World War I and served as a captain of infantry, commanding Company I, 365th Infantry, and as a trial judge advocate of the Ninety-Second Division. His civil rights leadership included service as president of the Atlanta Branch of the NAACP, national vice president of the NAACP, and member of its board of directors and legal committee. Walden founded the Atlanta Negro Voters League and was the first president of the Gate City Bar Association. He played a leading role in a number of prominent civic and business organizations, including serving as president and general counsel for the Citizens Trust Company and director of the Mutual Federal Savings and Loan Association. He was the foremost community activist and civil rights lawyer in Georgia for more than forty years.

123. *Hunt v. Arnold*, Civil Action No. 5781, Complaint, filed by E. E. Moore Jr., Robert L. Carter, and Thurgood Marshall, attorneys for the plaintiffs, 8; see also Dyer, *University of Georgia*.

Chapter 3. Laying the Groundwork

1. Margaret Shannon, "January Edict Likely in School-Mixing Suit: Sloan Orders Written Data as Trial Ends," *Atlanta Journal*, December 12, 1958.

2. *Hunt v. Arnold*, Civil Action No. 5781, Complaint, filed by E. E. Moore Jr., Robert L. Carter, and Thurgood Marshall, attorneys for the plaintiffs, 8.

3. *Hunt v. Arnold*, 9.

4. *Hunt v. Arnold*, 10.

5. Margaret Shannon, "New Applicant in School Case: Negro Insurance Man Seeks to Join in Georgia State Plea," *Atlanta Journal*, December 11, 1958.

6. *Hunt v. Arnold*, 11-12; "Business College Entrance Suit Opens Monday Morning," *Atlanta Daily World*, December 7, 1958, 1; John Britton, "Negroes Have Qualifications to Enter College, One Regent Admits," *Atlanta Daily World*, December 9, 1958; "Negroes Ask School Entry," *Georgia State Signal*, October 5, 1956, 1, box 28, folder 357, George M. Sparks Collection, Georgia State University Special Collections. The plaintiffs in the lawsuit against the Georgia State College of Business asserted that college officials violated the provision for equal protection under the law guaranteed by the Fourteenth Amendment to the U.S. Constitution. See John R. Vile, *Encyclopedia of Constitutional Amendments, Proposed Amendments, and Amending Issues, 1789-1995* (Santa Barbara, Calif.: ABC-CLIO, 1996).

7. Achsah Nesmith, "Gunshot Is Fatal to Eugene Cook," *Atlanta Constitution*, April 15, 1967. Cook was a native of Wrightsville, Georgia, who attended Wrightsville public schools and later Mercer University. After serving as a solicitor and judge in the Johnson County City Court, he became solicitor general of the Dublin Judicial Court. Governor Ellis Arnall appointed him state revenue commissioner in 1942 and attorney general in 1945, and Governor Carl Sanders appointed him to serve on the Georgia Supreme Court bench in 1966. Cook died of a self-inflicted gunshot wound to the chest in April 1967. Friends of Cook reported that Cook had been despondent over the death of his wife less than a year earlier and was under a physician's care.

8. Eugene Cook, "The Southern View of Segregation: Usurpation of Legislative Power by Executive and Judicial Decree" (speech delivered to the Conservative Society, Yale Law School, New Haven, Connecticut, December 8, 1955).

9. Ibid.

10. Cook, "The Ugly Truth about the NAACP," speech delivered to the Fifty-Fifth Annual Convention of Peace Officers, Atlanta, October 19, 1955.

11. Ibid.

12. Jeff Woods, *Black Struggle, Red Scare: Segregation and Anti-Communism in the South, 1948–1968* (Baton Rouge: Louisiana State University Press, 2004), 58.

13. Ibid., 60.

14. Ibid., 62.

15. Ibid., 57.

16. Ibid., 59.

17. Louise T. Hollowell and Martin C. Lehfeldt, *The Sacred Call: A Tribute to Donald Hollowell—Civil Rights Champion* (Atlanta: Publishing Associates, 2006), 97; Maurice C. Daniels, *Horace T. Ward: Desegregation of the University of Georgia, Civil Rights Advocacy, and Jurisprudence* (Atlanta: Clark Atlanta University Press, 2001), 79–80.

18. Jesse Hill Jr., interview with author, Atlanta, December 17, 1996.

19. *Hunt v. Arnold*, Civil Action No. 5781, trial transcript, December 1958, 823.

20. Ibid.

21. Margaret Shannon, "January Edict Likely."

22. *State v. Willie Nash*, Fulton County Superior Court, Clerk's No. 70024-26, November 10, 1953.

23. George M. Coleman, "Judge Declares Mistrial in 'Lover's Lane' Murder Case," *Atlanta Daily World*, January 15, 1954.

24. Vernon E. Jordan Jr., interview with author, Atlanta, February 28, 1997.

25. Howard Moore Jr., "Tenth Black Lawyer in Georgia," *Widener Law Journal* 13 (2003): 214.

26. For a study of civil rights lawyers who worked in the era of segregation, see Kenneth W. Mack, *Representing the Race: The Creation of the Civil Rights Lawyer* (Cambridge, Mass.: Harvard University Press, 2012).

27. Liz Babiarz, "Quiet Courage," *Georgia State University Magazine*, Fall 2009, 2.

28. *Georgia State Signal*, October 5, 1956, 4.

29. Numan V. Bartley, *The Rise of Massive Resistance: Race and Politics in the South during the 1950s* (Baton Rouge: Louisiana State University Press, 1969), 13.

30. Ibid., 13.

31. "Four Negroes Acting Unwise," *Georgia State Signal*, July 12, 1957.

32. Ibid.

33. See Louis R. Harlan, *Booker T. Washington: The Making of a Black Leader, 1856–1901* (New York: Oxford University Press, 1972).

34. David Levering Lewis, *W. E. B. Du Bois: Biography of a Race, 1868–1919* (New York: Henry Holt, 1993), 175.

35. Ibid.

36. James D. Anderson, *The Education of Blacks in the South, 1860–1935* (Chapel Hill: University of North Carolina Press, 1988), 44.

37. Ibid., 198, 273.

38. Ibid., 105. Other black leaders who endorsed "racial equality, political enfranchisement, equal civil rights, and higher education of black teachers and leaders" included William Monroe Trotter, Charles Chesnutt, John S. Durham, John Hope, Bishop Alexander Walters, Bishop Henry M. Turner, Ida Wells-Barnett, and Calvin Chase.

39. W. E. B. Du Bois, *The Souls of Black Folk* (New York: Dover, 1994), 35. First published by A. C. McClurg, Chicago, 1903.

40. Derrick P. Alridge, *The Educational Thought of W. E. B. Du Bois* (New York: Teachers College Press, 2008), 53.

41. W. E. B. Du Bois, *Souls of Black Folk*, 30.

42. Alridge, *Educational Thought of W. E. B. Du Bois*, 55.

43. Lewis, *W. E. B. Du Bois*, 258.

44. Richard Lentz, *Symbols, the News Magazines and Martin Luther King* (Baton Rouge: Louisiana State University Press, 1990), 35-36; Daniels, *Horace T. Ward*, 66.

45. John N. Popham, "'Breathing Spell' for Adjustment Tempers Region's Feelings," *New York Times*, May 18, 1954, 1, 20.

46. John Britton, "Witness Asks If Lawyer in School Case Is Klansman," *Atlanta Daily World*, December 11, 1958, 1.

47. *Hunt v. Arnold*, Civil Action No. 5781, motion of defendants to dismiss, Federal Records Center, East Point, Ga., February 1957.

48. See Constance Baker Motley, *Equal Justice Under Law: An Autobiography* (New York: Farrar, Strauss & Giroux, 1998); Mark V. Tushnet, *The NAACP's Legal Strategy Against Segregated Education, 1925-1950* (Chapel Hill: University of North Carolina Press, 1987); Jack Greenberg, *Crusaders in the Courts: How a Dedicated Band of Lawyers Fought for the Civil Rights Revolution* (New York: Basic Books, 1994); Maurice C. Daniels, *Saving the Soul of Georgia: Donald L. Hollowell and the Struggle for Civil Rights* (Athens: University of Georgia Press, 2013). By the time of *Hunt v. Arnold* the NAACP had won a number of court cases, including U.S. Supreme Court cases, in which judges or justices had ruled that segregation in higher education was unconstitutional. See *Gaines v. Canada*, 305 U.S. 337, 352, 59 S. Ct. 232, 238 (1938); *Lucy v. Adams*, 350 U.S. 1, 76 S. Ct. 33 (1955); *McLaurin v. Oklahoma*, 339 U.S. 637-642 (1950); *Pearson et al. v. Murray*, Court of Appeals of Maryland 592 (1936); *Sipuel v. Board of Regents of University of Oklahoma*, 332 U.S. 631, 68 S. Ct. 299 (1948); *Sweatt v. Painter*, 339 U.S. 629 (1950).

49. *Hunt v. Arnold*, Civil Action No. 5781, pretrial order, June 1957; Gene Britton, "First Negro School Suit Trial Nears," *Atlanta Journal*, December 7, 1958.

50. "School Suit Held Lacking in Faith," *Atlanta Journal*, October 13, 1958.

51. Deposition of J. H. Calhoun, *Hunt v. Arnold*, Atlanta, September 26, 1958, 73-77.

52. Ibid., 88; A Longtime Fighter for Rights in South," *New York Times*, May 10, 1988.

53. Stephen G. N. Tuck, *Beyond Atlanta: The Struggle for Racial Equality in Georgia, 1940-1980* (Athens: University of Georgia Press, 2001), 91.

54. *Hunt v. Arnold*, Civil Action No. 5781, pretrial order, October 29, 1958, p. 5-6.

55. Ibid.

56. *Hunt v. Arnold*, trial transcript, 410.

57. Gene Britton, "White Minister's Role Hit at College Trial," *Atlanta Constitution*, December 11, 1958.

58. *Revenue Commissioner of Georgia v. The National Association for the Advancement of Colored People et al.*, No. 1-58654, motion by defendant requesting court to vacate $25,000 payment for contempt charge, frame 0922, reel 2, part 22, Legal Department Administration Files, NAACP Papers. See also *NAACP, Inc. et al. v. Williams, Revenue Commissioner of Georgia*, 98 Ga. App. 74, 104 S.E. 2d. 923 (1958).

59. Hollowell and Lehfeldt, *Sacred Call*, 114–15; Charles Pou, "NAACP Head Here Ordered Put in Jail: Organization Draws Fine of $25,000 for Contempt," *Atlanta Journal*, December 14, 1956.

60. Pou, "NAACP Head."

61. Ibid.

62. Hollowell and Lehfeldt, *Sacred Call*, 116.

63. Robert L. Carter to Donald L. Hollowell, April 21, 1960, frame 0922, reel 2, part 22, Legal Dept. Administration files, NAACP Papers.

64. Deposition of John Calhoun, *Hunt v. Arnold*, Atlanta, September 26, 1958, 82.

65. "Plaintiff Quits Georgia College Entry Suit Here," *Atlanta Daily World*, December 4, 1958.

66. Ibid.

67. "NAACP May Appeal Va. School Integration Delay," *Jet Magazine*, August 21, 1958, 23.

68. Deposition of Russell T. Roberts, *Hunt v. Arnold*, Atlanta, August 18, 1958.

69. Ibid., 49–51.

70. Ibid., 54.

71. Ibid., 62–63.

72. Ibid., 69–70.

73. Ibid., 55.

74. Ibid., 6.

75. Ibid., 5–7, 60.

76. Ibid., 72.

77. See *Holmes v. Danner*, trial transcript, vol. 1, 69–71.

78. Ibid., 69–71, 92–94, 108; see also Daniels, *Horace T. Ward*, 130.

79. Motley, *Equal Justice under Law*, 141.

80. See Greenberg, *Crusaders in the Courts*; Motley, *Equal Justice under Law*; Daniels, *Saving the Soul of Georgia*.

81. Report of D. L. Hollowell, Legal Redress Committee, Chairman, to the Fifteenth Annual Convention, Georgia State Conference of Branches, NAACP, December 8, 1956, NAACP Papers.

82. Ibid.

83. Ibid.

84. Ibid.

85. Letter from John Calhoun to Thurgood Marshall, December 14, 1956, NAACP Papers.

86. Pou, "NAACP Head."

87. Letter from John H. Calhoun to Roy Wilkins, March 7, 1958, NAACP Papers.

88. Ibid.; "Dixie Trends," *INS Release*, March 8, 1958, Advance for Sunday AMS, March 9, 1958.

89. Letter from Calhoun to Wilkins, March 7, 1958.

90. Letter from John H. Calhoun to Roy Wilkins, May 20, 1958, NAACP Papers.

91. Woods, *Black Struggle, Red Scare*, 68.

92. Letter from Roy Wilkins to John H. Calhoun, March 31, 1958, NAACP Papers.

93. Howard Moore Jr., "Black Barrister at the Southern Bar," in *Radical Lawyers: Their Role in the Movement and in the Courts*, ed. Jonathan Black (New York: Avon Books, 1971), 153–58; Daniels, *Saving the Soul of Georgia*, 72.

94. Constance Baker Motley, interview with author, New York City, March 30, 1995; Motley, *Equal Justice under Law*, 141.

95. "Plaintiff Quits."

96. Myra Elliott Dinsmore, interview with author, Atlanta, February 19, 1997. In Dinsmore's interview, she indicated that she did not recall how she had encountered E. E. Moore. During her August 22, 1958, deposition, Iris Mae Welch stated that J. E. Jordan referred the applicants to Moore.

Chapter 4. Hunt v. Arnold

1. The case was not a jury trial; Sloan was the sole arbiter. *Hunt v. Arnold*, Civil Action No. 5781, trial transcript, December 1958; Gene Britton, "First Negro School Suit Trial Nears," *Atlanta Journal*, December 7, 1958.

2. G. Britton, "First Negro School Suit"; Jack Nelson, "Ruling Expected in Georgia State Suit by Jan. 12: Integration Trial Ends in U.S. Court," *Atlanta Constitution*, January 13, 1958.

3. G. Britton, "First Negro School Suit."

4. "Business College Entrance Suit Opens Monday Morning: 3 Plaintiffs Attack Tests as 'Unreasonable,'" *Atlanta Daily World*, December 7, 1958.

5. Ibid.

6. Ibid.

7. Margaret Shannon, "No Race Line, Arnold Says: Regent Head Testifies in Suit of Negroes Seeking GSC Entrance," *Atlanta Journal*, December 8, 1958.

8. Ibid.

9. John Britton, "Negroes Have Qualifications to Enter College, One Regent Admits," *Atlanta Daily World*, December 9, 1958, 1. See also Louise Hollowell and Martin C. Lehfeldt, *The Sacred Call: A Tribute to Donald Hollowell—Civil Rights Champion* (Winter Park, Fla.: Four-G, 1997).

10. J. Britton, "Negroes Have Qualifications."

11. Gene Britton, "3 in State College Suit Deny Aid by NAACP," *Atlanta Constitution*, December 10, 1958.

12. *Hunt v. Arnold*, Civil Action No. 5781, trial transcript, December 1958, 142–43.

13. J. Britton, "Negroes Have Qualifications."

14. Ibid.

15. Ibid.

16. Ibid.

17. Ibid.

18. Myra Elliott Dinsmore, interview with author, Atlanta, February 19, 1997. In a striking contrast to the inhospitable reception Myra Dinsmore received at Georgia State in 1956 when the registrar refused her an application, Cleon Arrington, Georgia State's first African American vice president, arranged for the author to interview Dinsmore in the president's conference room.

19. J. Britton, "Negroes Have Qualifications." See also Billie Speed, "Businessman Robert O. Arnold Dies," *Atlanta Constitution*, January 26, 1983. Arnold served on the University System of Georgia Board of Regents from 1948 to 1962. The successful businessman and army veteran served as chairman of the board of directors of the Mobile Gas Service Corporation and on the board of directors of the Atlanta Gas Light Company and the Piedmont Investment Company. Arnold was also a longtime member and deacon of the First Baptist Church of Covington, Georgia.

20. Testimony of Robert Arnold, *Hunt v. Arnold*, trial transcript, 62.

21. Ibid., 65–66.

22. In 1989, the Capital City Club opened its doors to the iconic entrepreneur Herman J. Russell, who "became the first Black Atlantan invited to join an exclusive local country club" (Renée D. Turner, "Atlanta: Gone with the Winds of Change," *Ebony*, August 1989, 38–45, here 40). For a review of Russell's building success and struggle to overcome racial barriers, see Herman J. Russell, *Building Atlanta: How I Broke through Segregation to Launch a Building Empire* (Chicago: Chicago Review Press, 2014).

23. Letter from Robert O. Arnold to J. Alton Hosch, February 25, 1952, Horace T. Ward case folder, J. Alton Hosch Papers, Hargrett Rare Book and Manuscript Library / University of Georgia Libraries; "Students Turn Thumbs Down to Negro Seeking Entrance," *Red and Black*, February 22, 1952.

24. Maurice C. Daniels, *Horace T. Ward: Desegregation of the University of Georgia, Civil Rights Advocacy, and Jurisprudence* (Atlanta: Clark Atlanta University Press, 2001), 101.

25. "NAACP Backing Suit, Court Told," *Atlanta Constitution*, December 12, 1958.

26. Testimony of Charles Bloch, *Hunt v. Arnold*, trial transcript, 744.

27. "Charles Bloch Dead at 80," *Atlanta Constitution*, August 29, 1974.

28. Charles J. Bloch Biographical File, Georgiana Collection, Hargrett Rare Book and Manuscript Library / University of Georgia Libraries, Athens, Georgia; Daniels, *Horace T. Ward*, 108.

29. Jason Morgan Ward, *Defending White Democracy: The Making of a Segregationist Movement and the Remaking of Racial Politics, 1936–1965* (Chapel Hill: University of North Carolina Press, 2011), 113.

30. Charles J. Bloch, "We Need Not Integrate to Educate," distributed by States' Rights Council of Georgia, Inc., Atlanta, March 2, 1959, Charles J. Bloch Biographical File, Georgiana Collection, Hargrett Rare Book and Manuscript Library / University of Georgia Libraries, Athens, Georgia.

31. Clive Webb, *Fight against Fear: Southern Jews and Black Civil Rights* (Athens: University of Georgia Press, 2011), 137, 141.

32. Harold Davis, "A Self-Made Person: When Charles Bloch Debates, the Nation's Leaders Listen," *Atlanta Journal*, April 3, 1960; Webb, *Fight against Fear*, 137.
33. Webb, *Fight against Fear*, 137.
34. Testimony of Charles Bloch, *Hunt v. Arnold*, 739.
35. Ibid., 735.
36. J. Britton, "Negroes Have Qualifications."
37. Ibid.
38. Testimony of Charles Bloch, *Hunt v. Arnold*, 751.
39. Ibid.
40. Daniels, *Horace T. Ward*, 88.
41. Ibid., 88–89.
42. Testimony of Charles Bloch, *Hunt v. Arnold*, 757–58.
43. Margaret Shannon, "January Edict Likely in School-Mixing Suit: Sloan Orders Written Data as Trial Ends," *Atlanta Journal*, December 12, 1958.
44. "NAACP Backing Suit, Court Told."
45. Testimony of Harmon Caldwell, *Hunt v. Arnold*, trial transcript, 780.
46. Ibid., 796.
47. Letter from Harmon Caldwell to Charles J. Bloch, February 7, 1952, folder: Horace T. Ward case, J. Alton Hosch Papers, Hargrett Rare Book and Manuscript Library / University of Georgia Libraries.
48. Testimony of Judge Eugene Gunby, *Hunt v. Arnold*, trial transcript, 650–54.
49. Thomas Dyer, *The University of Georgia: A Bicentennial History, 1785–1985* (Athens: University of Georgia Press, 1985), 317; Deposition of Myra Elliott Dinsmore, *Hunt v. Arnold*, Atlanta, September 26, 1958, 25, 30, 40.
50. J. Britton, "Negroes Have Qualifications."
51. Shannon, "No Race Line."
52. J. Britton, "Negroes Have Qualifications."
53. Shannon, "No Race Line."
54. "GSU's First President," *Georgia State University Magazine*, April 2013.
55. John Britton, "Written Arguments to Climax College Suit," *Atlanta Daily World*, December 13, 1956.
56. Testimony of George Blair, *Hunt v. Arnold*, trial transcript, December 1958, 863.
57. Nelson, "Ruling Expected."
58. Testimony of George Blair, *Hunt v. Arnold*, 864.
59. Shannon, "January Edict Likely."
60. Testimony of George Blair, *Hunt v. Arnold*, 882–83.
61. J. Britton, "Negroes Have Qualifications."
62. G. Britton, "3 in State College Suit."
63. Testimony of Rev. Samuel Williams, *Hunt v. Arnold*, trial transcript, 420.
64. Ibid., 413; Margaret Shannon, "Red Query Stirs Row in School Suit: Witness, Attorney Trade Barbs As Tempers Flare," *Atlanta Journal*, December 10, 1958.
65. Quoted from the testimony of Edward Clemons, *Hunt v. Arnold*, trial transcript, 599.
66. Testimony of L. R. Siebert, *Hunt v. Arnold*, 83.

67. University System of Georgia, Board of Regents Minutes, July 12, 1950, 20.
68. Testimony of Harmon Caldwell, *Hunt v. Arnold*, 785.
69. Testimony of L. R. Siebert, *Hunt v. Arnold*, 93.
70. University System of Georgia Board of Regents Minutes, August 11, 1943, italics added.
71. Testimony of L. R. Siebert, *Hunt v. Arnold*, 97.
72. Daniels, *Horace T. Ward*, 81.
73. Testimony of Harmon Caldwell, *Hunt v. Arnold*, 799.
74. Dyer, *University of Georgia*, 317-18; Shannon, "January Edict Likely."
75. Daniels, *Horace T. Ward*, 92.
76. Testimony of Harmon Caldwell, *Hunt v. Arnold*, 799.
77. Donald Hollowell, interview with author, Atlanta, August 27, 1993.
78. Quoted in Calvin Trillin, *An Education in Georgia: Charlayne Hunter, Hamilton Holmes, and the Integration of the University of Georgia* (New York: Viking Press, 1964), 42.
79. Shannon, "No Race Line."
80. Testimony of Robert Arnold, *Hunt v. Arnold*, 61.
81. The U.S. Commission on Civil Rights, *The Unfinished Business: Twenty Years Later...* (Washington, D.C.: U.S. Commission on Civil Rights, 1977), 47.
82. Benjamin E. Mays, *Born to Rebel: An Autobiography* (New York: Charles Scribner & Sons, 1971), 206.
83. Testimony of Rev. Samuel Williams, *Hunt v. Arnold*, 464; see also Jeff Woods, *Black Struggle, Red Scare: Segregation and Anti-Communism in the South, 1948-1968* (Baton Rouge: Louisiana State University Press, 2004), 58.
84. Shannon, "Red Query Stirs Row."
85. Testimony of Rev. Samuel Williams, *Hunt v. Arnold*, 464.
86. Shannon, "Red Query Stirs Row."
87. John Britton, "Witness Asks If Lawyer in School Case Is Klansman," *Atlanta Daily World*, December 11, 1958, 1.
88. "Witness Clashes with Ga. Attorney in School Suit," *Jet*, December 25, 1958.
89. Testimony of Rev. Samuel Williams, *Hunt v. Arnold*, 465.
90. Ibid.
91. Shannon, "Red Query Stirs Row"; Gene Britton, "White Minister's Role Hit at College Trial," *Atlanta Constitution*, December 11, 1958.
92. J. Britton, "Witness Asks."
93. Deposition of Rev. Dr. Samuel Williams, *Hunt v. Arnold*, September 26, 1958, 98-99.
94. Maurice C. Daniels, *Saving the Soul of Georgia: Donald L. Hollowell and the Struggle for Civil Rights* (Athens: University of Georgia Press, 2013), 106-7. Samuel Woodrow Williams earned an AB degree from Morehouse College and bachelor's and master's degrees in divinity from Howard University. In addition to his activism with the NAACP, in 1963 he cofounded the progressive Atlanta Summit Leadership Conference, which collaborated with a number of other civil rights organizations to fight racism and social injustice in Atlanta. He served as pastor of the Friendship Baptist Church from 1954 until his death in 1970. See Martin Luther King Papers Project—MBU, box

117, Martin Luther King Jr. Research and Education Institute, Stanford University, Stanford, Calif.

95. Rosa Marie Wells, "Samuel Woodrow Williams, Catalyst for Black Atlantans, 1946-1970," MA thesis, Atlanta University, Atlanta, Georgia, August 1975, 14, Electronic Theses & Dissertations Collection for Atlanta University Center, Robert W. Woodruff Library, Atlanta.

96. Mays, *Born to Rebel*, 186.

97. Harry G. Lefever, *Undaunted by the Fight: Spelman College and the Civil Rights Movement, 1957-1967* (Macon, Ga.: Mercer University Press, 2005), 97.

98. J. Britton, "Witness Asks."

99. Margaret Shannon, "NAACP Link in Suit Told," *Atlanta Journal*, December 9, 1958, A1; *Hunt v. Arnold*, trial transcript, 236.

100. *Hunt v. Arnold*, trial transcript, 235-36.

101. Shannon, "NAACP Link in Suit Told," A15.

102. Testimony of Barbara Hunt, *Hunt v. Arnold*, trial transcript, 243, 245.

103. Ibid., 248, 250, 253.

104. Testimony of Marian McDaniel, *Hunt v. Arnold*, trial transcript, 550.

105. Ibid.

106. Gene Britton, "3 in College Suit Deny NAACP Aid," *Atlanta Constitution*, December 10, 1958.

107. Dinsmore, interview.

108. Liz Babiarz, "Quiet Courage," *GSU Magazine*, Fall 2009, 2.

109. *Hunt v. Arnold*, trial transcript, 832; Shannon, "January Edict Likely."

110. Testimony of John Calhoun, *Hunt v. Arnold*, trial transcript, 838; Deposition of Barbara Hunt, *Hunt v. Arnold*, August 18, 1958, Atlanta, 26.

111. "NAACP Backing Suit, Court Told."

112. Testimony of Barbara Hunt, *Hunt v. Arnold*, trial transcript, 212-15.

113. Ibid., 214-15; G. Britton, "White Minister's Role."

114. G. Britton, "3 in State College Suit."

115. Constance Baker Motley, *Equal Justice under Law: An Autobiography* (New York: Farrar, Strauss & Giroux, 1998), 141.

116. Deposition of Edward Jacob Clemons, *Hunt v. Arnold*, Atlanta, December 10, 1958, 162-63; Margaret Shannon, "New Applicant in School Case: Negro Insurance Man Seeks to Join in Georgia State Plea," *Atlanta Journal*, December 11, 1958.

117. "NAACP Backing Suit"; Shannon, "New Applicant in School Case."

118. G. Britton, "White Minister's Role Hit."

119. Ibid.

120. bid.

121. *Hunt v. Arnold*, 271.

122. J. Britton, "Written Arguments"; Shannon, "New Applicant in School Case"; "NAACP Backing Suit, Court Told."

123. J. Britton, "Written Arguments."

124. "NAACP Backing Suit, Court Told."

125. Shannon, "January Edict Likely."

126. Ibid.; Nelson, "Ruling Expected."

152 NOTES TO CHAPTERS FOUR AND FIVE

127. Shannon, "New Applicant in School Case."
128. "NAACP Backing Suit, Court Told."
129. Motley, *Equal Justice under Law*, 141.
130. *Hunt v. Arnold*, 299–300.
131. J. Britton, "Written Arguments."
132. Ibid.
133. "3 Negroes Sum Up in College Suit," *Atlanta Journal and Constitution*, January 1, 1959; "Court Asked to Void Controversial State School Requirements: Plaintiffs Say Rules Designed against Race," *Atlanta Daily World*, January 1, 1959.
134. "3 Negroes Sum Up."
135. "Court Asked to Void."
136. Ibid.
137. Ibid.
138. "3 Negroes Sum Up."
139. Dyer, *University of Georgia*, 318; Nelson, "Ruling Expected. Murphy questioned the plaintiffs extensively regarding the fact that transcripts of their high school and previous college academic records had not been submitted to Georgia State College at the time they attempted to apply for admission. In an effort to discredit the plaintiffs' applications on academic grounds, Murphy emphasized that "an official transcript giving a complete record of work done in secondary schools and colleges previously attended [was] required of each registrant." See Testimony of Myra Dinsmore, *Hunt v. Arnold*, 405. In an exchange with Hunt, she responded that she had requested a transcript from Clark College, but her application was "turned down before the transcript was received." See Testimony of Barbara Hunt, *Hunt v. Arnold*, 208.
140. Nelson, "Ruling Expected."
141. Nelson, "Ruling Expected."

Chapter 5. "The Higher Dictates of Justice and Equity"

1. James M. Washington, *A Testament of Hope: The Essential Writings and Speeches of Martin Luther King, Jr.* (New York: Harper Collins, 1986), 292.
2. *Hunt v. Arnold*, 172 F. Supp. 847 (N.D. Ga. 1959), 7.
3. "Georgia Decision Imposes Reality," *Atlanta Constitution*, January 12, 1959.
4. *Hunt v. Arnold*, 172 F. Supp. 847 (N.D. Ga. 1959), 6.
5. Ibid., 7.
6. Ibid.
7. Margaret Shannon, "Negroes Win Right to Seek Admission," *Atlanta Journal*, January 10, 1959.
8. Claude Sitton, "U.S. Judge Orders Georgia College to End Negro Ban," *New York Times*, January 11, 1959.
9. *Hunt v. Arnold*, 172 F. Supp. 847 (N.D. Ga. 1959), 8.
10. Ibid., 6.
11. Jack Nelson, "Ruling Expected in Georgia State Suit by Jan. 12: Integration Trial Ends in U.S. Court," *Atlanta Constitution*, December 13, 1958.
12. *Hunt v. Arnold*, 172 F. Supp. 847 (N.D. Ga. 1959), 6.
13. Maurice C. Daniels, *Horace T. Ward: Desegregation of the University of Geor-

gia, Civil Rights Advocacy, and Jurisprudence (Atlanta: Clark Atlanta University Press, 2001), 115.

14. Gene Britton, "White Minister's Role Hit at College Trial," *Atlanta Constitution*, December 11, 1958.

15. "Court Asked to Void Controversial State School Requirements: Plaintiffs Say Rules Designed against Race," *Atlanta Daily World*, January 1, 1959.

16. *Hunt v. Arnold*, 172 F. Supp. 847 (N.D. Ga. 1959), 2.

17. Danielle L. McGuire, *At the Dark End of the Street: Black Women, Rape, and Resistance—A New History of the Civil Rights Movement from Rosa Parks to the Rise of Black Power* (New York: Alfred A. Knopf, 2010), xxi; Maurice C. Daniels, *Saving the Soul of Georgia: Donald L. Hollowell and the Struggle for Civil Rights* (Athens: University of Georgia Press, 2013), 58–59.

18. Confidential Informant Report on Mary Frances Early, Walter N. Danner Subject File, 1959–1960, Hargrett Rare Book and Manuscript Library / University of Georgia Libraries; Mary Frances Early, interview with the author, Atlanta, February 19, 1997; Maurice C. Daniels, executive producer, *Mary Frances Early: The Quiet Trailblazer*, Georgia Public Broadcasting airing, Foot Soldier Project for Civil Rights Studies, University of Georgia, 2018.

19. Daniels, *Horace T. Ward*, 117.

20. Myra Elliott Dinsmore, interview with author, Atlanta, Georgia, February 19, 1997.

21. *Hunt v. Arnold*, 172 F. Supp. 847 (N.D. Ga. 1959), 6.

22. "Judge Kills Racial Bar of Georgia School," *Chicago Sunday Tribune*, January 11, 1959.

23. Constance Baker Motley, "Remarks on Holmes-Hunter Lecture," *Harvard Blackletter Journal* 5 (Spring 1988): 3; Constance Baker Motley, interview with author, New York City, March 30, 1995. President Harry S. Truman nominated Boyd Sloan to the U.S. District Court, Northern District of Georgia, in 1951. Prior to his federal judicial appointment, Sloan served on the bench of the city court of Hall County, Georgia, and on the Superior Court of Georgia, Northeast Judicial Circuit.

24. University System of Georgia Board of Regents Minutes, August 11, 1943; June 4 and 5, 1944; and November 8, 1944.

25. *Hunt v. Arnold*, 172 F. Supp. 847 (N.D. Ga. 1959), 7.

26. Gene Britton, "First Negro School Suit Trial Nears," *Atlanta Journal*, December 7, 1958.

27. Shannon, "Negroes Win Right."

28. Sitton, "U.S. Judge Orders Georgia College."

29. "Judge Kills Racial Bar"; "Ga.'s School Laws Ripped by Rulings," *Pittsburgh Courier*, January 17, 1959.

30. "Ga.'s School Laws."

31. "Judge Sloan Rules Entrance Regulation at Ga. State Invalid," *Georgia State Signal*, January 23, 1959.

32. Letter from Phil Davis to Barbara Hunt, January 10, 1959, Barbara Hunt personal papers.

33. David Wayne Nunnery, "The Attempted Integration of Georgia State College of

NOTES TO CHAPTER FIVE

Business Administration in 1956: A Significant Step toward the Withdrawal of Georgia from the Massive Resistance Stance" (honors thesis, College of Arts and Sciences, Georgia State University, 1995), 20.

34. "Reactions Varied to Sloan's Ruling," *Atlanta Journal*, January 11, 1959, 1.

35. "Desegregation Suit Plaintiffs Are Feted Here," *Atlanta Daily World*, January 27, 1959; Juan Williams, "Little Known Wiley Branton," *Washington Post*, December 19, 1988; Jack Greenberg, *Crusaders in the Courts: How a Dedicated Band of Lawyers Fought for the Civil Rights Revolution* (New York: Basic Books, 1994), 37, 557.

36. "Desegregation Suit Plaintiffs Are Feted."

37. Constance Baker Motley, *Equal Justice under Law: An Autobiography* (New York: Farrar, Strauss & Giroux, 1998), 141.

38. John Pennington and Homer Meaders, "State Officials Silent on Ruling," *Atlanta Journal*, January 10, 1959.

39. Pennington and Meaders, "State Officials Silent on Ruling."

40. Sitton, "U.S. Judge Orders Georgia College."

41. Pennington and Meaders, "State Officials Silent on Ruling."

42. "Reactions Varied to Sloan's Ruling," 18.

43. Ibid.

44. "Open College to Negroes, Georgia Told," *Washington Post and Times Herald*, January 11, 1959; "Reactions Varied to Sloan's Ruling," 18.

45. "Judge Kills Racial Bar."

46. Ibid.

47. "Reactions Varied to Sloan's Ruling," 18.

48. Motley, *Equal Justice under Law*, 141.

49. Ibid.

50. University System of Georgia Board of Regents Minutes, April 22, 1959, University System of Georgia Board of Regents, Atlanta. During 1956–57, the regents awarded 2,105 "Negro" students scholarship aid grants for graduate and professional work at seventy-nine institutions. *Hunt v. Arnold*, 172 F. Supp. 847 (N.D. Ga. 1959), 3.

51. Emilye Crosby, ed., *Civil Rights History from the Ground Up: Local Struggles, a National Movement* (Athens: University of Georgia Press, 2011), 5.

52. Nunnery, "Attempted Integration," preface.

53. See Daniels, *Horace T. Ward*; Daniels, *Saving the Soul of Georgia*; Maurice C. Daniels, executive producer, *Foot Soldier for Equal Justice: Horace T. Ward and the Desegregation of the University of Georgia*, Georgia Public Television Broadcast (Athens: University of Georgia Center for Continuing Education, 2000); Charlayne Hunter-Gault, *In My Place* (New York: Vintage Books, 1993); Robert Pratt, *We Shall Not Be Moved: The Desegregation of the University of Georgia* (Athens: University of Georgia Press, 2002); Calvin Trillin, *An Education in Georgia: Charlayne Hunter, Hamilton Holmes, and the Integration of the University of Georgia* (New York: Viking Press, 1964).

54. Nunnery, "Attempted Integration," 1–2.

55. Daniels, *Horace T. Ward*, 115.

56. Jesse Hill Jr., interview with author, Atlanta, December 17, 1996.

57. Louise Hollowell and Martin C. Lehfeldt, *The Sacred Call: A Tribute to Donald Hollowell—Civil Rights Champion* (Winter Park, Fla.: Four-G, 1997), 121.

58. Hollowell and Lehfeldt, *The Sacred Call*, 121–22.

59. Juan Williams, *Eyes on the Prize: America's Civil Rights Years, 1954–1965* (New York: Penguin Books, 1988), 38.

60. Ibid., 34.

61. Dinsmore, interview. Dinsmore worked for the Atlanta Life Insurance Company until 1961. After job opportunities with the federal government became more available for blacks during the administration of President John Fitzgerald Kennedy, Dinsmore secured a job with the Atlanta Army Depot in July 1961. She later transferred to the Federal Aviation Administration, where she worked until 1981. She also worked for a few years at the Prudential Insurance Company before her retirement in 1993. She currently resides in Atlanta. Dinsmore noted that she is extremely proud that blacks today do not face the resistance and opposition she encountered in 1957–58 at the Georgia State College of Business.

62. Liz Babiarz, "Quiet Courage," *GSU Magazine*, Fall 2009, 35.

63. Georgia House Bill 1735, March 7, 2014; "Barbara Pace Hunt: Quiet Courage, the Civil Rights Struggle of a Heroine," *La Vida News: The Black Voice*, March 27–April 2, 2014.

64. Gordon Dickson, "Woman Was Secretary to Civil Rights Leader," *Star-Telegram*, March 11, 2005.

65. Alice Bernstein, "Barbara Pace Sears: Activist and Person," *Tennessee Tribune*, March 2005; "Barbara Pace Hunt."

66. Dickson, "Woman Was Secretary."

67. Georgia House Resolution, 1735, March 7, 2014; Babiarz, "Quiet Courage," 1–3.

68. "Barbara Pace Hunt: Quiet Courage."

69. Quotation from Dinsmore, interview; see also Deposition of Russell T. Roberts, *Hunt v. Arnold*, Atlanta August 18, 1958, 21; Testimony of Myra Dinsmore, *Hunt v. Arnold*, trial transcript, 348–60.

70. Dinsmore, interview.

71. Stephen G. N. Tuck, *Beyond Atlanta: The Struggle for Racial Equality in Georgia, 1940–1980* (Athens: University of Georgia Press, 2001), 3–4.

72. Robin D. G. Kelley and Earl Lewis, *To Make Our World Anew: A History of African Americans* (New York: Oxford University Press, 2000), 212.

73. See Motley, *Equal Justice under Law*; Constance Baker Motley, interview; Daniels, *Horace T. Ward*, 79, 106.

74. Tomiko Brown-Nagin, *Courage to Dissent: Atlanta and the Long History of the Civil Rights Movement* (New York: Oxford University Press, 2011), 308.

75. Testimony of John Calhoun, *Hunt v. Arnold*, trial transcript, 842–43.

76. Letter from John Calhoun to Thurgood Marshall, May 12, 1956, NAACP Papers. Calhoun also wrote to NAACP assistant counsel Robert L. Carter on June 16, 1956. The letter reveals Calhoun's key role as a liaison between the NAACP national office and the Atlanta branch in addressing procedural and legal questions related to the Georgia State case (NAACP Papers).

77. Letter from Calhoun to Marshall, May 12, 1956. See also letter from John H. Calhoun to Thurgood Marshall, December 14, 1956, in which Calhoun advises Marshall that the Atlanta Branch education committee is "preparing applicants for the Ga. State College of Business Adm. (Old University Evening School)" (NAACP papers).

78. Letter from Calhoun to Marshall, May 12, 1956.

79. Ibid.

80. Daniels, *Saving the Soul of Georgia*, 56. In addition to the black attorneys in Atlanta, the small fraternity of black lawyers across the state also demonstrated their commitment to the cause of civil rights. As Donald Hollowell emerged as Georgia's chief civil rights attorney in the 1950s and early 1960s, the attorneys worked closely with him and the NAACP on civil rights cases ranging from challenging state-sanctioned racial discrimination in voting and schools to representing black criminal defendants in the racially hostile legal system. Hollowell served as counsel on civil rights cases with black attorney C. B. King in Albany; Eugene Gadsden and B. Clarence Mayfield in Savannah; Thomas Jackson in Macon; and John Ruffin and John D. Watkins in Augusta. Despite Walden's long tenure as a black lawyer dating back to the early 1900s, by 1940, there were only seven black lawyers in Georgia—three in Atlanta, two in Savannah, and one each in Macon and Augusta. Walden blamed "racism in the law and tradition" for the dearth of black lawyers. For information on black lawyers, see J. Clay Smith Jr., *Emancipation: The Making of the Black Lawyer, 1844–1944* (Philadelphia: University of Pennsylvania Press, 1993), 191–201.

81. Daniels, *Horace T. Ward*, 195.

82. Tuck, *Beyond Atlanta*, 3.

83. *Hunt v. Arnold*, 172 F. Supp. 847 (N.D. Ga. 1959), 3; Deposition of Russell T. Roberts, *Hunt v. Arnold*, Atlanta, Georgia, August 18, 1958, 12.

84. *Hunt v. Arnold*, 172 F. Supp. 847, 854 (N.D. Ga. 1959); Deposition of Iris Mae Welch, *Hunt v. Arnold*, Atlanta, August 22, 1958, 31–32.

85. Margaret Shannon, "Red Query Stirs Row in School Suit: Witness, Attorney Trade Barbs as Tempers Flare," *Atlanta Journal*, December 10, 1958; *Hunt v. Arnold*, 172 F. Supp. 847, 854 (N.D. Ga. 1959); Deposition of Iris Mae Welch, *Hunt v. Arnold*, August 22, 1958, 18–19; *Hunt v. Arnold*, trial transcript, 312.

86. *Hunt v. Arnold*, 172 F. Supp. 847, 854 (N.D. Ga. 1959); Deposition of Iris Mae Welch, *Hunt v. Arnold*, August 22, 1958, 28–29.

87. Testimony of Iris Welch, *Hunt v. Arnold*, trial transcript, 303, 312, 336.

88. Ibid., 303.

89. "Four Negroes Acting Unwise," *Georgia State Signal*, July 12, 1957.

90. Harold Paulk Henderson, *The Politics of Change in Georgia: A Political Biography of Ellis Arnall* (Athens: University of Georgia Press, 1991), 139; William Anderson, *The Wild Man from Sugar Creek: The Political Career of Eugene Talmadge* (Baton Rouge: Louisiana State University Press, 1975), 210.

91. See Molly O'Brien, "Discriminatory Effects: Desegregation Litigation in Higher Education in Georgia," *William & Mary Bill of Rights Journal* 8, no. 1/2, 19.

92. Daniels, *Horace T. Ward*, 150, 152.

93. Robert Cohen, "G-men in Georgia: The FBI and the Segregationist Riot at the

University of Georgia, 1961," *Georgia Historical Quarterly* 83 (1999): 3, 508–38; Daniels, *Horace T. Ward*, 152, 160.

94. Testimony of Iris Welch, *Hunt v. Arnold*, trial transcript, 347.

95. Testimony of Edward Clemons, *Hunt v. Arnold*, trial transcript, December 1958, 611, 624.

96. Daniels, *Horace T. Ward*, 113; Hill, interview.

97. Deposition of J. H. Calhoun, Atlanta, September 26, 1958, 62.

98. Brown-Nagin, *Courage to Dissent*, 79–80.

99. Ibid., 80.

100. Hill, interview.

101. Robert Brisbane, interview with author, Atlanta, January 19, 1995.

102. Ibid.

103. Jack Lamar Walker, *Sit-Ins in Atlanta* (New York: McGraw Hill, 1964), 13.

104. "Atlanta Grabs Six Bus Riding Negro Pastors," *Chicago Tribune*, January 11, 1957; Herman "Skip" Mason Jr., *Politics, Civil Rights, and Law in Black Atlanta, 1870–1970* (Charleston, S.C.: Arcadia, 2000), 76; Bruce Galphin, "Negroes End Bus Push Here, Plan Court Test," *Atlanta Constitution*, January 11, 1957.

105. Quotation from *Williams v. Georgia Public Service Commission et al.*, U.S. District Court, N.D. Ga. Atlanta Division, C.A. No. 6067, January 1959; see also Galphin, "Negroes End Bus Push Here."

106. *Browder v. Gayle*, 352 U.S. 903 (1956); Benjamin E. Mays, *Born to Rebel: An Autobiography* (New York: Charles Scribner and Sons, 1971), 286.

107. *Williams v. Georgia Public Service Commission et al.*, U.S. District Court, N.D. Ga. Atlanta Division, C.A. No. 6067, January 1959.

108. "Trolley Decision Is Test for Community," *Atlanta Journal*, January 9, 1959; "Georgia Decision Imposes Reality," *Atlanta Constitution*, January 12, 1959.

109. Margaret Shannon, "Bus Desegregation Ruled Illegal Here," *Atlanta Journal*, January 9, 1959.

110. Howell Raines, *My Soul is Rested: Movement Days in the Deep South Remembered* (New York: G. P. Putnam & Sons, 1977), 83–93.

111. Walker, *Sit-Ins in Atlanta*, 6; Tuck, *Beyond Atlanta*, 111; Lonnie King, interview with author, Atlanta, December 20, 2011; Julian Bond, interview with author and Derrick P. Alridge, Charlottesville, Va., October 21, 2004.

112. In *Bell et al. v. Fulton-DeKalb Hospital Authority et al.* (1964) and *Bell v. Georgia Dental Association* (1964), the plaintiffs' actions resulted in the desegregation of the nursing school at Grady Hospital, the addition of black physicians and dentists to the staff at Grady, and the enrollment of black physicians as members of the medical associations. In the housing discrimination case against the City of Atlanta for erecting barricades separating black and white neighborhoods, Fulton County Superior Court judge George P. Whitman ruled the barriers unconstitutional. In the cases of *George Willis, Jr., Woodrow T. Lewis, and Albert L. Dunn, Plaintiffs, Robert F. Kennedy, Attorney General, Intervenor v. The Pickrick Restaurant, a Corporation, and Lester G. Maddox, Defendants*, 234 F. Supp. 179, (D.C. N.D. Ga. 1964) and *Heart of Atlanta Motel v. United States*, 379 U.S. 241 (1964), the courts issued rulings prohibiting racial discrimination in public accommodations.

113. In the 1960 case of *H. D. Coke v. the City of Atlanta*, Federal District Court judge Boyd Sloan ruled that the Dobbs House airport restaurant's refusal to serve blacks except on a segregated basis violated Coke's rights as a black citizen.

114. Kenneth W. Mack, *Representing the Race: The Creation of the Civil Rights Lawyer* (Cambridge, Mass.: Harvard University Press, 2012), 6–7.

115. Ibid., 6–7.

116. James Melvin Washington, ed., *A Testament of Hope: The Essential Writings and Speeches of Martin Luther King, Jr.* (New York: HarperCollins, 1986), 225.

Chapter 6. The Struggle Continues

1. "NAACP supports Negroes' GSC bid," *Atlanta Journal*, May 14, 1959, A1.

2. Robert A. Pratt, *We Shall Not Be Moved: The Desegregation of the University of Georgia* (Athens: University of Georgia Press, 2002), 71.

3. S. Bill 3, Georgia Laws 1959 Session, I General Acts and Res. 20–21(1959). See also Anne S. Emanuel, "Turning the Tide in the Civil Rights Revolution: Elbert Tuttle and the Desegregation of the University of Georgia," *Michigan Journal of Race and Law* 5, no. 1 (1999): 6.

4. Molly O'Brien, "Discriminatory Effects: Desegregation Litigation in Higher Education in Georgia," *William & Mary Bill of Rights Journal*, 8, no. 1 (1999): 19.

5. *Hunt v. Arnold*, 172 F. Supp. 847 (N.D. Ga. 1959), 6.

6. Harold P. Henderson, *Ernest Vandiver, Governor of Georgia* (Athens: University of Georgia Press, 2000), 96.

7. Ibid.

8. Kenneth Coleman, *A History of Georgia* (Athens: University of Georgia Press, 1991), 365.

9. S. Bill 3, Georgia Laws 1959 Session, I General Acts and Res. 20–21(1959), 20. The bill also prohibited the admission of any person to Georgia's public college or universities "after such person has reached twenty-five (25) years of age: Provided, however, that any person engaged in teaching or instructing in any elementary or high school, in this state, public or private, and who desires to pursue courses of study to better qualify himself therefor, may be admitted to any college, undergraduate or graduate, or professional school of the University of Georgia or any of its branches, notwithstanding his age, subject, however to such limitations or regulations as the Board of Regents may prescribe."

10. U.S. Commission on Civil Rights, *The Unfinished Business: Twenty Years Later . . .* (Washington, D.C.: U.S. Commission on Civil Rights, 1977), 47.

11. See *Calhoun et al. v. Members of the Board of Education, City of Atlanta et al.*, Civ. A. No. 6298, 188 F. Supp. 401, U.S. Dist. (1959).

12. "Open College to Negroes, Georgia Told," *Washington Post and Times Herald*, January 11, 1959.

13. Claude Sitton, "U.S. Judge Orders Georgia College to End Negro Ban," *New York Times*, January 11, 1959; "Georgia Halts College Entry," *Washington Post and Times Herald*, January 12, 1959.

14. "Open College to Negroes."

15. "Georgia Halts College Entry."

16. Jeff Roche, *Restructured Resistance: The Sibley Commission and the Politics of Desegregation in Georgia* (Athens: University of Georgia Press, 2010), 73–74.

17. Ibid., 74.

18. Pratt, *We Shall Not Be Moved*, 70–71.

19. Paul E. Mertz, "'Mind Changing Time All Over Georgia': HOPE, Inc. and School Desegregation, 1958–1961," *Georgia Historical Quarterly* 77, no. 1 (Spring 1993): 43; Maurice C. Daniels, *Horace T. Ward: Desegregation of the University of Georgia, Civil Rights Advocacy, and Jurisprudence* (Atlanta: Clark Atlanta University Press, 2001), 151; Thomas Dyer, *The University of Georgia: A Bicentennial History, 1785–1985* (Athens: University of Georgia Press, 1985), 318. Though Vandiver considered closing all black schools in the face of court-ordered desegregation, some white officials feared such action would make it easier for blacks to push for entrance to white schools.

20. Bruce Galphin, "State Is Prepared to Shut Colleges, Vandiver Warns," *Atlanta Constitution*, May 7, 1959.

21. Roy Wilkins, "Georgia Plan to Close Schools Denounced by NAACP Secretary," NAACP press release, January 14, 1960, NAACP Papers.

22. Wilkins, "Georgia Plan to Close Schools Denounced by NAACP Secretary."

23. Wilkins, "Georgia Plan to Close Schools."

24. Charles J. Bloch, "We Need Not Integrate to Educate," States' Rights Council of Georgia, Inc., Atlanta, March 2, 1959, 1, Bloch Papers, University of Georgia Hargrett Rare Book and Manuscript Library.

25. Daniels, *Horace T. Ward*, 119.

26. Confidential Informant Report on Hamilton Holmes, Walter N. Danner Subject File, 1959–60, Hargrett Rare Book and Manuscript Library / University of Georgia Libraries.

27. Confidential Informant Report on Charlayne Hunter, Walter N. Danner Subject File, 1959–60, Hargrett Rare Book and Manuscript Library/University of Georgia Libraries. University of Georgia officials also spied on Mary Frances Early. Early entered the university in June 1961, a few months after the admission of Holmes and Hunter, and became UGA's first black graduate. Early observed that university officials investigated her and her parents and even accused her of being a prostitute during an admissions interview. See Confidential Informant Report on Mary Frances Early, Walter N. Danner Subject File-Integration, Hargrett Rare Book and Manuscript Library / University of Georgia Libraries; Mary Frances Early, interview with author, Atlanta, February 19, 1997.

28. Donald Hollowell, interview with author, Atlanta, August 27, 1993; Jesse Hill Jr., interview with author, Atlanta, December 17, 1996.

29. For a review of the Holmes court record and Bootle's ruling ordering the admission of Holmes and Hunter, see *Hamilton E. Holmes et al. v. Walter N. Danner et al.*, Civil Action No. 450, Federal Records Center, East Point, Georgia, December 1960; Daniels, *Horace T. Ward*; Maurice C. Daniels, *Saving the Soul of Georgia: Donald L. Hollowell and the Struggle for Civil Rights* (Athens: University of Georgia Press, 2013); and Pratt, *We Shall Not Be Moved*.

30. Daniels, *Horace T. Ward*, 117.

31. Mertz, "'Mind Changing Time,'" 60; Ernest Vandiver Jr., interview with author, Sky Valley, Georgia, August 14, 1996.

32. Vandiver, interview.

33. Ibid.

34. Constance Baker Motley, *Equal Justice under Law: An Autobiography* (New York: Farrar, Strauss & Giroux, 1998), 187.

35. Richard Kluger, *Simple Justice: The History of* Brown v. Board of Education *and Black America's Struggle for Equality* (New York: Alfred A. Knopf, 1975), xi.

36. "Georgia State Admits First Negro," *Atlanta Inquirer*, June 23, 1962, 1; Liz Babiarz, "Quiet Courage," *GSU Magazine*, Fall 2009, 3. Hall taught history, social studies, and science in Georgia's public schools until she retired in August 1970. She died on December 10, 1995, at the age of eighty-seven from Alzheimer's disease. See "Annette Lucille Hall: The Quiet Warrior," in the article "Quiet Courage."

37. Babiarz, "Quiet Courage," 3.

38. Ibid.; Michelle Hiskey, "Investment in Education Vital for Atlanta's Pioneering Hall-Long Family," *Saporta Report*, October 2012.

39. Babiarz, "Quiet Courage," 36.

40. Ibid., 4.

41. Clinton Warner also spearheaded the challenge to housing discrimination in Atlanta that ultimately led to a successful lawsuit against residential segregation in the city in 1963. See Howard Moore, interview with author, Atlanta, June 10, 2004; Louise Hollowell and Martin C. Lehfeldt, *The Sacred Call: A Tribute to Donald Hollowell—Civil Rights Champion* (Winter Park, Fla.: Four-G, 1997); "Peyton Wall Now Tumbled," *Atlanta Inquirer*, March 9, 1963.

42. David Smith Jr., *Georgia State University: An Institutional History, 1913–2002* (self-pub., CreateSpace, 2010), 221.

43. University System of Georgia Board of Regents Semester Enrollment Report, Spring 2018, Board of Regents, University System of Georgia, Atlanta

44. Richard Fausset, "Georgia State, Leading U.S. in Black Graduates, Is Engine of Social Mobility," *New York Times*, May 15, 2018.

45. Benjamin Elijah Mays, *Born to Rebel: An Autobiography* (New York: Charles Scribner & Sons, 1971), 286.

BIBLIOGRAPHY

Books and Articles

Allen, Frederick. *Atlanta Rising: The Invention of an International City, 1946–1996.* Atlanta: Longstreet Press, 1996.

Alridge, Derrick P. *The Educational Thought of W. E. B. Du Bois: An Intellectual History.* New York: Teachers College Press, 2008.

Anderson, James D. *The Education of Blacks in the South, 1860–1935.* Chapel Hill: University of North Carolina Press, 1988.

Anderson, William. *The Wild Man from Sugar Creek: The Political Career of Eugene Talmadge.* Baton Rouge: Louisiana State University Press, 1975.

Bartley, Numan V. *The Rise of Massive Resistance: Race and Politics in the South during the 1950s.* Baton Rouge: Louisiana State University Press, 1969.

Bauerlein, Mark. *Negrophobia: A Race Riot in Atlanta, 1906.* San Francisco: Encounter Books, 2001.

Black, Jonathan. *Radical Lawyers: Their Role in the Movement and in the Courts.* New York: Avon Books, 1971.

Brown-Nagin, Tomiko. *Courage to Dissent: Atlanta and the Long History of the Civil Rights Movement.* New York: Oxford University Press, 2011.

———. "Reconstructing Civil Rights Legal History from the Bottom Up." *Virginia Journal* 13 (2010): 7–16.

Brundage, W. Fitzhugh. *Lynching in the New South: Georgia and Virginia, 1880–1930.* Urbana: University of Illinois Press, 1993.

Buchanan, S. E. "The Effects of the Abolition of the Georgia County-Unit System on the 1962 Gubernatorial Election." *Southeastern Political Review* 25, no. 4 (1997): 687–704.

Bullock, Charles S., Scott E. Buchanan, and Ronald K. Gaddie. *The Three Governors*

Controversy: Skullduggery, Machinations, and the Decline of Georgia's Progressive Politics. Athens: University of Georgia Press, 2015.

Bunie, Andrew. *Robert L. Vann of the* Pittsburgh Courier: *Politics and Black Journalism*. Pittsburgh: University of Pittsburgh Press, 1974.

Carson, Clayborne, ed. *The Papers of Martin Luther King, Jr*. Vol. 4: *Symbol of the Movement, January 1957–December 1958*. Berkeley: University of California Press, 2000.

Carson, Clayborne, Tenisha Armstrong, Susan Carson, Adrienne Clay, and Kieran Taylor, eds. *The Papers of Martin Luther King, Jr*. Vol. 5: *Threshold of a New Decade, January 1959–December 1960*. Berkeley: University of California Press, 2005.

Clark, E. Culpepper. *The Schoolhouse Door: Segregation's Last Stand at the University of Alabama*. New York: Oxford University Press, 1993.

Cohen, Robert. "G-Men in Georgia: The FBI and the Segregationist Riot at the University of Georgia, 1961." *Georgia Historical Quarterly* 83, no. 3 (Fall 1999): 508–38.

———. "Two, Four, Six, Eight, We Don't Want to Integrate: White Student Attitudes toward the University of Georgia's Desegregation." *Georgia Historical Quarterly* 80 (1996): 616–45.

Cohen, Robert, and David J. Snyder, eds. *Rebellion in Black and White: Southern Student Activism in the 1960s*. Baltimore: John Hopkins University Press, 2013.

Coleman, Kenneth. *A History of Georgia*. Athens: University of Georgia Press, 1991.

Cook, James F. *The Governors of Georgia, 1754–1995*. Macon: Mercer University Press, 1995.

Crosby, Emilye, ed. *Civil Rights History from the Ground Up: Local Struggles, a National Movement*. Athens: University of Georgia Press, 2011.

Daniels, Maurice C. *Horace T. Ward: Desegregation of the University of Georgia, Civil Rights Advocacy, and Jurisprudence*. Atlanta: Clark Atlanta University Press, 2001.

———. *Saving the Soul of Georgia: Donald L. Hollowell and the Struggle for Civil Rights*. Athens: University of Georgia Press, 2013.

Daniels, Maurice C., and Cameron Van Patterson. "(Re)Considering Race in the Desegregation of Higher Education." *Georgia Law Review* 46, no. 3 (Spring 2012): 521–56.

Dittmer, John. *Local People: The Struggle for Civil Rights in Mississippi*. Urbana: University of Illinois Press, 1994.

Dorsey, Allison. *To Build Our Lives Together: Community Formation in Black Atlanta, 1875–1906*. Athens: University of Georgia Press, 2004.

Du Bois, W. E. B. *The Souls of Black Folk*. Chicago: A. C. McClurg, 1903; rpt., New York: Dover Publications, 1994.

Dyer, Thomas G. *The University of Georgia: A Bicentennial History, 1785–1985*. Athens: University of Georgia Press, 1985.

Eagles, Charles W. *The Price of Defiance: James Meredith and the Integration of Ole Miss*. Chapel Hill: University of North Carolina Press, 2009.

Emanuel, Anne S. *Elbert Parr Tuttle: Chief Jurist of the Civil Rights Revolution*. Athens: University of Georgia Press, 2011.

———. "Turning the Tide in the Civil Rights Revolution: Elbert Tuttle and the Desegregation of the University of Georgia." *Michigan Journal of Race & Law* 5, no. 1 (1999): 1–30.

Endersby, James W., and William T. Horner. *Lloyd Gaines and the Fight to End Segregation*. Columbia: University of Missouri Press, 2016.

Eskew, Glenn T. *But for Birmingham: The Local and National Movements in the Civil Rights Struggle*. Chapel Hill: University of North Carolina Press, 1997.

Feimster, Crystal Nicole. *Southern Horrors: Women and the Politics of Rape and Lynching*. Cambridge, Mass.: Harvard University Press, 2009.

Finder, Henry. *The 60s: The Story of a Decade*. New York: Random House, 2016.

Fisher, Ada Lois Sipuel, and Danney Goble. *A Matter of Black and White: The Autobiography of Ada Lois Sipuel Fisher*. Norman: University of Oklahoma Press, 1996.

Gasman, Marybeth, and Christopher L. Tudico, eds. *Historically Black Colleges and Universities: Triumphs, Troubles, and Taboos*. New York: Palgrave Macmillan, 2008.

Gellman, Erik S. *Death Blow to Jim Crow: The National Negro Congress and the Rise of Militant Civil Rights*. Chapel Hill: University of North Carolina Press, 2012.

Godshalk, David Fort. *Veiled Visions: The 1906 Atlanta Race Riot and the Reshaping of American Race Relations*. Chapel Hill: University of North Carolina Press, 2005.

Greenberg, Jack. *Crusaders in the Courts: How a Dedicated Band of Lawyers Fought for the Civil Rights Revolution*. New York: Basic Books, 1994.

Griffin, Marvin. *Interposition Address of Governor Marvin Griffin*. Atlanta: Georgia Commission on Education, 1956.

Gurr, Charles S. *The Personal Equation: A Biography of Steadman Vincent Sanford*. Athens: University of Georgia Press, 1999.

Harlan, Louise R. *Booker T. Washington: The Making of a Black Leader, 1856–1901*. New York: Oxford University Press, 1972.

Henderson, Alexa Benson. *Atlanta Life Insurance Company: Guardian of Black Economic Dignity*. Tuscaloosa: University of Alabama Press, 1990.

Henderson, Harold P. *Ernest Vandiver, Governor of Georgia*. Athens: University of Georgia Press, 2000.

Henderson, Harold Paulk. *The Politics of Change in Georgia: A Political Biography of Ellis Arnall*. Athens: University of Georgia Press, 1991.

Hine, Darlene Clark. *The Rise and Fall of the White Primary in Texas*. Columbia: University of Missouri Press, 1979.

Hobson, Maurice J. *The Legend of the Black Mecca: Politics and Class in the Making of Modern Atlanta*. Chapel Hill: University of North Carolina Press, 2017.

Hollowell, Louise, and Martin C. Lehfeldt. *The Sacred Call: A Tribute to Donald Hollowell, Civil Rights Champion*. Winter Park, Fla.: Four-G, 1997.

Holsaert, Faith S., Martha Prescod Norman Noonan, Judy Richardson, Betty Garman Robinson, Jean Smith Young, and Dorothy M. Zellner, eds. *Hands on the Freedom Plow: Personal Accounts by Women in SNCC*. Urbana: University of Illinois Press, 2010.

Hunter-Gault, Charlayne. *In My Place*. New York: Vintage Books, 1993.

Jordan, Clarence. *The Substance of Faith and Other Cotton Patch Sermons*. Edited by Dallas Lee. New York: Association Press, 1972.

Jordan, Vernon E., Jr., and Annette Gordon-Reed. *Vernon Can Read! A Memoir*. New York: Basic Civitas Books, 2003.

Kelley, Robin D. G., and Earl Lewis. *To Make Our World Anew: A History of African Americans*. New York: Oxford University Press, 2000.

Kennedy, Stetson. *The Klan Unmasked*. Boca Raton: Florida Atlantic University Press, 1954.

Kluger, Richard. *Simple Justice: The History of* Brown v. Board of Education *and Black America's Struggle for Equality*. New York: Knopf, 1976.

Kruse, Kevin Michael. *White Flight: Atlanta and the Making of Modern Conservatism*. Princeton, N.J.: Princeton University Press, 2005.

Lavergne, Gary M. *Before Brown: Heman Marion Sweatt, Thurgood Marshall, and the Long Road to Justice*. Austin: University of Texas Press, 2010.

Lefever, Harry G. *Undaunted by the Fight: Spelman College and the Civil Rights Movement, 1957–1967*. Macon, Ga.: Mercer University Press, 2005.

Lentz, Richard. *Symbols, the News Magazines, and Martin Luther King*. Baton Rouge: Louisiana State University Press, 1990.

Lewis, David L. *W. E. B. Du Bois*. Vol. 1: *Biography of a Race, 1868–1919*. New York: H. Holt, 1993.

———. *W. E. B. Du Bois*. Vol. 2: *The Fight for Equality and the American Century, 1919–1963*. New York: H. Holt, 2000.

Lewis, David L., and Charles W. Eagles, eds. *The Civil Rights Movement in America: Essays*. Jackson: University Press of Mississippi, 1986.

Litwack, Leon F. *Trouble in Mind: Black Southerners in the Age of Jim Crow*. New York: Knopf, 1998.

Mack, Kenneth Walter. *Representing the Race: The Creation of the Civil Rights Lawyer*. Cambridge, Mass.: Harvard University Press, 2012.

Martin, Charles H. "Racial Change and 'Big Time' College Football in Georgia: The Age of Segregation, 1892–1957." *Georgia Historical Quarterly* 80, no. 3 (1996): 532–62.

Martin, Harold H. *William Berry Hartsfield: Mayor of Atlanta*. Athens: University of Georgia Press, 1978.

Mason, Jr., Herman "Skip." *Politics, Civil Rights, and Law in Black Atlanta, 1870–1970*. Charleston: Arcadia, 2000.

Mays, Benjamin E. *Born to Rebel: An Autobiography*. New York: Scribner, 1971.

McGuire, Danielle L. *At the Dark End of the Street: Black Women, Rape, and Resistance—a New History of the Civil Rights Movement from Rosa Parks to the Rise of Black Power*. New York: Alfred A. Knopf, 2010.

McNeil, Genna Rae. *Groundwork: Charles Hamilton Houston and the Struggle for Civil Rights*. Philadelphia: University of Pennsylvania Press, 1983.

Mertz, Paul E. "'Mind Changing Time All over Georgia': HOPE, Inc. and School Desegregation, 1958–1961." *Georgia Historical Quarterly* 77, no. 1 (1993): 41–61.

Mixon, Gregory. *The Atlanta Riot: Race, Class, and Violence in a New South City*. Gainesville: University Press of Florida, 2005.

Moore, Howard, Jr. "Black Barrister at the Southern Bar." In *Radical Lawyers: Their Role in the Movement and in the Courts*, edited by Jonathon Black. New York: Avon Books, 1971.

———. "The Tenth Black Lawyer in Georgia." *Widener Law Journal* 13 (2003): 210–16.

Motley, Constance Baker. *Equal Justice under Law: An Autobiography*. New York: Farrar, Straus and Giroux, 1998.
———. "Remarks on Holmes-Hunter Lecture." *Harvard Blackletter Journal* 5 (1988): 1–11.
National Association for the Advancement of Colored People. *Thirty Years of Lynching in the United States, 1889–1918*. New York: NAACP, 1919.
O'Brien, Molly. "Discriminatory Effects: Desegregation Litigation in Higher Education in Georgia." *William & Mary Bill of Rights Journal* 8, no. 1 (1999): 1–51.
Pratt, Robert A. *We Shall Not Be Moved: The Desegregation of the University of Georgia*. Athens: University of Georgia Press, 2002.
Raines, Howell. *My Soul Is Rested: Movement Days in the Deep South Remembered*. New York: Bantam Books, 1978.
Ransby, Barbara. *Ella Baker and the Black Freedom Movement: A Radical Democratic Vision*. Chapel Hill: University of North Carolina Press, 2003.
Roche, Jeff. *Restructured Resistance: The Sibley Commission and the Politics of Desegregation in Georgia*. Athens: University of Georgia Press, 2010.
Russell, Herman J. *Building Atlanta: How I Broke through Segregation to Launch a Building Empire*. Chicago: Chicago Review Press, 2014.
Smith, David, Jr. *Georgia State University: An Institutional History, 1913–2002*. N.p.: CreateSpace, 2010.
Smith, J. Clay. *Emancipation: The Making of the Black Lawyer, 1844–1944*. Philadelphia: University of Pennsylvania Press, 1993.
Sullivan, Patricia. *Lift Every Voice: The NAACP and the Making of the Civil Rights Movement*. New York: New Press, 2009.
Tolnay, Stewart Emory, and E. M. Beck. *A Festival of Violence: An Analysis of Southern Lynchings, 1882–1930*. Urbana: University of Illinois Press, 1995.
Trillin, Calvin. *An Education in Georgia: Charlayne Hunter, Hamilton Holmes, and the Integration of the University of Georgia*. Athens: University of Georgia Press, 1991.
Tuck, Stephen G. N. *Beyond Atlanta: The Struggle for Racial Equality in Georgia, 1940–1980*. Athens: University of Georgia Press, 2001.
Tushnet, Mark V. *Making Civil Rights Law: Thurgood Marshall and the Supreme Court, 1936–1961*. New York: Oxford University Press, 1994.
———. *The NAACP's Legal Strategy against Segregated Education, 1925–1950*. Chapel Hill: University of North Carolina Press, 1987.
U.S. Commission on Civil Rights. *The Unfinished Business: Twenty Years Later.* . . . Washington, D.C.: U.S. Commission on Civil Rights, 1977.
Walker, Jack Lamar. *Sit-Ins in Atlanta*. New York: McGraw-Hill, 1964.
Ward, Jason Morgan. *Defending White Democracy: The Making of a Segregationist Movement and the Remaking of Racial Politics, 1936–1965*. Chapel Hill: University of North Carolina Press, 2011.
Washington, James M. *A Testament of Hope: The Essential Writings and Speeches of Martin Luther King, Jr.* New York: Harper Collins, 1986.
Webb, Clive. *Fight against Fear: Southern Jews and Black Civil Rights*. Athens: University of Georgia Press, 2011.

Wexler, Laura. *Fire in a Canebrake: The Last Mass Lynching in America*. New York: Scribner, 2003.
White, Walter Francis. *A Man Called White: The Autobiography of Walter White*. New York: Viking Press, 1948.
Williams, Juan. *Eyes on the Prize: America's Civil Rights Years, 1954–1965*. New York: Penguin Books, 1988.
Williams, Roger M. *The Bonds: An American Family*. New York: Athenum, 1971.
Williamson, Joy Ann. *Radicalizing the Ebony Tower: Black Colleges and the Black Freedom Struggle in Mississippi*. New York: Teachers College Press, 2008.
Woods, Jeff. *Black Struggle, Red Scare: Segregation and Anti-Communism in the South, 1948–1968*. Baton Rouge: Louisiana State University Press, 2004.

Documentaries

Foot Soldier for Equal Justice: Horace T. Ward and the Desegregation of the University of Georgia. Maurice C. Daniels, executive producer; Janice Reaves, producer; George Rodrigues, coproducer; Derrick P. Alridge, academic adviser. Georgia Public Television Broadcast. Athens: University of Georgia Center for Continuing Education, 2000.
Mary Francis Early: The Quiet Trailblazer. Maurice C. Daniels, executive producer; Michelle Garfield Cook, coexecutive producer; Bobby Mitchell, editor; Greg Morrison, LaGeris Underwood Bell, Janice Reaves, producers. Georgia Public Television Broadcast. Athens: Foot Soldier Project for Civil Rights Studies, 2018.

Newspapers and Periodicals

Atlanta Constitution
Atlanta Daily World
Atlanta Inquirer
Atlanta Journal
Atlanta Journal and Constitution
Augusta Courier
Chicago Tribune
Ebony
Georgia State Signal
Georgia State University Magazine
Jet Magazine
La Vida News: The Black Voice
Life
Macon Telegraph
New York Times
Pittsburgh Courier
Saporta Report (Atlanta)
Savannah Evening Press
Savannah Tribune
Southern Negro Youth Congress News Bulletin

Star-Telegram (Fort Worth)
Tennessee Tribune
Washington Post
Washington Post and Times Herald

Interviews

Bell, Charles. Interview by the author, Atlanta, Ga., June 13, 2002.
Bond, Julian. Interview by the author and Derrick P. Alridge, Charlottesville, Va., October 21, 2004.
Bootle, William A. Interview by the author, Macon, Ga., June 14, 2000.
Brisbane, Robert. Interview by the author, Atlanta, Ga., January 19, 1995
Dinsmore, Myra E. Interview by the author, Atlanta, Ga., February 19, 1997
Early, Mary Frances. Interview by the author, Atlanta, Ga., February 19, 1997, October 21, 2009.
Early, Mary Frances. Interview by Greg Morrison in conjunction with the Foot Soldier Project for Civil Rights Studies, Athens, Ga., January 17, 2017.
Hill, Jesse. Interview by the author, Atlanta, Ga., December 17, 1996.
Hollowell, Donald L. Interview by the author, Atlanta, Ga., July 27, 1993, August 22, 1994.
Holmes, Gary. Interview by the author, Atlanta, Ga., June 15, 2001.
Holmes, Hamilton E. Interview by the author, Atlanta, Ga., February 24, 1995.
Holmes, Isabella. Interview by the author, Atlanta, Ga., June 15, 2001.
Holmes, Lauren. Interview by Derrick P. Alridge, New York, N.Y., May 8, 2002.
Hunter-Gault, Charlayne. Interview by the author, Atlanta, Ga., June 14, 2006.
Johnson, Leroy. Interview by the author, Atlanta, Ga., December 17, 1996.
Jordan, Jr., Vernon E. Interview by the author, Atlanta, Ga., February 28, 1997.
King, Lonnie. Interview by the author, Atlanta, Ga., December 20, 2011.
Manners, George. Interview by Lee Hough, Atlanta, Ga., 1985.
McCracken, William. Interview by the author, Augusta, Ga., January 13, 1997.
McIntyre, Edward. Interview by the author, Augusta, Ga., January 13, 1997.
Moore, Howard, Jr. Interview by the author, Atlanta, Ga., June 10, 2004; Berkeley, Calif., June 11, 2011, June 25, 2011.
Motley, Constance Baker. Interview by the author, New York, N.Y., March 30, 1995.
Phipps, Herbert. Interview by the author, Atlanta, Ga., June 22, 2004.
Pickett, Albert. Interview by the author, Augusta, Ga., January 1977.
Vandiver, Ernest. Interview by the author, Sky Valley, Ga., August 14, 1996.
Ward, Horace T. Interview by the author, Atlanta, Ga., August 22, 1994.

Archival and Manuscript Collections

Atlanta History Center, Atlanta, Ga.: A. T. Walden Papers.
Auburn Avenue Research Library on African American Culture and History, Atlanta-Fulton Public Library System, Atlanta, Ga.: Jesse Hill Jr. Papers, Archives Division; Donald L. Hollowell Papers; Samuel W. Williams Papers.
Barbara Hunt Personal Papers, Atlanta, Ga.

Georgia State University Special Collections, Atlanta, Ga.: George Sparks Papers.
Hargrett Rare Book and Manuscript Library, University of Georgia Libraries, Athens, Ga.: O. C. Aderhold Papers; Charles J. Bloch File, Georgiana Collection; Harmon Caldwell Papers; Walter N. Danner Subject file; J. Alton Hosch Papers; University Archives and Records Management.
Library of Congress, Washington, D.C.: Papers of the NAACP, The Campaign for Educational Equality: Legal Department and Central Office Records, 1913–1950, 1951–1955, 1956–1965.
NAACP Legal Defense and Educational Fund, Inc. Archives, New York.
National Archives and Records Administration, Washington, D.C.: Department of Justice, Federal Bureau of Investigation Files.
National Archives--Southeast Region, Federal Records Center, East Point, Ga.: *Hamilton E. Holmes et. al. v. Walter N. Danner et al.*, Civil Action no. 450 (December 1960); *Horace T. Ward v. Regents of the University System of Georgia*, Civil Action no. 4355 (1956); *Hunt v. Arnold*, Civil Action no. 5781 (December 1958).
Pittsburgh Courier Archives, Pittsburgh, Pa.
Richard B. Russell Library for Political Research and Studies, University of Georgia Libraries, Athens, Ga.: Donald L. Hollowell Collection, Foot Soldier Project for Civil Rights Studies; Richard B. Russell Jr. Collection.; Horace T. Ward Collection, Foot Soldier Project for Civil Rights Studies.
Robert W. Woodruff Library, Atlanta University Center, Atlanta, Ga.: William Madison Boyd Papers, Archives Research Center; John H. Calhoun Papers, Archives Research Center; Southern Regional Council's Voter Education Project Files.
Simon Schwob Memorial Library, Columbus State University, Columbus, Ga.: Primus King Papers.
Tamiment Library, New York University, New York: James E. Jackson and Esther Cooper Jackson Papers, Wagner Archives.

Government Documents

General Acts and Resolutions. Vol. 1, no. 97, House Resolution 232–743r, December 10, 1953.
General Appropriations Act. Secs. 8, 9. Ga. Laws 1951, 425.
General Appropriations Act. Secs. 8, 9. Ga. Laws Jan.–Feb. Sess. 1953, 154.
General Appropriations Act. Secs. 8. 9. Ga. Laws 1956, 762.
Georgia House Resolution, 1735, March 7, 2014.
The Southern Manifesto, 102nd Congressional Record 4515–16, 1956.
University System of Georgia Board of Regents' minutes. Archives, Office of the Board of Regents, Atlanta, Ga.
University System of Georgia Board of Regents Annual Report for the Fiscal Year 1958–1959. July 1, 1959. Archives, Office of the Board of Regents, Atlanta, Ga.
University System of Georgia Board of Regents Semester Enrollment Report, Spring 2018. Board of Regents, University System of Georgia, Atlanta, Ga.

INDEX

activists. *See* grassroots activists; local activists
Adams, Samuel, 41–42
Adams, William, 25
Aderhold, O. C., 2
African American economy. *See* black-owned businesses
African American higher education. *See* black higher education
African American higher education institutions. *See* black colleges
African American lawyers. *See* black lawyers
African American women, 4–5, 109–10, 111
Alabama State College, 49, 50
Albany State College, 21, 22, 23
Alcorn, James L., 20
Alcorn University, 20
Allen University, 24
Alridge, Derrick, 35, 61
alumni certification requirements: court certification and, 30, 31, 32, 62, 79, 80, 91; Georgia State case and, 3, 7, 8, 45–46, 47, 53–54, 62, 73–76, 78, 80–82, 90–91, 93–94, 96–97, 99–100, 139–40n50; at Georgia State College of Business Administration, 7, 30–31, 32, 39–40, 41–42, 43–44, 73, 104, 105, 140n67; *Meredith v. Fair* and, 3, 124; social contact between blacks and whites and, 53, 74–76, 78, 97; University of Georgia and, 29, 31, 39, 42, 44, 62, 73, 75, 77, 79, 81, 100, 105, 140n67; University System of Georgia and, 30–31, 32, 39, 41, 42, 46, 73, 74–76, 77, 78–79, 82, 94, 96–97, 99–100, 105; Ward and, 28–29, 31, 39, 73, 78, 79, 81, 105; *Ward v. Regents* and, 62, 63, 83
American Bar Association, 77
Anderson, James D., 23, 61, 138n25; *An Education of Blacks in the South*, 20–21
"Appeal for Human Rights, An" (petition), 116
Arnall, Ellis, 13, 113, 131n19, 143n7
Arnold, Robert O., 24–25, 75–76, 79, 84–85, 120, 148n19
Atlanta Board of Education, 119–20
Atlanta Committee for Cooperative Action (ACCA), 38, 139n28
Atlanta Compromise, 60. *See also* Cotton States and International Exposition
Atlanta Constitution, 43, 91, 92, 116
Atlanta Daily World (ADW), 31, 36, 40, 41–42, 65, 72–73, 74, 77–78, 87, 93, 98, 102, 116
Atlanta Division of the University of Georgia, 11, 44. *See also* Georgia State College of Business Administration
Atlanta Journal, 19, 22, 24, 43, 57, 65, 72, 85, 92, 101, 116

INDEX

Atlanta Junior College, 106
Atlanta Life Insurance Company, 35, 36, 38–39, 49, 71, 106, 112, 155n61
Atlanta Negro Voters League, 137n130, 143n122
Atlanta Public Schools, 119, 120–21, 159n19
Atlanta Race Riot, The (Mixon), 36–37
Atlanta Student Movement, 86–87
Atlanta student sit-ins, 51, 116, 129n2
Atlanta University, 6, 20, 27, 28, 34, 48, 83, 112, 125, 139n28, 143n122; Political Science Department and, 37–38, 71
Auburn Avenue, 32, 33, 34, 36, 38, 48, 49–50, 113. *See also* black-owned businesses

Bagby, George T., 119
Baker, Ella, 109
Banks, Carolyn Long, 125
barratry laws, 69–70
Bauerlein, Mark, 36
Beyond Atlanta (Tuck), 109
Bilbo, Theodore G., 18
black codes, 20
black colleges, 5–6, 20–25, 27, 37–38, 113, 135n90, 138n25; Albany State College, 21, 22, 23; Allen University, 24; Boggs Academy, 49, 88; Fort Valley State College, 21; Gamma Theological Seminary, 37; Howard University, 16, 111, 150–51n94; Lane College, 24; Lincoln University, 89; Meharry Medical College, 83; Morris Brown College, 37; Savannah State College, 18–20, 21–22, 23; Tuskegee Institute, 60, 83. *See also* Atlanta University; Clark College; Morehouse College; Spelman College
black higher education, 9, 33; black-owned businesses and, 34, 36, 37, 49–50. *See also* black colleges; U.S. Supreme Court
black institutions, 5, 114, 137n130, 143n122; Atlanta Committee for Cooperative Action (ACCA), 38, 139n28. *See also* National Association for the Advancement of Colored People
black lawyers, 24, 31–32, 44–45, 116, 137n130, 143n122; *Hunt v. Arnold* and, 4–5, 29–30, 71, 108–9, 110, 111, 125, 129n2; NAACP and, 3, 4, 7, 17–18, 29–30, 31, 32, 44, 45, 50–52, 65, 70, 108, 109–10, 111, 155n76,

156n80; Robinson, S. S., 45, 111; Thomas, R. Edwin, Jr., 45, 111; *Ward v. Regents* and, 3, 4, 6, 9, 29, 30, 50, 129n2. *See also* Carter, Robert L.; civil rights movement; Hollowell, Donald L.; local black lawyers; Marshall, Thurgood; Moore, E. E., Jr.; Motley, Constance Baker; Walden, A. T.; Ward, Horace T.
black-owned businesses, 7, 27, 44; civil rights work, 35, 38–39, 71, 113–14; higher education and, 34, 36, 37, 49–50; Pilgrim Life Insurance Company, 16; support for Georgia State case, 5–6, 112, 113–14, 125. *See also Atlanta Daily World (ADW)*; Atlanta Life Insurance Company; Auburn Avenue; North Carolina Mutual Insurance Company; *Pittsburgh Courier*
Black Struggle, Red Scare (Woods), 56
Blair, George, 31, 41, 43, 44, 54, 79–82, 112
Bloch, Charles, 76–77, 78, 79, 121
Boggs Academy, 49, 88
Bond, Julian, 26–27, 86, 116
Boone, Mae Thelma, 11, 30, 34, 42, 81, 111, 126, 140n56
Bootle, William Augustus, 1, 2, 3, 105, 113, 123, 124
Borders, William Holmes, 115
Born to Rebel (Mays), 126
Boyd, William Madison, 37–38, 50, 71
Branton, Wiley, 102
Brisbane, Robert, 114
Britton, Gene, 43, 72
Britton, John, 78, 87
Browder v. Gayle, 115
Brown, Ernestine, 118
Brown, Paul, 48
Brown, R. Jess, 124, 130n13
Brown-Nagin, Tomiko, 5, 36, 37, 51, 110; *Courage to Dissent*, 4
Brown v. Board of Education, 11, 12, 16, 25, 26, 55, 62, 101, 106, 109
Brumby, Bebe, 2
Brumby, Otis A., 2
Bussey, Howard, 115

Caldwell, Harmon W., 54, 78–79, 83, 84
Calhoun, John, 8, 30, 47–48, 63–65, 70, 87, 88, 89, 103, 110–11, 113–14, 155n76
Callaway, Howard, 73, 78

INDEX

Capital City Club, 75–76, 148n22
Carmichael, Floyd, 37
Carter, Robert L., 1, 7, 29, 50, 51–52, 65, 109, 110, 155n76
Chicago Tribune, 101
Citizens' Councils of America, 14
Civil Rights Bill, 76
Civil Rights History from the Ground Up (Crosby), 5
civil rights lawyers. *See* black lawyers; Carter, Robert L.; local black lawyers; Marshall, Thurgood; Motley, Constance Baker
civil rights movement: black lawyers and, 4–5, 24, 29–30, 31–32, 44–45, 50–51, 57–58, 70, 71, 116, 129n2, 137n130, 143n122, 156n80; black students and, 22–24, 50–51, 86–87, 116, 135n90; direct-action campaign, 116, 157n112, 158n113; grass-roots campaigners, 5, 6–7, 107, 116–17, 126–27; NAACP and, 51, 62, 63, 87, 132n41; segregation and, 15, 25–27, 35, 38–39, 44–45, 68–69, 99–102, 113–14, 116–17, 121; voting rights and, 16, 18, 31, 51, 132n41, 137n130; women and, 109–10, 111
Clark College, 37, 48, 90, 112, 139n28, 140n56, 152n139
Clemons, Edward Jacob, 42, 92, 93, 102, 111, 112, 126, 140n56; enrollment process, 11, 30, 34, 43, 44, 81, 90–91, 113
Cocking, Walter Dewey, 28
Cohen, Robert, 35, 113
Coke, H. D., 116, 117, 158n113
Communism, 7, 8, 43, 55–56, 59, 62, 85–86
Congressional Record, 116
Cook, Eugene, 7, 8, 47, 54–56, 62–63, 69, 72, 85, 89, 94, 104, 143n7; "The Southern View of Segregation," 54–55; "The Ugly Truth about the NAACP," 55–56
Cotton States and International Exposition (Washington address), 7, 59, 60–61
Courage to Dissent (Brown-Nagin), 4
Crosby, Emilye, 5
Current, Gloster, 63

Daniels, Maurice, 35
Davis, Phil, 101–2
Dees, Morris, 107
DeKalb Community College, 106
Dennis, William, 22, 23

desegregation. *See* civil rights movement; Georgia State College of Business Administration; National Association for the Advancement of Colored People; racial equality; University of Georgia; University System of Georgia; U.S. Supreme Court; white supremacy
Dinsmore, Adolphus, Jr., 49, 98
Dinsmore, Adolphus, III, 49
Dinsmore, Myra E.: discrediting during trial, 83, 84, 88, 89–90, 92, 98, 99, 102; enrollment process, 11, 30, 33, 34, 38, 39, 40, 45, 71, 79, 81, 108; legacy of, 5, 106–7, 123, 125, 126, 148n18, 155n61; preparing for court case, 7, 48, 49, 53, 71, 111, 147n96; trial, 8, 74, 77, 78, 108–9, 113; trial verdict, 2, 96, 101–2, 106, 119
Dodd, Bobby, 14
Dorsey, Allison, 37, 113
Dorsey, George, 13, 113
Dorsey, Mae Murray, 13, 113
Du Bois, W. E. B., 23–24, 60, 61–62; *The Souls of Black Folk*, 61
Dungee, Roscoe, 17
Durham, W. J., 17

Early, Mary Frances, 27, 99, 159n27
Eastland, James, 106
Education in Georgia, An (Trillin), 38
Education of Blacks in the South, The (Anderson), 20–21
Emancipation Proclamation, 36
Empire Real Estate Board, 114
Equal Justice under Law (Motley), 68, 89–90, 124
Espy, Henry, 17

Fight against Fear (Webb), 77
Fisher, Albert Franklin, 115
Fort Valley State College, 21
Fourteenth Amendment, 3, 17, 26, 54, 63, 94, 96, 100, 106, 115, 123, 124, 143n6
Freedmen's Bureau, 36, 138n25
Freeman, Crystal, 108
French, Frank, 57

Gaines, Lloyd, 17, 33, 100
Gaines v. Canada, 17, 32, 33, 100, 137n140
Gamma Theological Seminary, 37

Gasman, Marybeth, 21
George, Walter F., 26
Georgia Bureau of Investigation (GBI), 42
Georgia Commission on Education, 25–26
Georgia General Assembly, 2, 9, 12, 26, 28, 46, 54–55, 70, 85, 120, 121
Georgia House of Representatives, 14, 26, 70, 107, 108
Georgia Institute of Technology, 6, 14–15, 125, 132n22, 140n67
Georgia Institute of Technology, Evening School of Commerce, 11, 43–44, 46–47
Georgia State College of Business Administration: aftermath of trial, 9, 103, 104–5, 106, 115, 116, 118–19, 120–21, 122; alumni certification requirements, 30–31, 32, 39–40, 41–42, 43–44, 99–100, 104, 105, 140n67; alumni certification requirements mentioned at trial, 3, 7, 8, 45–46, 47, 53–54, 62, 73–76, 78, 80–82, 90–91, 93–94, 96–97; Atlanta Division of the University of Georgia, 11, 44; black enrollment process, 6–7, 11–12, 34–36, 38–44, 49, 50, 62, 87, 88, 90, 112, 113, 152n139; court certification, 30, 31, 32, 62, 79, 80, 91; denial of support for segregation, 46, 47, 74, 80, 100; desegregation, 9, 125–26, 127; founding and history of, 6, 11, 43–44; *Hunt v. Arnold* and, 2–3, 4–5, 8, 11, 29–30, 45–46, 47–48, 50, 51–52, 62–63, 72–73, 110, 117, 123, 143n6; impeding black applicants, 7, 30–31, 32–33, 39, 42, 44, 53–54, 106, 118–19, 121, 125, 158n9; lack of alumni in first year of existence, 43, 81; out-of-state aid to black students, 32–33, 79, 97, 99, 100; as separate college, 6, 11, 43, 47, 81; state financial support, 46, 73, 101, 120–21; trial verdict, 2, 8–9, 96–98, 101, 104–5, 106, 118, 119, 120–21, 122, 123, 124; University System of Georgia Evening School, 11, 44; white student opposition to black enrollments, 58–60, 62. *See also* Georgia State University; University System of Georgia
Georgia State Senate, 26, 43, 70
Georgia State Signal, 7, 58–60, 62, 101, 112
Georgia State University, 2, 9, 10, 108, 126–27. *See also* Georgia State College of Business Administration

Georgia State University (Smith), 125
Georgia Supreme Court, 65, 143n7
Gore, Albert, Sr., 26
grassroots activists, 5, 6–7, 107, 112, 113, 116–17, 126–27. *See also* Boone, Mae Thelma; civil rights movement; Clemons, Edward Jacob; Dinsmore, Myra E.; Hunt, Barbara Pace; Knight, Charlie Mae; local activists; Roberts, Russell T.; Welch, Iris Mae
Greenberg, Jack, 1, 109, 130n13
Grier, Bobby, 14
Griffin, Cheney, 15
Griffin, Marvin, 12, 13, 14–15, 16, 25–26, 28, 33, 41, 62, 63
Grooms, J. Harlan, 25
Gunby, Eugene, 31, 32, 79, 91

Hall, Amos T., 17
Hall, Annette Lucille, 125, 126, 160n36
Hall, Robert, 43
Hall, Robert H., 54
Hamer, Fannie Lou, 126
Hamilton Earl Holmes (documentary), 35
Harlan, Louis, 61
Harris, George, 15
Harris, Roy V., 14, 15–16, 18–20, 21–22, 23, 24, 56
Hartsfield, William B., 12, 27, 28, 115
Hill, Jesse, Jr., 6, 35–36, 38–39, 49, 57, 58, 71, 105, 113, 114, 118, 121, 123
Hine, Darlene Clark, 16
Hobson, Maurice J., 36, 37, 45; *The Legend of the Black Mecca*, 5
Holland, Jocelyn Elaine, 49
Holland, Myretta June, 49
Holland, Robert Joseph, 49
Hollowell, Donald L.: aftermath of trial, 97, 99, 102–4, 105, 106, 118, 119; civil rights work, 4, 24, 44, 50, 51, 57–58, 64–65, 68–69, 70, 111, 116, 129n2, 139n28, 156n80; *Holmes v. Danner*, 1, 2, 67–68, 121, 122, 123; *Hunt v. Arnold* involvement, 4, 24, 30, 108–9, 111, 129n2; *Hunt v. Arnold* preparation, 50, 57, 64, 66, 90, 112, 113; *Hunt v. Arnold* trial, 8, 72, 73, 74, 77, 78, 80–81, 82, 83, 84, 85–86, 87, 88, 90, 91, 92–95
Holmes, Alfred "Tup," 44–45, 141n75
Holmes, Hamilton, 35–36, 45, 86, 113;

desegregation court case, 1, 2, 3, 4, 105, 122–23, 124, 125, 126, 159n27; discrediting in court, 67–68, 122
Holmes, Hamilton Mayo, 44–45
Holmes, Isabella, 35
Holmes, Oliver Wendell, 44–45
Holmes v. City of Atlanta, 45, 111, 141n75
Holmes v. Danner, 1–3, 8, 51, 105, 121–23, 125, 129n2; discrediting of plaintiffs, 67–68, 122–23; University of Georgia and, 1, 2, 4, 105, 113, 121–24
Hooper, Frank, 115, 119
Hoover, J. Edgar, 56
Hosch, J. Alton, 1, 2, 76
Hose, Sam, 37
Houston, Charles Hamilton, 16, 17
Howard University, 16, 111, 150–51n94
Hughes, Langston, 23
Hunt, Barbara Pace: discrediting during trial, 83, 84, 86, 87–88, 89, 90, 92, 98, 99, 102, 152n139; enrollment process, 34, 40–41, 45, 79, 81, 87; legacy of, 5, 107–8, 123, 125, 126; preparing for court case, 7, 47–48, 53, 70–71, 89, 111; trial, 8, 74, 77, 78, 112, 113; trial verdict, 2, 96, 101–2, 119
Hunt, Eldridge F., Jr., 48, 98
Hunter, Charlayne, 4, 35–36, 113, 125, 159n27; desegregation court case, 1, 2, 3, 86, 105, 124, 126; discrediting in court, 122–23; *In My Place*, 35
Hunt v. Arnold, 11, 50, 57, 119, 143n6, 145n48, 155n76; alumni certification requirements, 3, 7, 8, 53–54, 62, 73–76, 77, 78–79, 80–82, 90–91, 93–94, 139–40n50, 140n67; alumni certification requirements verdict, 96–97, 99–100, 104, 105; beginning of trial, 72–74, 75, 77–79, 147n1; court certification, 79, 80; discrediting NAACP, 62, 63–65, 69, 70, 85–86, 87–89, 97, 107, 110; discrediting plaintiffs, 7–8, 9–10, 62, 66–67, 83, 85, 86, 87–88, 89–91, 92, 94, 98–99, 102, 104, 152n139; filing as class-action suit, 91–93; filing of suit, 7, 32, 48, 51–52; legacy of, 2–3, 4, 8–10, 106–8, 123, 124–25; local black lawyers and, 4–5, 29–30, 108–9, 110, 111, 125, 129n2; out-of-state aid to black students and, 82–83, 84, 97, 99, 100; Roberts's withdrawal, 65–67, 68, 70–71, 89; seeking dismissal of case, 62–63;

support from black-owned businesses, 5–6, 112, 113–14, 125; verdict, 2, 4, 8–9, 96–98, 101, 104–5, 106, 118, 119, 120–21, 122, 123, 124; white colleges' denial of support for segregation and, 79–80, 81–83, 84–85; written closing arguments, 93–95. *See also* Georgia State College of Business Administration; Hollowell, Donald L.; Marshall, Thurgood; Moore, E. E., Jr.; Motley, Constance Baker; Murphy, B. D.; National Association for the Advancement of Colored People; Sloan, Boyd; University System of Georgia; Walden, A. T.; Williams, Samuel W.
Hurley, Ruby, 32, 50

In My Place (Hunter-Gault), 35
Interposition Resolution, 25, 26, 33, 58

Jackson, Esther Cooper, 23
Jackson, Maynard Holbrook, 86
Jenkins, Herbert, 115
Jet Magazine, 66, 85
Johnson, Joseph, 115
Johnson, Lyndon B., 26
Johnson, R. O., 20
Johnston, Olin D., 18
Jordan, Clarence, 42–43, 44
Jordan, J. E., 49–50, 71, 112, 147n96
Jordan, Vernon E., Jr., 1, 2, 51, 57–58
Journal of Negro Education, 20

Kefauver, Estes, 26
King, Lonnie, 87, 116
King, Martin Luther, Jr., 12, 62, 86, 87, 107, 116, 117; "Letter from a Birmingham Jail," 96
King, Primus, 31
King v. Chapman, 16
Kluger, Richard, 124
Knight, Charlie Mae, 11, 30, 34, 38, 39, 49, 111, 126
Koinonia Farm, 42–43
Ku Klux Klan, 8, 13, 20, 31, 42–43, 51, 85, 107, 112, 113

Lane College, 24
Langdale, Noah, Jr., 80
La Vida News, 107

Law, Westley Wallace, 21, 134n69
Legend of the Black Mecca, The (Hobson), 5
"Letter from a Birmingham Jail" (M. L. King), 96
Leverett, E. Freeman, 54, 69
Lewis, David Levering, 61–62
Lincoln University, 89
Little Rock public school case, 102
local activists, 71, 116, 125; Early, Mary Frances, 27, 99, 159n27; Jordan, Clarence, 42–43, 44; Young, Whitney M., Jr., 27, 71, 139n28. *See also* black lawyers; Calhoun, John; civil rights movement; grassroots activists; Hill, Jesse, Jr.; Jordan, J. E.; Welden, James L.; Williams, Samuel W.
local black lawyers, 9, 17–18, 44–45, 111. *See also* Hollowell, Donald L.; *Hunt v. Arnold*; Moore, E. E., Jr.; National Association for the Advancement of Colored People; Walden, A. T.; Ward, Horace T.; *Ward v. Regents*
Lockett, Marthenia, 67
Long, Ralph, Jr., 125
Lucy, Autherine, 3, 25
lynching, 13, 37, 43, 113

Mack, Kenneth, 5, 116–17; *Representing the Race*, 116
Malcom, Dorothy Dorsey, 13, 113
Malcom, Roger, 13, 113
Manners, George, 46, 47
Marshall, Thurgood, 5, 56; civil rights work, 1, 16, 17, 30, 31, 38, 44, 45, 50, 109, 116, 117, 132n41; *Hunt v. Arnold*, 7, 29, 51–52, 110, 111, 112
Mays, Benjamin Elijah, 23, 28, 85, 86; *Born to Rebel*, 126
McClure, Joseph Howard, 126
McCracken, J. Roy, 16, 118
McDaniel, Marian, 34, 39–40, 45, 48, 64, 87, 88, 111, 112, 126
McGhee, Rosalyn Virginia, 11, 30, 34, 38, 39, 49, 111, 126, 139–40n50
McIntyre, Ed, 16
McLaurin, G. W., 17
McLaurin v. Oklahoma, 17
Meharry Medical College, 83
Mercer University, 77, 143n7
Meredith, James, 3, 124

Meredith v. Fair, 3, 124, 125, 130n13
Mixon, Gregory, 36
Moore, E. E., Jr.: aftermath of trial, 97, 102, 103–4, 119; civil rights work, 44–45; *Hunt v. Arnold* involvement, 4, 7, 111, 147n96; *Hunt v. Arnold* preparation, 50, 51–52, 53–54, 64, 65, 66, 69, 71, 88, 90; *Hunt v. Arnold* trial, 8, 72, 73, 74, 75, 78, 79, 80, 81, 84, 93–94, 99, 108–9, 113; initial support for black applicants, 45–46, 47–48, 112
Moore, Howard, Jr., 51, 58
Morehouse College, 23, 27, 28, 37, 38, 85, 86–87, 114, 115, 116, 150–51n94
Morris Brown College, 37
Motley, Constance Baker: aftermath of trial, 97, 100, 102; civil rights work, 1, 25, 31, 70; *Equal Justice under Law*, 68, 89–90, 124; extent of desegregation cases and, 3, 109–10; *Hunt v. Arnold* involvement, 3, 4–5, 29, 50, 68, 111; *Hunt v. Arnold* trial, 8, 72, 78, 84, 89–90, 91, 92, 93–94, 99, 104; *Meredith v. Fair*, 3, 124, 130n13
Murphy, B. D.: *Hunt v. Arnold* discrediting NAACP and, 8, 85–86, 87–89, 97, 103, 107; *Hunt v. Arnold* discrediting plaintiffs and, 87–89, 92, 94, 97, 98, 107, 152n139; *Hunt v. Arnold* preparation, 54, 56–57, 64, 65, 66–67; *Hunt v. Arnold* trial, 72, 78, 90–91

NAACP. *See* National Association for the Advancement of Colored People
Nabrit, James M., Jr., 17
Nash, Willie, 57
National Association for the Advancement of Colored People (NAACP), 38, 60, 134n69, 143n122, 150–51n94; aftermath of trial, 99, 102, 103, 104, 118, 121; civil rights work, 51, 62, 63, 87; desegregation campaign, 3, 4, 6, 7, 10, 16, 21–22, 24–25, 45, 99, 104, 117, 118, 145n48; *Holmes v. Danner*, 4, 122; *Hunt v. Arnold*, 2, 3, 4, 10, 91–92, 94, 108, 109, 110–11, 112, 155n76; *Hunt v. Arnold* discrediting of plaintiffs and, 62, 63–65, 83, 85, 87–89, 97, 103, 107, 110; *Hunt v. Arnold* preparation, 29–30, 32, 35–36, 39–40, 44, 47–48, 50, 51–52, 53, 63, 71, 113; legal harassment and, 4, 69–70, 103, 111, 114; local black lawyers and, 3, 4, 7, 17–18, 29–30, 31, 32, 44, 45, 50–52, 108, 110, 111,

156n80; voting rights, 16, 132n41; *Ward v. Regents*, 4, 63, 83–84; white harassment of, 7, 8, 20, 55–56, 59, 62, 63–65, 83–84, 85–86, 121

National Association for the Advancement of Colored People Legal Defense and Educational Fund (NAACP LDF): desegregation campaign, 3, 5, 9, 16, 17–18, 68–69, 106, 109–10, 116, 119, 124, 130n13, 132n41; extent of cases, 68–69, 70; founding of, 130n14; *Hunt v. Arnold*, 7, 29, 70, 102, 109, 112; local black lawyers and, 3, 4, 7, 17–18

National Urban League, 27, 139n28

Negrophobia (Bauerlein), 36

New York Times, 27, 101, 116, 120

North Carolina A&T, 23

North Carolina Mutual Insurance Company, 50, 90, 112, 113, 140n56

North Texas State University, 107

Northwestern University School of Law, 1–2

Oklahoma School of Law, 17

Parks, Rosa, 107

Payne, William K., 21–22, 23

Peace Officers Association of Georgia, 55

Phelps, Morris O., 67

Pierce, Joe, 116

Pilgrim Life Insurance Company, 16

Pittsburgh Courier, 48, 71, 101, 112, 142n100

Pope, Roslyn, 116

Porter, John Thomas, 115

Powell, Adam Clayton, Jr., 23

Powell, Romae, 111

Princeton University, 59

public school desegregation, 25–26

Pye, Durwood, 64–65

racial equality, 61–62, 116, 123–24, 125, 157n112, 158n113, 160n41; *Hunt v. Arnold* verdict and, 96–98, 102, 115; Koinonia Farm and, 42–43; sport and, 15, 44–45, 111, 132n22, 141n75. *See also* civil rights movement; National Association for the Advancement of Colored People; U.S. Supreme Court

racial violence, 13, 15, 19, 20, 36–37, 42–43, 112–13

racism: black students in dormitories and, 2, 35–36, 122; death threats, 85, 107, 112; laws maintaining segregation, 46, 54–55, 57, 81, 85, 94, 118–19, 120–21, 123–24, 125, 158n9; racial hatred, 12–13, 14, 15, 18, 19, 26, 56, 57–60, 62, 76, 131n19, 140n60; segregation, 18–22, 24–29, 76–77, 91, 102, 113–14, 115–16, 119–21, 123–24, 157–58nn112–13, 159n19, 160n41; segregation in sport, 14–15, 44–45, 111, 132n22, 141n75; social contact between blacks and whites, 53, 74–76, 78, 97; threatening phone calls, 34, 41, 113

Radicalizing the Ebony Tower (Williamson), 20

Red and Black, 76

Redmond, Sidney, 17

Representing the Race (Mack), 116

Roberts, Russell T., 90, 112, 126; enrollment process, 11, 30, 34, 40, 41, 45, 50, 111; preparing for court case, 7, 47, 48, 53; withdrawal from case, 65–67, 68, 70–71, 89

Robeson, Paul, 23, 24

Robinson, S. S., 45, 111

Rogers, Mary, 118

Roosevelt, Eleanor, 23

Russell, Richard, 2, 26, 29, 76, 102

Sanders, Carl, 124, 143n7

Savannah State College, 18–20, 21–22, 23

Savannah Tribune, 19, 22

Screws, Claude, 43

Searcy, E. R., 40, 41, 139–40n50

segregation. *See* civil rights movement; Georgia State College of Business Administration; National Association for the Advancement of Colored People; racism; University of Georgia; University System of Georgia; U.S. Supreme Court; white supremacy

Shannon, Margaret, 57, 92, 101

Shorts, Robert, 115

Siebert, L. R., 78, 81, 82, 83

Simple Justice (Kluger), 124

Sipuel, Ada Lois, 17

Sipuel v. Board of Regents of the University of Oklahoma, 17

Sitton, Claude, 101, 120

Sloan, Boyd, 153n23, 158n113; *Hunt v. Arnold*, 57, 63, 64, 65, 72, 78, 86, 87, 88, 91,

Sloan, Boyd (*continued*)
  92–93, 94, 95, 147n1; verdict, 8–9, 96–100, 102, 103, 104–5, 106, 115, 118, 119, 120, 121, 122, 123
Smith, David, Jr., 125
Smith v. Allwright, 16, 18, 31, 132n41
Souls of Black Folk, The (Du Bois), 61
Southern Christian Leadership Conference (SCLC), 107, 112
Southern Manifesto, 26, 33, 55, 58
Southern Negro Youth Congress (SNYC), 23–24
Southern Poverty Law Center, 107
"Southern View of Segregation, The" (Cook speech), 54–55
Sparks, George, 43, 45–47, 54, 80, 82
Spelman College, 37, 49, 116, 125
States' Rights Council of Georgia, 12, 14, 18, 21, 33, 76
states' rights doctrine, 63
St. Louis University, 125
Student Nonviolent Coordinating Committee (SNCC), 109
Sweatt, Heman Marion, 17, 18
Sweatt v. Painter, 17

Talmadge, Eugene, 12–13, 28, 29, 131n19
Talmadge, Herman, 13, 28–29, 57, 91, 102, 104, 106
Thomas, R. Edwin, Jr., 45, 111
Trillin, Calvin, 38
Tuck, Stephen, 109
Tudico, Christopher, 21
Tuskegee Institute, 60, 83
Tuskegee Institute High School, 50
Tuttle, Elbert, 1, 123
Twitty, Frank, 124

"Ugly Truth about the NAACP, The" (Cook speech), 55–56
University of Alabama, 3, 25, 109
University of Georgia, 25, 84, 99, 132n22; alumni certification requirements, 29, 31, 39, 42, 44, 73, 75, 77, 79, 81, 100, 105, 140n67; desegregation, 1, 2, 4, 9, 35–36, 105, 109, 113, 123–24, 126, 159n27; *Holmes v. Danner*, 1, 2, 4, 105, 113, 121–24; Ward and, 28–29, 31, 38, 39, 46, 73, 76, 78, 79, 81, 85, 114, 121; *Ward v. Regents*, 1, 6, 57, 62, 77, 83, 92, 94, 100

University of Georgia School of Law, 1, 28–29, 31, 39, 73, 76, 77, 78, 79, 81, 92, 100
University of Michigan, 99, 143n122
University of Mississippi, 3, 20, 109, 124
University of Missouri, 17
University of Oklahoma, 17, 18
University of Pittsburgh, 14
University of Texas, 17, 18, 107
University System of Georgia: aftermath of trial, 102–3, 105, 120; alumni certification requirements, 30–31, 32, 39, 41, 42, 46, 73, 74–76, 77, 78–79, 82, 94; alumni certification requirements verdict, 96–97, 99–100, 105; black colleges and, 18–19, 20–22; Board of Regents, 15, 18, 20, 21, 24–25, 28, 32, 34, 54, 78–80, 120, 148n19; court certification, 30, 31, 32, 62; denial of support for segregation, 74, 78–80, 81–83, 100; diversity, 126–27; Georgia State as separate college, 6, 11, 43, 47, 81; *Hunt v. Arnold*, 51–52, 54, 62, 92, 94, 99, 100; out-of-state aid to black students, 32–33, 79, 82–83, 84, 97, 99, 100, 105, 137n137, 137n140, 154n50; state financial support, 46, 120–21; *Ward v. Regents*, 92, 123
University System of Georgia Evening School, 11, 44. *See also* Georgia State College of Business Administration
U.S. Fifth Circuit Court of Appeals, 1, 3, 45, 124
U.S. Supreme Court: desegregation and, 16, 45, 54, 106, 109–10, 115, 141n75; higher education desegregation and, 1, 3, 6, 9, 17–18, 20, 25, 26, 33, 63, 97, 100, 105, 123, 145n48

Vandiver, Ernest, 120–21, 123–24, 159n19
voting rights, 16, 18, 31, 51, 60–61, 131n19, 132n41, 137n130, 145n38

Walden, A. T.: aftermath of trial, 103–4, 119; black enrollment process, 33, 42, 79; civil rights work, 4, 31–32, 50–51, 116, 137n130, 143n122, 156n80; *Hunt v. Arnold*, 4, 30, 102, 108–9, 111; NAACP and, 64–65, 70, 102, 111, 143n122; *Ward v. Regents*, 29, 30
Ward, Horace T., 1–2; alumni certification requirements, 28–29, 31, 39, 62, 63, 73, 78, 79, 81, 83, 105; civil rights work, 51, 116; enrollment process, 38, 46, 76, 85, 114, 121;

Holmes v. Danner, 1, 2; *Ward v. Regents*, 1, 6, 30, 50, 62, 77, 83–84, 85, 92, 94, 100
Ward v. Regents, 77, 85, 123; alumni certification requirements, 62, 63, 83; local black lawyers and, 3, 4, 6, 9, 29, 30, 50, 129n2; NAACP and, 4, 63, 83–84; trial verdict, 1, 57, 92, 94, 100
Warner, Clinton, 126, 160n41
Warner, Marybelle Reynolds, 125–26
Washington, Booker T., 7, 59–62
Washington University (St. Louis), 125
Webb, Clive, 77
W. E. B. Du Bois (Lewis), 61–62
Welch, Iris Mae: discrediting during trial, 83, 84, 98; enrollment process, 34, 40, 45, 48, 49–50, 74, 79, 112; legacy of, 5, 123, 125, 126; NAACP and, 111, 112; preparing for court case, 7, 48, 53, 71, 147n96; trial, 8, 74, 77, 78, 79, 112, 113; trial verdict, 2, 96, 98, 101–2, 103, 119
Welden, James L., 42, 43, 44, 81, 91, 93
West, Michael, 61
White Citizens' Council, 107
white supremacy, 5, 6, 7, 10, 24, 42, 62, 83; desegregation and, 3, 18, 25–29, 33, 104–5, 117; laws maintaining segregation and, 46, 47, 54–55, 57
Wilkins, Roy, 24–25, 56, 70, 121
Williams, Everett, 73–74
Williams, Hosea, 15
Williams, J. A., 35
Williams, Ray H., 115
Williams, Samuel W.: black enrollment process, 40–41, 43, 44, 74, 81, 82; civil rights work, 87, 114, 115, 139n28, 150–51n94; *Hunt v. Arnold*, 6, 38, 40–41, 81–82, 85–87, 118
Williams, T. V., 64
Williamson, Joy Ann, 22–23; *Radicalizing the Ebony Tower*, 20
Woodruff, Robert, 27
Woods, Jeff, 56
Woodson, Carter G., 23
Wright, Fielding, 18
Wyche, Alice, 118

Yale Law School, 54
Young, Whitney M., Jr., 27, 71, 139n28

www.ingramcontent.com/pod-product-compliance
Lightning Source LLC
Chambersburg PA
CBHW010719250426
43672CB00033B/2979